The Development of
International Markets

The Development of International Markets

John Walmsley

Graham & Trotman
A member of the Kluwer Academic Publishers Group
LONDON/DORDRECHT/BOSTON

Graham & Trotman Limited
Sterling House
66 Wilton Road
London SW1V 1DE
UK

Graham & Trotman
Kluwer Academic Publishers Group
101 Philip Drive
Assinippi Park
Norwell, MA 02061
USA

© J. Walmsley, 1989
First published in 1989

British Library Cataloguing in Publication Data
Walmsley, J. (John), 1937–
    The development of international markets.
    1. International marketing
    I. Title
    658.8′48

    ISBN 1–85333–279–8

Library of Congress Cataloging-in-Publication Data
Walmsley, John.
    The development of international markets / John Walmsley.
        p.   cm.
    Includes index.
    ISBN 1–85333–279–8
    1. Export marketing—Handbooks, manuals, etc.   I. Title.
HF1416.W35   1989
658.8′48—dc20

89–33464
CIP

Typeset in Baskerville by Wyvern Typesetting Ltd, Bristol
Printed and bound in Great Britain by Billing & Sons Ltd, Worcester

Contents

Preface

There is a sub-theme to this book which is consistent with the content of my other books on joint ventures—it concerns people—the essential and unavoidable business 'ingredient' or, if you will the marketing man's fifth 'P'. Throughout there is the recurring theme of empathy in working relationship in the market place; it even merits a picture on page 149.

The change in attitudes at work have been nothing short of a cultural revolution. The customer, the employee, and even the shareholders with their 'glossies' and a fistful of perks have all benefited. It would seem, however, that the business to business relationships have not received so much attention and, relatively speaking, remain up a back water.

In a broad way I have tried to stick on the side of my personal business wagon a much loved phrase from Drucker: 'Adversarial power relationships work only if you never have to work with the bastard again!' Naturally I will have to grin and bear it if any workaday colleague claims that my writing to practice ratio is out of sync. Perhaps we can all accept that it is not easy to build and retain good relationships particularly so when they have to endure across language, cultural, national and business frontiers. I am convinced beyond reasonable doubt that people understanding and international success are particularly strong bed fellows.

It is impossible to divorce business issues from salient world issues and the hopes, frustrations and national feelings of the people involved. Therefore, relationship failures can have very nasty side effects! Export salesmen or global business diplomats, whichever they prefer to be called, need both a head and a heart; the first to secure good work procedures and the second for a 'multiplier effect'.

As I have no great pretensions to academia and write from within the rough and tumble of industrial life, my advice to readers remains unchanged. As there are no magic formulas and often many more good practical solutions than wrong ideas, the reader requires only two more things before proceeding to the text. The first requirement is the advice of one of my earlier managers: 'Be sure that you do not let the sparks from the grinding of the axes set alight to the cotton wool being pulled over your eyes!' and the second a pencil to attack the text with—I know there are many improvements that can be made and many other ideas that would be of benefit. In a good and sensible business relationship being open to discussion and listening are fundamentals; in a shrinking world with expanding markets we will need to keep improving ourselves in these areas.

John Walmsley
England, U.K.

July 1989

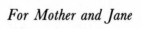
For Mother and Jane

Acknowledgements

I would like to thank the many business associates, both at home and overseas who are too numerous to mention, for their advice and information, as well as those who have corresponded thoughtfully on the earlier works on joint ventures. To those who have attempted translations a particular thank you—it all contributes to current thoughts. Specifically, I would like to thank John Townsend of Business International Corporation Geneva for making available a personal copy of *Investing, Licensing and Trading Conditions Abroad*. As always a thank you to the family for tolerance and Tim for helping with the proofs. For completeness shoe manufacturers should also get a mention for providing me with the only sure means of field research.

1

The Natural Order of Things

The development of overseas markets is a matter of concern for many companies. To some companies already working in an international environment the struggle is second nature. For others, where the effort is more token and not supported by any depth of understanding which leads to consistent policies, the development of international markets becomes an increasingly difficult problem. The fight for exports, the penetration of overseas markets, and the maintenance of a long-term and established position is common ground, with the general acceptance by business that easy markets no longer exist. Failure, lost markets, unfair competition, requests for new strategic approaches, and the revision of time-honoured policies are the frequent summary of overseas expeditions. Contact lost with agents, lower conversion quotation-to-order ratios, weak margins, lower volumes, fractious telex exchanges, and strict financial control of overseas budgets are not uncommon experiences.

It is not considered possible that any discussion of international markets will be able to correct all the problems, but it is hoped that by co-ordinating some overseas understanding and practical experiences a sharper focus can be created which will prompt a more detailed evaluation of today's problems and policies and that a more meaningful, sustained, and systematic longer-range attack on international markets will emerge.

To achieve this, the broad outline of the background to world trading patterns will be examined and note taken of the factors causing change. The opportunities which are thought to exist within the changing patterns will also be examined. Wherever possible, emphasis will be placed on practical considerations and the ways and means of implementing overseas arrangements. Such considerations will, where possible, be set against a backcloth of the more important and ever-increasing trade rules and regulations: such edicts and their interpretations have growing influence on the quality of international opportunities that are available.

WORLD INTERDEPENDENCE

Trade, industry, and commerce do not exist in a purist vacuum. They are closely aligned to, and constantly influenced by, world politics and governments, national considerations, the generality of perceived norms by business communities, and local aspirations and prejudices. In a wide sense, therefore, an appropriate starting-point is the consideration of what might sensibly be called the natural order of international activity, whereby the world's manufacturing resources have tended to be grouped together in Europe and North America, and, more recently, Japan. Traditionally, raw materials have flowed to these areas, which are colloquially called 'the North', and, after conversion, some of the manufactured goods have been circulated to the less developed areas of the world, which are usually known as 'the South'.

In more recent times the mould has been broken to the extent that some countries, such as India, Brazil, and Iran, have made steady progress towards industrial development. Other smaller countries have moved forwards at a more spectacular pace; countries like South Korea, Taiwan, Hong Kong, and Singapore have earned themselves the 'NIC' accolade (newly industrialized countries) and a fearsome reputation in price competitiveness, often beyond their practical ability to supply and their actual export volumes.

Over and above these developments, 'oil shock' has gripped the world, particularly in 1973 and 1977, and succeeded in imposing a firm distinction between the oil-rich countries and the oil-importing countries. The oil-rich, combined in membership of the wealthy OPEC club, have struggled for a common policy, particularly as the trump card of shortage weakened in the early 1980s, but by and large these countries have succeeded in becoming at least industrial micro-meccas, attracting considerable attention from the North. Other countries have had to progress through their own initiative with what aid they can obtain and have generally shown a tendency to drop back in development terms despite a welter of increasing moral support. The commercial nature of these 'have-not' countries can be remarkably different, dependng upon the development policies that they have chosen. In broad terms, some have adopted 'basic need' strategies, generally in favour of agriculture, although not repudiating eventual industrialization, others have sought appropriate technology or lower levels of technology likely to produce many workplaces and high employment. Some countries have had policies centring on achieving isolation from the international economy as far as possible—as is the case of, say, Algeria or Cuba. Alternatively, there have been straightforward imitative policies of Western development albeit with attempts to avoid the most harmful side effects.

The obvious disparities of wealth, the moral implications, the consequences for world politics and for changing affiliations and alignments, with the consequent threats to world order, are but some of the substantial problems that stem from the situation outlined. Such arguments are complex and often disturbing subjects in their own rights. Businessmen, however, have to exercise practical judgements to find profitable paths. Certainly, business judgement on risks and opportunities will be conditioned by reactions to such arguments and their likely effects. A way forward, however, has to be found if there is a general acceptance of the argument that the North can only move away from industrial stagnation through the growth of the less developed countries in the South. Given the existing extent of industrial development in the North as well as the shrinkage and erosion of traditional markets, the requirement for the South to develop and to be the North's 'motor of growth' is a strong argument. Part of the South's own development, however, requires that Northern markets remain open and readily accessible. The extent to which such trade interchanges affect the existing industrial base, particularly for simpler low-added-value products which are most susceptible to third world competition, is another important factor which companies have to take into account when considering their future international strategies.

Equally, companies which have no overseas presence or aspirations may well find that in tomorrow's markets the combined effect of competitors and equipment and raw material suppliers implementing *their* overseas strategies will have an effect upon the home market which forces strategic and structural changes on their own businesses. Clearly, there are many ways of handling such threats. At one extreme, stated simply, are the "endgame" strategies such as, for example, securing market leadership, exercising more market control for above-average profits, and "harvesting" or "divestment" strategies. At the other extreme is the implementation of a long-term overseas manufacturing strategy to optimize the opportunities in some or all of many diverse and fluctuating overseas markets. In this way it can be seen that international business is not, as a broad concept, a narrow specialist field, but rather a strong conditioning influence on business which can affect even those who seek to eschew it.

That this should be so is the result in broad terms of two main opposing international global forces: on the one hand, the power of what has been graphically described as the 'gravitational effect'—consolidating and giving new strengths to the business interests of the North—in the third world (or in the South), on the other hand, there is the drive for largely imitative development, often closely bound up with national minimum requirements for the security of self-sufficiency and the provision of jobs to bring living standards up above subsistence level.

THE COHESION OF THE NORTH

The statistics of cohesion within the so-called gravitational effect mentioned above and underlined by the Brandt report with its reference to the privileged inner circle of wealth, are that 20 per cent of the North's foreign investment is in foreign hands and this is largely owned by other Northern

Table 1.1. Net Inward Direct Investment to the United Kingdom by Area of Investor (£m)

	1975	1976	1977	1978	1979
European Community	95.7	176.5	267.2	309.9	267.4
EFTA	112.5	81.6	169.7	122.1	252.2
USA	310.0	549.9	635.7	807.1	991.9
Japan	−40.4	−15.7	98.9	−19.7	45.0
Other Countries	136.0	5.7	154.5	72.7	261.8
Total Investment	613.8	798.0	1326.0	1292.1	1818.3

Source: Table adapted from Kenneth Fleet, *Investment into United Kingdom by Third Countries*, Study Commissioned by European League of Economic Co-operation.

investors and that the 25 per cent of the domestic industrial requirements that are imported also come largely from Northern countries.

The generalized pattern of development appears to·have followed three clearly defined phases: between 1945 and 1960 through general investment in industrialized countries; from 1960 to 1972 during which time investment was largely centred on Western Europe's manufacturing sectors; and then from 1973 onwards when the United States of America was the host country for investment following the oil price hike and the subsequent decline of the dollar.

There are many national case histories of foreign investment in the North since host governments are sensitive to the ownership of their industry and keep a watchful eye on trends. Investment in the United Kingdom can serve as an example and the pattern of investment between 1975 and 1979 is shown in Table 1.1.

As a rough and ready comparison with the investment levels in the third world reference can be made to the total investment under various OECD schemes. In 1977 the level of investment was $5,748 m (£3,380 m). That is to say that OECD countries invested about half as much in an island with sixty million inhabitants as they invested in the third world with its combined population of around 3,500 million people.

It is hardly surprising, with such a pattern of investment, that there is a strong correlated pattern of export activity. This is well illustrated in the '*Economist* World Survey' (Fig. 1.1).

The snapshot of exports in Figure 1.1 does not show, however, the impact that developing countries, and the newly developed countries (NICs) in particular, have had in reducing the developed world's share of the export trade. The success stories of countries such as Taiwan, Singapore, Korea, and Hong Kong have open testament in most High Streets and are doubtless enshrined in many overseas representatives' competition reports. The statistical effect of success is, however, generally obscured in global analysis by the fact that NIC exports' values start at very low base levels. Table 1.2 is included to show this development in terms of manufactured goods. The impact of Japan, often described as the original NIC, on two

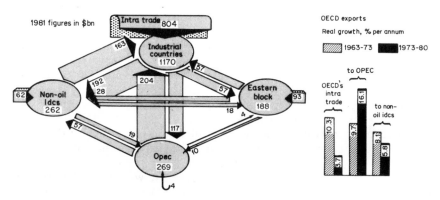

Figure 1.1. How Exports Flow

Source: 'Economist World Survey', *Economist,* 24 Sept. 1983.

Table 1.2. Trade in Manufactured Goods (% Share)

	1961	1969	1978
Japan	5.0	8.3	11.5
UK	12.7	8.6	7.0
USA	17.9	15.5	11.5
Other OECD	33.9	35.0	37.1
Total OECD	69.5	67.4	67.1
Rest of World	30.5	32.6	32.9

Source: Table adapted from *Cambridge Economic Policy Review,* No. 5, Apr. 1979 (Department of Applied Economics, University of Cambridge).

major exporters, the United Kingdom and the United States, is clearly shown, but, equally, the growth in percentage terms of trade from the rest of the world is not particularly noticeable.

The cohesion of the North is partially due to traditional and apparently unshakeable views on investment which give strong weight overall to risk reduction. The devil you know is considered less risky. In such terms the North offers a very sound proposition for there is a general similarity between the Northern countries with regard to markets, purchasing, selling and distribution methods, manufacturing and design techniques, personnel policies, accounting practices, and the underlying principles of business. Japan is, of course, a noticeable exception to the rule.

Further, the setting up of a plant or the revising of production facilities is relatively easy to organize and essential services are readily available. The Legal framework, commercial codes of practices, and product standards and specifications, despite many differences in detail, appear readily recognizable and, as such, hold less fear and therefore less risk.

Within the North the annotation of market values is often done with reference to penetrating a particular segment of an existing market and key decisions concern market share and competitive strengths rather than the more difficult exercise of risk judgement for total market innovation. When investment is a strategic move to protect a market well known through long-term trading as an exporting activity, the risk element may also be considered low.

On the practical side, production costs are readily discernible, the quality of raw materials easily assessed, and a skilled or adaptable labour force at a known cost is available. Overall, factors concerning management and union rituals are also well-enough established to be taken in one's stride.

Credit risk can be reduced because there are well-established records concerning potential customers and ways and means of enforcing terms of trade exist. The cost of money, the machinery of financing, and the impact of taxation are generally well known, understandable, reasonably fair, and consistent.

The foregoing recital of attributes of Northern markets serves to contrast with the obviously higher overall risks of investing in a development country where few of the above factors can be so readily understood, where overall experience is limited, and where risks other than purely commercial ones have to be taken into account.

Alluring as this incestuous Northern investment club can be shown to be, consideration should, however, be given to some of the weaknesses which are beginning to be more apparent. The value which one is prepared to give to such weaknesses and the judgement made of their impact in the longer term will have a strong influence on determining long-term international strategies.

THE WEAKNESSES OF THE NORTH AND THE FALLACY OF EFFICIENCY

The major Northern weakness which has been exposed in the early 1980s is that world industrial interdependence has reached a point where the similarities between markets, which appeared so alluring during growth, have led to severe weaknesses in recession when Northern industrialists have found themselves victims of their own markets and their methods of manufacture to serve them. The concepts of volume and mass production are vulnerable and weighed down by high overheads, expensive capital equipment, and high service costs to improve efficiency in shrinking markets.

Further, the products from such systems are geared to local Northern markets in both price and standards. As such they are often reliant on high-run volumes and lacking in possibilities for range reduction. They therefore cannot be readily switched to alternative markets or respond to alternative strategies at short notice. For these reasons new phrases have crept into commercial terminology as desperation has paraphrased 'exporting' as 'distress selling'.

Once again, within OECD it is Japan that has proved the exception to the rule. In a very telling analysis, Theodore Levitt explains this type of success in terms of companies changing their emphasis from customizing items to offering globally standardized products that are advanced technically, functionally reliable, and low priced. The pace at which such global strategies can be developed and the practicalities preventing companies from pursuing such strategies, once the financial structure is weakened by a crumbling home base and the extent of the risk in competitive markets, will prevent rapid transition—however valid the argument and dire the warning that 'companies that do not adapt to new global realities will become victim of those that do'.

The North's weakness has been accentuated for many companies because prices orientated primarily towards those markets have absorbed the costs of local raw materials which have often turned out to be higher than those available to similar manufacturers in developing countries. Northern industry's skills in efficient production have frequently turned out to be inadequate, particularly in medium- or low-added-value products, to overcome the burden of higher material costs and the inadequacies of physical distribution (internal and external) which often turns out to be the Achilles' heel.

It is possible to argue that Northern industries, in pursuing marketing and production excellence, have paid inadequate attention to the effect of achieving a small percentage saving on the puchasing bill. While pursuing time and cost improvements on the production line, reduction in costs in moving goods has also received insufficient attention. The extent to which these weaknesses are apparent is the price paid for pursuing excellence by specialization, when perhaps a more perceptive judgement would have considered balanced efficiency throughout the whole business.

THE BURDEN OF INNOVATION

After efficiency, innovation is probably considered as the next most important attribute of Northern industry. There are two main aspects to innovation: research and implementation, which perhaps in a more general way is often described as business development.

Supremacy in innovation and technological development is perhaps, on closer examination, however, a prejudiced judgement and there is no natural or national order of intelligence in such matters. In any case, of course common parlance traces many inventions back to earlier Chinese civilizations. The point is perhaps more aptly demonstrated in modern times by just glancing at Appendix I which sets out some of the more important licences in the medical, energy, and metallurgical fields which have been sold by Comecon countries to the United States. John Kiser, who carried out the research, estimated that the number of licences exchanged between Eastern and Western countries since 1965 was, approximately, 1,500 licences and between Western and Eastern countries, 2,500 licences.

This summary is particularly important since the motivation to innovate is clearly based on different business principles in the respective areas.

The high cost of research to Northern companies, and its highly competitive nature, is leading to a more questioning attitude towards the traditional 'hide-and-hold' approach. Ryan and Ford, for example, have analysed the trends and argue strongly that the time has come for companies to consider more seriously marketing technology independently of product application.

The main arguments advanced for developing a company's expertise to exploit the sale of technology are generally considered as:

- Within the time scale necessary for development and application companies' overall strategies can change thereby reducing the value of the research investment.
- Protection of new technology is frequently based on patents which in practice give only limited protection since, given time, most technologies can be copied.
- If a company does not sell technology but if a competitor is prepared to do so, then the company faces competitive challenge without compensating royalty.
- The funds for organizing production capacity for full exploitation when a new technology is ready may not be available from either internal resources or risk financiers.
- It is unlikely that many companies can fully exploit new technologies in world markets as they will face practical difficulties of tariff barriers and cheaper local production.
- Anti-trust legislation may prevent the development of a monopoly position.

Further, there is concern that the costs of research and its implementation may be in conflict with shareholders' views regarding acceptable shorter-term financial returns. In order to justify a full-scale research programme, companies may well have to give value to their technology not only through sales but also through the value of royalties from licences, turnkey deals, and joint ventures. Any shrinkage in the volume available for product sales intensifies the problem; the 1980/3 period was for example, characterized by reducing volumes.

The balanced view between selling or holding technology during the important growth stage of development is given in Table 1.3. Innovation respects no boundaries and is vulnerable to being used uniquely to support products. Dispersal of technology will have a weakening effect on many Northern countries' present-day strategies.

With regard to the profitable application of new technology, or business development, there is no shortage of either commercial or editorial comment or erudite text. The central theme of the writing covers the problems faced by large companies (often claimed to be short of ideas) in trying to be entrepreneurial, and small companies (often claimed to be full of ideas) in trying to handle growth. Business development is fast turning into the

Table 1.3. The Critical Timing Decision During Growth Stage of Development

Factors for Early Sale	Factors against Early Sale
Difficulty of developing new market alone	Low value of technology until proved
Lack of process or support technologies in company	High initial investment by developer
Cash shortage	Need to use production facilities
Importance of achieving standardization	High value added in production
Wide potential application for technology	

Source: Chris Ryan and David Ford, 'Taking Technology to the Market', *Harvard Business Review* (Mar./Apr. 1981). Reprinted by permission of Harvard Business Review. Copyright © 1981 by the President and Fellows of Harvard College; all rights reserved.

modern alchemy of management science with the search for a foolproof method of achieving development progress either by the restructuring of the organization or by the careful ferreting out of suitable people (who are in curiously short supply) who will succeed despite the organization. Once again the comment has to be made that it is the Japanese who have found the most successful formulas for innovation and many texts examine this phenomenon.

A non-exclusive but representative list of written approaches towards successful business development might include:

- Assigning managers on the basis of the stage in the life-cycle that a product has reached.
- Selecting and keeping corporate entrepreneurs.
- Overcoming barriers to product innovation in small firms.
- Using the middle manager as an innovator.
- Designing an innovatory organization.
- Connecting creativity to the corporation.
- Innovation as the source of long-term economic growth.

Practical business people are, of course, aware of the problem and will probably be able to recall more failures than successes in the business development area.

It is therefore clear that the North is faced with problems in the key area of bringing its technology from the test-tube and drawing-board to the market-place.

FINANCIAL PROBLEMS

Attention should finally be drawn towards global financing, since the North has the bulk of the world's monetary resources at its disposal. In simpler terms, one might argue, whatever the other problems are, if you have money you can find a way forward.

Viewed from within its own boundaries it can be argued that the North, by presiding over varying degrees of inflation since the 1960s and then stimulating severe retrenchment to reverse the process, has made little headway in providing a sound economic structure to support a wealth-producing economy which concerns investment in manufacturing, production, jobs, and the overall standard of living and the quality of life. OECD's 34 million unemployed people (1983) were surely sufficient testament in themselves to justify the contention that the North had found no formula for long-term economic effectiveness. The measure of the problem is in business confidence to regenerate and maintain sufficient momentum to achieve adequate growth to underwrite the North's continued development. For reasons mentioned earlier concerning the interdependence of the North and the South, it remains a very open question as to whether or not the North can sustain a growth rate of 3 or 4 per cent in the long term, necessary to enable the South to develop sufficiently to keep pace with the requirements of its natural population growth.

The misuse of financial resource is not, however, confined within the North since in broad terms there can be little doubt that the Northern banks' scramble to lend money to the poor exceeded their prudence. It is possible that the effects of this indiscretion were not even fully recognized since the pace to lend was only blunted in response to the real fear that repayments would not be made and not in response to any logical evaluation. Nevertheless, the IMF's managing director, Dr de Larosiere, and the World Bank president, Mr Tom Clausen, commented, respectively: 'that [some of the larger debtor countries] are fast approaching the limits of social and political tolerance of their adjustment efforts' and 'the economic distress of the poorest nations is a time bomb ticking away'. The fact that there has been more debt rescheduling in the 1982/9 period than in the preceding 25 years further points to the fundamental problems that have to be faced.

The London *Economist* estimated that in the years 1978 to 1981 the poor South received US$28 m more than it was paying to the rich North in interest and capital. In 1982, when the threat of repayment problems was properly recognized, the positive transfer balance shrank back to US$6.6 m. In 1983, however, the transfer balance was reversed with the South paying the North US$11 m when borrowings were around US$88 m but interest and capital repayments totalled US$96 m. In other words, the day of reckoning had arrived—but then it was inevitable that it would. If there is any grain of truth in the argument that the North needs the South to develop to buy its products and to act as its motors of growth, then there can hardly have been a more counter-productive policy and it is difficult to argue that this is a hindsight judgement.

In summary, an attempt has been made to explain the cohesion of the first of the major global forces to be examined—the North. The strengths of the North are self-apparent in comparison with the South and contribute to the cohesion. To improve understanding particular attention has been paid to Northern weaknesses as these constitute threats to the future. The

North's inability to respond to changing markets due to inflexible methods of capital-intensive production has been examined and the difficulties in funding research and implementing new technology have been highlighted. The use of the North's financial muscle, both at home and abroad, appears inadequate and the inability to see the effect of upsetting the balance of interdependence between North and South is a shortcoming. Attention can now be given in equally broad terms to the nature of the other global force—the South.

THE SOUTH

Various labels are applied to the South including 'the Third World', 'the developing world', 'the group of 77' or, more simply, 'the have-nots'. Within such a wide-ranging and different set of states there are, of course, sub-groupings; the most obvious—the oil-producing countries (OPEC) and the non-oil-producing countries (NOPEC)—form the main distinction within the broader Southern grouping. While clearly the economic conditions are not always similar, the South may be identified by the fact the various nations are prepared to co-ordinate their views in seeking to establish a world economic order which they consider to be more just and equitable. A recent book, *The Struggle for Change in International Economic Relations*, by K. B. Lall, Chairman of the Indian Council for Research on International Economic Relations, gives a valuable insight into the development of the thought processes on this subject over the years:

> Their shared historical experience, their persisting backwardness in one sector or another, their subordinate role in world economy and in the prevailing economic system, their common inability to influence its operation or contain its adverse impact, combine them together in the struggle to secure structural change in the international economic order.

This co-ordination of the Southern viewpoint is not wholly self-motivating since the North has been prepared to notify the world at large, during the Bretton Woods Conference in 1944, for example, that there was merit in organizing international economic relations. The conference, taking place before the end of the 1939–45 War, was clearly influenced by a vision of peace. Equally, War governments were in full control of their economies and in international relations, therefore, they foresaw little difficulty in negotiating world economic relationships to mutual benefit. Against a backcloth of low inflation and fixed exchange rates and the hopes for a better world, Maynard Caines and Harry Dexter White negotiated a new world easier to pursue in the 1950s and 1960s but more difficult to maintain in the ensuing age of economic uncertainty.

It would be out of place to consider in detail the month-by-month development of North/South relations. Other writers have covered the subject well since Barbara Ward published her now seminal work on global inequality, *The Rich Nations and the Poor Nations*, in 1962. More recently, of course, there is the Brandt Report and the Trade Policy Research Centre's *Global Strategy for Growth*. Between them, the authors of these works and many others offer reading that goes deep and wide over descriptions, major issues, and possible strategies and reaches peaks of eloquence and erudition for what in both moral as well as economic terms is claimed to be a worthy cause.

In Appendix II, Lall's chronology of main events is given, together with a list of abbreviations, as a set of stepping-stones for the reader who may not be conversant with the full scope of activity or who may wish to place some event in historical perspective.

A broader brush is needed to give substance to the international backcloth in the 1980s. Important is the so-called hard-line Southern view, which has tended to be most strongly argued at times when oil price rises have put the North under greatest stress—stress which has given the South the courage and confidence to state its case clearly and unequivocally. There are three main areas of contention:

Commodities
That the South should have a large share in the processing and marketing of their commodities and that ways and means should be found to stabilize prices. Some limited progress has been made through the international programme for commodities.

Trade
That there should be freedom of trade and access to Northern markets and the dismantling of protectionism.

Finance
That world finances should be restructured to increase resources to meet the South's need to give a greater measure of control over international financial conditions. Specifically, less conditionality over IMF loans, increased allocation of special drawing rights (SDRs), and quotas to the less developed countries.

It is immediately apparent how such demands interact harshly with the North's own problems. Solutions to inflation and recession have a strong relationship upon the volume and prices of commodities. Free trade, the opening of Northern markets, the transfer of technology, and the withdrawal from commodity processing are not easy concepts to follow in the face of actual unemployment (or, in political terms, with the threat of possible unemployment). The allocation of finance for unconditional use is not easy to offer from an overtaxed North where there are businesses which might have to bear the brunt of lost volume from subsidized manufacture from new industries overseas.

In consequence, in the mid-1980s there is a consensus of opinion which concludes that the economic outlook for the South is bleak. This bleakness is all the more important because it marks a halt to progress.

If, as is alleged, the tendency toward Northern right-wing governments pursuing narrow nationalistic policies stops the general progress of the South, the ensuing difficulties will be considerable. The South now attracts around 18 per cent of the world GDP, 28 per cent of world exports, and has seen its gross domestic investment rise to 27 per cent, as well as achieving substantial improvements in saving ratios. But a crucial difference for the South now is that the urban population is about to reach parity with the developed world, following persistent drifts away from the land. In such circumstances, any reversal of the development process will cause hardship and political difficulties on a new scale as city dwellers no longer have the opportunity to alleviate some of the problems of subsistence living by making best use of the land.

An attempt has been made, quite deliberately, to simplify the issues rather than to perpetrate the arrid intellectual debates on world economic order. Also, it is hoped that no undue emphasis has been given to the moral and social issues; in any case they are apparent. What is more important for the international strategist is to have a feeling for the general perspective of the North/South issues as these considerations will shape the policies that will affect future world markets in the widest sense. It is, however, important not to accept the North/South discussion as a monolithic interaction because there are other important forces at work within the framework.

SPECIFIC CO-OPERATION AGREEMENTS BETWEEN NORTHERN AND SOUTHERN COUNTRIES

The EEC, for example, has long offered assistance to countries through the LOME convention. This agreement between 'the Ten' and sixty-six other countries in Africa, the Pacific, and the Caribbean has been in progress for ten years. The negotiations leading up to the renewal in 1985 showed all the signs of strain. General criticism from the North is that aid money is ill-spent and does not reach the poorest countries. There is also a desire to see more commitment to human rights in return for giving aid. The South, on the other hand, feels that aid proposals fluctuate and that aid is declining in real terms as the number of convention countries increases. Further, access to EEC markets leaves much to be desired and the single market of 1992 intensifies the fear. Equally, it is thought that the convention is about economic development and that it is not the correct place to introduce political issues which will cause further delay and distortion to progress.

These charges may be somewhat difficult for the Brussels Headquarters staff to accept as they keep a skilful watch for new industry in many third world countries through their antennae and make a very practical effort to determine business opportunities and assist in their development, often by stimulating joint venture agreements.

Generaly, it is the International Finance Corporation (IFC) which is considered as being the only truly multinational public investment corporation. There would appear to be general acceptance that it is the most active of all corporations of its type, both in terms of the volume of annual commitments and also as regards the association of private investors from developed and developing countries and the number of countries in which it operates. The OECD describes the IFC's activities thus:

> It was set up in 1956 by member countries of the World Bank Group with the purpose of 'furthering economic development by encouraging the growth of productive private enterprise in member countries'. A United Nations Agency like the World Bank, the Corporation is an independent legal entity with its own subscribed capital (some $107 million as of 1st October 1974, subscribed by 100 countries) and its own management and operating staff. Its president and board of directors (20 directors representing the member countries) are the same as the World Bank's. Projects are approved by the Corporation's board of directors. The Corporation has also an advisory board, a panel of six prominent investment bankers from United States, European and Japanese private firms. The panel, which is purely advisory, meets once a year and discusses general policy issues.
>
> The IFC's resources are relatively large and allow considerable financial flexibility in the Corporation's loan operations and in its equity investments. In addition to its share capital, the Corporation is able to borrow from the World Bank for its lending operations up to four times its unimpaired share capital and surplus.* In 1971, the Netherlands government extended a special loan of $5 million to the Corporation on terms that allow it to be used for equity investment. Finally, in recent years, repayments to the Corporation of its own investments, profits from operations and the Corporation's sales of parts of its portfolio to participants have resulted in a relatively high level of internal resources.
>
> During the first decade of its history, the volume of IFC's operations remained at relatively modest levels, largely because until 1961 the Corporation's character prevented direct equity investments. The expansion of IFC's operations was subsequently facilitated by two amendments of its Articles of Agreement. The first amendment, in 1961, removed a restriction on investing in capital stock, thus giving IFC an unusual position among public international institutions. The second amendment, in 1965, permitted IFC to borrow from the World Bank (see preceding paragraph). Thus, in its second decade, IFC had the resources as well as the experience to sustain a higher level of operations and to meet more diversified demands. Since 1965, total annual commitments have increased sharply. Commitments during the financial years 1972, 1973 and 1974 were respectively $115.6 million, $146.7 million and $203.4 million. Several of the Corporation's new investments during these years exceeded $20 million.
>
> In recent years, IFC has been increasingly engaged in large and very large (particularly industrial) projects financed by a consortium of local and international sources (primarily private), where it has played a major role in appraising the projects and helping arrange for overall financing from various sources. It has helped establish, and has influenced the pattern of, a number of large projects (in the cost range of $20 to $245 million), in which local capital is largely associated. For instance, in fiscal year 1974, the Corporation's overall commitment of $203 million was matched by $571 million of commitments from other investors. Of the latter figure, $234 million was provided by

---

* That is, at present, about $690 million.

investors in capital exporting countries and $337 million by investors in developing countries.

Since the late sixties the Corporation has engaged in the direct promotion of prospective investments in priority sectors or countries (e.g. Indonesia). It can also join other investors in special pilot companies intended to initiate large-scale projects.

IFC is primarily committed to industry and agribusiness (approximately 91 per cent of total commitments to 30th June 1974), mining (1 per cent) and local development finance companies (8 per cent) which in turn, invest principally in industry and to a lesser extent in agriculture. Leading investments have taken place in cement, paper, textiles, fertilizers, steel, chemicals, and petrochemicals, machinery, food processing, motor vehicles and accessories, and tourism.

As regards the geographic distribution of its investments, IFC in its early years concentrated on Latin America and the Caribbean (which still took some 44 per cent of total commitments at 30th June 1974). More recently, however, a number of large investments have also been undertaken in Africa, Asia, and the Middle East.

It is IFC's policy not to undertake managerial responsibilities, and equity investments accordingly do not normally exceed 20 to 25 per cent; in large projects they can be well below these figures. IFC is not usually represented on the board of the companies in which it invests, except in the case of development finance companies. The Corporation does not normally provide organized technical and management assistance such as the British CDC, although it does provide on a continuing basis advice and know-how on technical and financial matters through its staff in liaison with its industrial partners.

Besides investing directly with industrial partners in its projects, the Corporation has developed an extensive relationship with international investment banks and financial institutions, which may either be associated directly in the original financing of projects or which may invest in IFC's own paper as 'participants;' to date, over 211 institutions (and over half of them repeatedly) have participated in IFC's own investments.

Finally, IFC has been traditionally concerned with the development of local capital markets and, with the need for the companies it assists, to obtain easier access to local financial resources. This has been done in association with the IBRD, with the development finance companies in which IFC has invested and through its contacts with local banks; through the sale of participations in its investments and through underwriting operations; or through various requirements in financial arrangements such as insistance that sponsors of a new project undertake to make shares available to local investors immediately or eventually. With a view to consolidating and developing its activities in this field, in March 1971, the Corporation set up a new Capital Markets Department which is "specifically designed as the focal point in the (World Bank) Group to encourage the growth of capital markets in the developing countries, "to facilitate the investment of local savings in the productive private enterprise."

Source: M. G. Hansen, *Investing in Developing Countries* (5th edn., 1982 OECD Publications: Paris).

There is also a variety of organizations such as ECOWAS in West Africa, ASEAN in South East Asia, and the Gulf Co-operation Council in the

Middle East, which seek to develop geographical regions. Generally, associations such as these are characterized by their informality in practical terms since national preoccupations tend to make each move a negotiated settlement rather than a response to pure business logic.

The strongest of the geographical associations is clearly the Eastern European grouping of Russia and its six East European allies: COMECON provides a good example of the difficulties of co-ordinating economic effort internationally, even when the political background is a dominant force and relatively stable. Figure 1.2 illustrates the dominance of one country, Russia, and therefore a source of imbalance despite years of planning. The intertrading and the price formulas based on previous years' averages do little to assist in building up hard currency with which to draw in products and/or advanced technology from the West, or to stimulate growth and competitiveness. Countries remain divided, depending upon their strengths and weaknesses, in favour of a tougher planning regime or liberalization.

As one way to solve the problem, Russia has signed trade treaties with countries such as India, in rupee terms. Another, more common, procedure is the countertrade formula which often acts as an impediment when suppliers can find markets with less onerous responsibilities.

Of a less specific nature is the third world Group of 77, which could be considered to represent 'the poor'. It has, however, become clear in recent years that in the deprived areas there are both the poor and the very poor, say thirty-four countries with a GNP per person of less than $410. This has given rise to suggestions that self-help within the group could be more meaningful than North/South help. India, for example, can claim (and with some justification) that it knows more than any Northern country about developing poor economies—India is the seventeenth poorest country in the world and grapples with the problems daily. Significant moves in such alignment of resources within the South could seriously affect Northern growth aspirations.

NATIONAL ECONOMIC PROGRESS

Finally, it is clear that the North/South argument should not be considered a monolithic one. There are many variations on the theme of North/South development and, of course, positive national drives to achieve economic progress through trade, fiscal policies, and by attracting invesment.

Sometimes it will be seen that the third world countries appear to act in concert by following a theme, such as the dislike of multinational companies (MNCs). It has often been considered that MNCs' overriding corporate interests are to the detriment of developing countries. In a limited sense this is undoubtedly true, but the realization is only just beginning to take shape that MNCs often have a better potential for setting up and running overseas businesses than smaller companies. Further, the emotional annoyance and frustration that third world countries feel over their

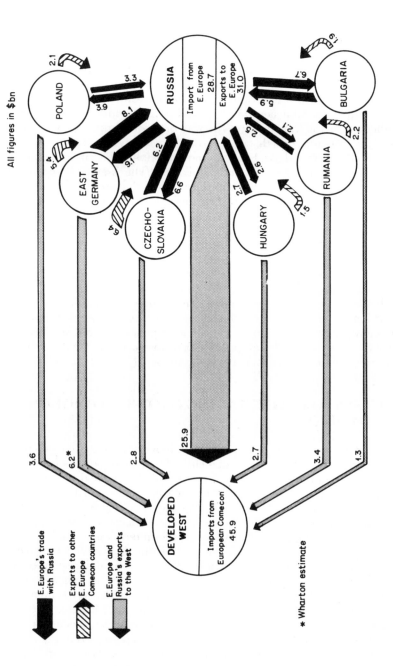

All figures in $bn

Figure 1.2. COMECON's Trade Trials, 1982

Source: Economist, 15 Oct. 1983.

E. Europe's trade
with Russia

Exports to other
E. Europe
Comecon countries

E. Europe and
Russia's exports
to the West

* Wharton estimate

lack of influence over transfer prices and export volumes, for example, are very "small beer" compared with the real and tangible gains in training, work experience, and absorption of the growing number of people trained under various State-sponsored education programmes. A B.Sc. graduate driving a bus, for example, might give rise to a moment's humour but the squandering of resources that this represents is clearly tragic. Further, the frustration from thwarted aspirations can become politically dangerous. The South's general disapproval of MNC's is a good example of how a synthetic principle can stand in the way of progress despite the genuine desire for economic growth.

Local economic and fiscal policies show no similar concensus of opinion. The 1983 World Bank Report makes this clear. The essence of the analysis revolves around price distortion and it is noted that some countries tend towards supporting local industry through restrictions and keeping exchange rates high to combat inflation, but this makes exporting unattractive and borrowing overseas relatively cheap. In broad terms, this was a course followed by Latin American countries and, to a lesser extent, by African countries (but only because they were unable to borrow so lavishly). Asian countries, on the other hand, choose the export path to growth and pay for their import needs out of export earnings.

The result of this analysis shows convincingly that the less the price distortion the greater the growth achievement. It can be argued that Asia was more successful not only because of its policies overall but because other countries had differing policies that, to a certain extent, left them more room to manœuvre in achieving exports.

POLICIES FOR STIMULATING GROWTH THROUGH INVESTMENT

Under either of the broad policies outlined above is the underlying theme of growth through industrial development. The range of policies to achieve this is varied and of considerable interest to the strategic development of international business. Most countries recognize that a portfolio of incentives can be a considerable asset in drawing industrial investors to their countries and this has become an international competitive situation. Usually the incentives are balanced by the imposition of various rules reflecting perceived local economic needs. Overall, there has been a general tendency to limit ownership to outsiders through reserving certain equity rights to local businessmen and giving finer tuning through increasing incentives according to the amount of regional guidance an intending investor will accept for the location of his factory and his commitments towards the export of finished products. Other key areas of concern have been the terms concerning technology transfer, rules governing domestic trading, and the support for local agents. Sometimes special export provisions have been made through the use of export processing zones (EPZs) which have now become a common feature in world trade.

To a lesser degree, industrialized countries have added to the intricacies of 'financial goading' to stimulate overseas investment. In the following Chapter these incentives and the attendant rules will be considered in more detail, as such information is the practical raw data, the considerations of which will influence appraisals of world trade in the future and therefore influence a company's strategy for international development.

In this introductory Chapter consideration has been given in general terms to the established business order as it is perceived by the participants.

Overall, the self-perpetuating and privileged North has been reviewed and some of its key weaknesses exposed in pertinent areas such as flexibility, efficiency, innovation, and development ability. Achievement through the wise use of its undoubted financial resources has also been questioned.

The South has also been considered, in equally broad terms, and its overall intentions to secure more control over world finance, the use of commodities and more freedom in world trade have been noted. Acknowledgement has been made of the fact that North/South considerations are important because of the interaction which is required between the two areas to sustain world economic progress and there are other social and political reasons for wanting to see such progress achieved.

The North/South argument is, however, not a monolithic debate susceptible to resolution through a single breakthrough formula. There are many interwoven and interacting themes that have ebbed and flowed with varying degrees of intensity and support since 1944. To stimulate adjustment of the world's industrial and wealth-producing resources there are many incentives, often tempered by rules reflecting a country's needs and views concerning international competitiveness. Such considerations are of crucial importance when considering international business in the future and, even for non-participants, such considerations can ultimately have an effect on their home-based operations.

Within the theories and rhetoric of the North/South dialogue there are hard practical issues which will grind away at the natural order of world business as it is perceived. Today's conditions do not allow a return to the overall succinctness of the Bretton Woods agreement in 1944: it is now necessary for each business to see its own future with broader horizons. The possible retreat by Northern governments from commitments to wider development issues, if not corrected, may ultimately be judged by history as an unwise political expedient. As chairmen and managing directors usually have a longer tenure of office than Prime Ministers, it would be unwise for them, perhaps, not to address themselves to these problems.

References

1 Leslie M. Dawson, 'Opportunities for Small Businesses in Third World Markets: A Market Segmentation Approach', *American Journal of Small Business*, 7 (1982).

2 Harrigan and Porter, 'End Game Strategies for Declining Industries', *Harvard Business Review* (July/Aug. 1983).

3 Jacqueline Grapin, ' "Gravitational Effect" Binds Economies of Rich Countries to One Another', *The Times Europa Supplement*, 3 Feb. 1981.

4 *North-South: A Programme for Survival*, Report of the Independent Commission on International Development (Pan Books: London, 1980) (Brandt Report).

5 *Investing in Developing Countries*. (4th edn. OECD Publications: Paris).

6 Theodore Levitt, 'The Globalization of Markets', *Harvard Business Review* (May/June 1983).

7 Ryan and Ford, 'Taking Technology to the Market', *Harvard Business Review* (Mar./Apr. 1981).

8 See Jeffrey Kerr, 'Assigning Managers on the Basis of the Life Cycle', *Journal of Business Strategy* (Antar Extract ZN75); H. E. Kierulff, 'Finding and Keeping Corporate Entrepreneurs', *Business Horizons* (Antar Extract SN65); Adam Adams, 'Barriers to Product Innovation in the Small Firm', *European Small Business Journal* 1.1 (Antar Extract AN94); K. J. Schmidt Tiedeman, 'A New Model for the Innovation Process', *Research Management* (Mar. 1982); R. M. Konter, 'The Middle Manager as Motivator', *Harvard Business Review* (July/Aug. 1982); J. R. Galbraith, 'Designing the Innovatory Organization', *Amacom: Division of American Management Association* (1982); E. B. Roberts and A. R. Fusfield, 'Staffing the Innovative Technology-Based Organization', *Sloan Management Review* (Spring 1981); D. R. Moody, 'The Corporate Creative Connection: Key to Innovation', *Mechanical Engineering* (June 1980); C. F. Ray, 'Innovation is the Source of Long Term Economic Growth', *Long Range Planning* (Apr. 1980).

9 'Beggering the Poor', *Economist* (19 Feb. 1984); 'Economist World Economic Survey', ibid. 24 Feb. 1984.

10 K. B. Lall, The Struggle for Change in International Economic Relations (Allied Publishers Private Ltd.).

11 (W. W. Norton: London, 1962).

12 See above n. 4.

13 *Global Strategy for Growth: A Report on North/South Issues*, Trade Policy Research Centre (London, 1981).

APPENDIX I[a]

Licences Recently Sold to United States by COMECON Countries

	Technology	Buyer	Seller
Medical biochemical	Surgical stapling guns	US Surgical 3M	USSR
	Soft contact lens	National Patent Development	Czechoslovakia
	Anticancer drugs	Bristol-Myers	USSR
	Cardiovascular drug	Squibb	German Democratic Republic
	Psychotropic drug	American Home Products	USSR
	Method for producing calcium pantothenate	Diamond Shamrock	German Democratic Republic
	Cardiovascular drug	DuPont	German Democratic Republic
	Vitride chemical reducing agent	National Patent Development	Czechoslovakia
Energy	In situ coal gasification	Texas Utilities Services	USSR
	Heller Forgo dry cooling process	Babcock and Wilcox	Hungary
	Method for making armoured drilling hoses	Gates Rubber	Hungary
	OSO dewatering screen for coal	National Standard	Poland
Metallurgy	Elactromagnetic casting of aluminium	Kaiser Aluminium & Chemical Reynolds Aluminium Alcoa	USSR
	Roller dies	Harrisburg Steel	Hungary
	Electromagnetic casting of copper	Olin	USSR
	Method for titanium nitriding of tool steels	Multiarc Vacuum Systems	USSR
	Magnetic impact bonding	Maxwell Laboratories	USSR
	Flash butt welding	J.R. McDermott	USSR
	Evaporative stave cooling of blast furnaces	Andco	USSR
Miscellaneous	Rock hammer Hefti	Joy Manufacturing	USSR
	Pneumatic trenching tool 'Hole Hog'	Allied Steel & Tractor	USSR
	Hydrocyclone 'Triclean'	Bird Manufacturing	Czechoslovakia
	Spray printing of carpets	Deering Mifliken	German Democratic Republic
	Inertial core crusher for extra hard rocks	Rexnord	USSR

[a] John N. Kiser III, 'Tapping Eastern Bloc Technology', *Harvard Business Review* (Mar./Apr. 1982). Reprinted by permission of *Harvard Business Review*. Copyright © 1982 by the President and Fellows of Harvard College; all rights reserved.

Appendix II[a]

Chronology of Main Events in International Economic Relations, 1955–1982

Year	Date and Month	Event
1955	17 Feb.	ECOSOC Resolution to establish a Permanent Advisory Commission on International Commodity Trade
	18–24 Apr.	Bandung Conference
1956	July	International Finance Corporation established under World Bank auspices
	13–19 July	Nehru–Tito–Nasser Conference at Brioni, Yugoslavia
1957	25 Mar.	Treaty signed in Rome by Belgium, France, Federal Republic of Germany, Luxembourg, Italy, and the Netherlands which later led to the formation of the Common Market
1958	1 Jan.	EEC (or the Common Market) established
	16 Nov.	Indo-Soviet Rupee Payment Trade Agreement signed; valid for five years
1959	8 Apr.	Trade Agreement with Japan comes into force
	20–1 July	Ministerial Conference of the Seven proposing formation of EFTA (Austria, Denmark, Norway, Portugal, Sweden, Switzerland, and the UK) Aid India Consortium formed
1960	3 May	EFTA formed
	Sept.	IDA established under the World Bank
	10 Sept.	OPEC established. First Conference in Baghdad, Iraq
	Nov.	BENELUX (Belgium, the Netherlands and Luxembourg) formed
1961	18 Feb.	Latin American Free Trade Association (LAFTA) formed
	Sept.	OEEC replaced by OECD; US and Canada join
	1–6 Sept.	Belgrade: First Summit of Non-Aligned countries
1962	Jan.	Establishment of the Indian Mission to the EEC
1963	25 May	OAU established
1964	23 Mar.–16 June	UNCTAD-I at Geneva
	4 May	Beginning of the Kennedy Round of Negotiations
	5–10 Oct.	Cairo: Second Summit of the Non-Aligned countries
	Nov.	OPEC Conference, Jakarta; OPEC Economic Commission formed
	Dec.	UN General Assembly adopted the Resolution, set up the Trade and Development Board as a permanent body
1965	5–30 Apr.	First Session of the Trade and Development Board Committee on Commodity Trade set up in pursuance of the General Assembly Resolution of 30 Dec. 1964 and the First Act adopted by UNCTAD-I
	Oct.	Asian Development Bank (ADB) established
1966	30 June	Kennedy Round Tariff Cuts Agreement, signed in Geneva by forty-six participating nations
1967	1 July	Merger of the three European Communities, namely ECSC, EEC and EAEC
	7 Aug.	ASEAN formed; replaces the ASA

[a] Adapted from K. B. Lall, *The Struggle for Change in International Economic Relations* (Allied Publishers Private Ltd.).

Year	Date and Month	Event
	25 Sept.	IMF meeting in Rio de Janeiro; agreement on the plan for creation of a new international monetary unit of SDRs
	24 Oct.	Charter of Algiers adopted by the Group of 77
1968	1 Feb.–29 Mar.	UNCTAD-II in New Delhi
	26 July	Arusha Agreement establishing an Association between EEC and the East African Community
	Sept.	OAPEC established
1969	Apr.–22 May	UN Conference on Law of Treaties. Vienna adopts the Vienna Declaration
	28 July	SDRs announced by IMF
	15 Sept.	*Partnership in Development:* Report of the Commission on International Development, headed by Lestor B. Pearson, submitted to President, International Bank for Reconstruction and Development
1970	1 Jan.	First allocation of SDRs made in total amount equivalent to US $3500 million
	8–10 Sept.	Lusaka: Third Summit of Non-Aligned countries
	Dec.	OPEC Conference, Caracas
	Dec.	Kabul Declaration on Asian Co-operation
1971	1 Jan.	Breakdown of Negotiations between OPEC and Oil Companies
	Feb.	OPEC Conference in Tehran: five-year agreement between six producing countries
	1–8 June	UNIDO-I, Vienna
	July	OPEC Conference, Vienna: Nigeria admitted
	16 Aug.	Second Trade and Transit Agreement signed with Nepal
	18 Dec.	Smithsonian Agreement providing for realignment of exchange rates among major currencies
1972	1 Jan.	Final reduction in tariffs (as per Kennedy Round) implemented
	Jan.	Meeting between OPEC and oil companies, Geneva (The Geneva Agreement)
	13 Apr.–21 May	UNCTAD-III. Santiago
1973	1 Jan.	UK, Ireland, and Denmark join EEC
	Apr.	OPEC meeting at Cairo; Second Geneva Agreement; Oil price raised by 11%
	5–9 Sept.	Fourth Non-Aligned Summit. Economic Declaration Action Programme for Economic Co-operation adopted
	12–14 Sept.	Declaration on Tokyo Round
	16 Oct.	OPEC Conference, Vienna. Rise in posted price by 70% from US $3.01 to $5.11 per barrel
	17 Dec.	India–EEC Commercial Co-operation Agreements effective from 1 Apr. 1974
	23 Dec.	OPEC Conference, Tehran. Further rise in price by 130% to US $11.65 a barrel
1974	1 Apr.	Indo-EEC Commercial Co-operation Agreement comes into force
	1 May	UN adopts Declaration on NIEO
	20–31 May	Sixth Sessions of the Special Committee on Preferences in Geneva. Discussion and second annual review of the operation and effects of GSP
	June	OPEC meeting, Quito. Rise in royalties of oil companies. IMF Oil Facility established
	15 Sept.	IMF provides Extended Fund Facility
	6 Nov.	UNCTAD Intergovernmental Group to evaluate progress of LDCs

Year	Date and Month	Event
	2 Dec.	Adoption of Charter of Economic Rights and Duties by the UN General Assembly
	5 Dec.	Economic and Social Council establishes a Commission on TNCs
1975	3–8 Feb.	Conference of Developing Countries on Raw Materials, Dakar, Senegal
	28 Feb.	Lome Convention between EEC and ACP countries, Togo
	12–26 Mar.	UNIDO-II, Lima, Peru
	17 Mar.	3rd Session on Law of the Sea, Geneva
	26 Mar.	Lima Declaration and Plan of Action on Industrial Development and Co-operation recommends setting up of the UN Industrial Development Fund
	9 Apr.	OPEC institutes US $25,000 million fund for mutual financial assistance and co-operation between OECD countries
	25 Aug.–16 Sept.	Seventh Session of the UN General Assembly endorses the Lima Declaration
	1 Nov.	Asian Clearing Union commences operations in Tehran
	3 Nov.	UN Centre on TNCs comes into existence
1976	26 Jan.	Third Ministerial meeting of the Group of 77 at Manila (Manila Declaration)
	28 Jan.	OPEC Special Fund established
	5–31 May	UNCTAD-IV, Nairobi
	May	Operations under IMF's Oil Facility conducted
	16–19 Aug.	Colombo; fifth Summit of the Non-Aligned countries
	6–19 Dec.	Conference on International Economic Co-operation (CIEC) at Paris
	Dec.	OPEC Conference, Qatar, 15% rise in price of oil
1977	7–8 Feb.	First Session of Committee on ECDC, Geneva
	Mar.–Apr.	UN Negotiating Conference on Common Fund
	2 June	Conclusion of CIEC, Paris
	29 Sept.	Meeting of Ministers of Foreign Affairs of Group 77 at New York
	Dec.	OPEC Conference, Caracas. Disagreement between the moderates (Saudi Arabia) and extremists (Libya) over oil price hike
1978	May	OPEC Conference, Saudi Arabia. Production ceilings of members lowered
	24 July–Aug.	Meeting of experts to examine the effects of World Inflationary Development, Geneva
	30 Aug.–12 Sept.	UN Conference on Technical Co-operation among Developing Countries, Buenos Aires
1979	Mar.–Apr.	Final stage of the Tokyo Round on Tariffs
	7 May–3 June	UNCTAD-V, Manila
	3 Sept.	Havana Summit of the Non-Aligned countries
	10 Dec.	International Energy Association, Ministerial Meeting, Paris; further steps to stabilize oil prices
	20 Dec.	North-South: A Programme for Survival, Report of the Independent Commission on International Development Issues under the chairmanship of Willy Brandt submitted
1980	1 Jan.	Tokyo Round Tariff reductions, as agreed upon by GATT, commenced
	21 Jan.–8 Feb.	UNIDO-III, New Delhi
	June-Oct.	UNCTAD's Common Fund programme for the Integrated Commodity Programme discussed and formulated
1981	1 Jan.	Proclamation by the UN of the Third Development Decade and formulation of an International Development Strategy
	23 June	Indo-EEC Economic Co-operation Agreement

Year	*Date and Month*	*Event*
	10–21 Aug.	Nairobi Conference on New and Renewable Sources of Energy
	1–14 Sept.	UN Conference on the 31 least developed countries, Paris. Adoption of a wide-ranging Substantial New Programme of Action (SNPA)
	5 Nov.	Cancun Summit
1982	22 Feb.	New Delhi consultations
	30 Apr.	Draft on the Law of the Sea finalized

Abbreviations

ADB	Asian Development Bank
ASEAN	Association of South East Asian Nations
CIEC	Conference on International Economic Co-operation
CMEA	Council for Mutual Economic Assistance
DAC	Development Assistance Committee (of OECD)
DCs	Developed Countries
DD	Development Decade
ECAFE	Economic Commission for Asia and the Far East
ECDC	Economic Co-operation among Developing Countries
ECLA	Economic Commission for Latin America
ECOSOC	Economic and Social Council (of the UN)
EEC	European Economic Community
EFTA	European Free Trade Association
ESCAP	Economic and Social Council for Asia and the Pacific
FAO	Food and Agriculture Organization
GATT	General Agreement on Trade and Tariffs
GNP	Gross National Product
GSP	Generalized System of Preferences
IAEA	International Atomic Energy Agency
IBRID	International Bank for Reconstruction and Development (World Bank)
IDA	International Development Agency
ILO	International Labour Organization
IMF	International Monetary Fund
ITO	International Trade Organization
LAFTA	Latin American Free Trade Association
MFA	Multi Fibre Agreement
MFN	Most Favoured Nation
MSACs	Most Seriously Affected Countries
MTN	Multilateral Trade Negotiations
NIEO	New International Economic Order
NPT	Nuclear Non-Proliferation Treaty
NTB	Non-Tariff Barriers
OAPEC	Organization of Arab Petroleum Exporting Countries
OAU	Organization of African Unity
ODA	Official Development Assistance
OEEC	Organization for European Economic Co-operation
TCDC	Technical Co-operation among Developing Countries
TNC	Transnational Corporations
UNCTAD	United Nations Conference on Trade and Development
UNDP	United Nations Development Programme
UNESCO	United Nations Educational Scientific and Cultural Organization
UNIDO	United Nations Industrial Development Organization

2

Incentives and Risks

In Chapter 1, the broad issues facing the world in which businesses have to operate were examined, and the convention of a wealthy and cohesive North, sometimes opposed to and sometimes understanding of the poorer South, was used.

This Chapter will consider the ways and means employed through investment and export incentives to redress or maintain the North/South balance.

INCENTIVES

Given that the South wants to encourage work-sharing with the North, which is a theme which ultimately has to affect the determination of business strategies, it is appropriate to consider the efforts which are being made to encourage established businesses to set up production facilities overseas.

The presentation in detail of all world investment conditions would be too cumbersome and specific for a book of this nature. Further, the subject-matter is constantly changing and heavily reliant on the careful weighting of government intent and local custom and practice proved through test cases. Detailed presentation is therefore better left to specialist reading-matter which offers readers frequent updating.

An alternative way of looking at investment incentives is through 'business eyes', by attempting to answer some basic questions which might be asked at an early stage, on a country-by-country basis. The questions that have been selected as being of most general value are:

1. What level of equity participation is available for a non-resident company?
2. Is it possible to remit profits freely?
3. What rates of corporation tax apply?

4. How easy is it to set up new businesses?
5. Are patents respected?
6. What incentives are available?
7. What is the interstate tax treaty situation? (dealt with in detail in Chapter 10)

Even in undertaking such a survey, there are considerable difficulties in making fair comparisons between countries, particularly when bureaucratic jargon, sometimes inadequately translated, is at variance with reported experience and when some Commercial Counsellors let political considerations overpower straightforward explanation. The comparison of 'lump sum taxes' against straightforward percentage taxes and the task of grouping the infinite variety of concessions (often drafted to allow for negotiation) also cause difficulties. It is therefore inevitable that a subjective view or intuitive judgement will intrude from time to time. The overall objective of showing the scope of both advantages and limitations in key business areas should, however, assist in understanding the forces that condition business appreciation.

The assumption is also made that, following the determination of interest in any area through this style of macro research, specific detailed analysis will be undertaken for a particular business and product, and that a determined effort will also be made to research and assess the effects of any likely changes. In this respect attention is particularly drawn to the considerations of risk outlined in the final part of this Chapter.

The most common specific incentives offered by countries to encourage overseas investors to set up in a territory can be divided into the following groups:

(1) Cash grants and interest-free loans;
    Subsidized loans;
    Interest payment subsidies;
    Investment guarantees, guarantees for finance and working capital;
    Interest-free loans converted to grants (in time).

(1a) Grants for energy-saving equipment;
    Grants for anti-pollution equipment;
    Grants for improved working conditions;
    Training grants;
    Production start-up grants;
    Relocation grants.

(2) Tax holidays (tax exemption);
    Reduced taxes;
    Reduction in tax for expatriates employed locally;
    Tax treaties with other countries;
    Carry forward of tax losses;
    Tax waiver on undistributed/reinvested profits;
    Favourable treatment for loan applications;
    Free import of equipment and/or raw materials;

Social security, etc. contribution waivers;
Investment allowances;
Tax credits;
Accelerated depreciation.

(3) Free or subsidized land;
Free or subsidized buildings;
Subsidized housing;
Subsidized energy.

(4) Tariff protection;
Preference for local manufacturers in government tenders.

(5) Assisted or free feasibility studies;
R & D grants, or allowable against tax.

(6) Transport grants;
Subsidized transport and rail freights.

These groups correspond to the circled numbers in Figure 2.1, which shows incentives to investors in countries divided into Northern and Southern areas. Where possible an indication is given (countries marked 'R') of those countries whose policy is only to provide incentives to investors accepting guidance on location.

Figure 2.2 shows the percentage of equity participation that an overseas investor is allowed to hold, together with an indication of the ease with which profits can be repatriated, and Figure 2.3 shows the rate of corporation tax applicable and the application of withholding tax to externalized dividends. On these same maps an indication is also given as to whether or not the country has organized its administrative facilities in such a way as to make it easy to set up in business, and whether or not patents are strongly protected.

When consideration is given to setting up a business overseas, the question as to whether the market can absorb the output of the plant, is crucially important, especially in view of the difficulty involved in effective market research in developing countries. Generally in such countries, more assumptions have to be made than is the case in better-defined and more mature markets. Moreover, where the perceived opportunity is geared to an early participation in an emerging or growing market, it is often the case that the size of the plant cannot be sensibly reduced further, and the market has to equal output if adequate returns are to be achieved. In such circumstances, easy local exports act as a strong incentive and safety-valve for the project as a whole.

In addition, host countries often attribute a high value in their order of economic priorities to export earnings which help to offset the currency outgoings for the industrialization process. This coincidence of policy requirements between businesses and governments leads to export incentives being a very active area.

The most common incentives available for export activity can be similarly divided into groups and the following groups correspond to the boxed numbers in Figure 2.1, which gives a good overall view of competition between countries both to attract exporters and protect their own industries.

[1] Overseas market entry support costs;
    Research grants;
    Grants for overseas promotional activity;
    Subsidy for employing export staff;
    Direct assistance from government offices overseas.

[2] Insurance cover and export credit schemes.

[3] Duty and tax exemption or remissions on goods exported;
    Duty and tax exemption or remission on equipment required for export manufacturing;
    Subsidized interest on bank loans for exports;
    Preferential bank loans;
    Rebates on FOB values;
    Exemption from social security payments;
    Special depreciation allowances;
    Double deduction of export expenses against tax;
    Special exchange rates;
    Tax bonus schemes.

[4] Retention of all export income for more export activity, e.g. purchase of imported raw materials;
    Insurance against increased manufacturing costs;
    Finance for stockholdings overseas;
    Guarantees on exchange rate tests for overseas stockholdings;
    Expansion/development grants and loans for export manufacture;
    Loans for foreign exchange and raw materials;
    Rights to hold overseas bank accounts;
    Higher percentages of equity holdings for high exporting companies.

The importance of the 'export incentive game' is clearly recognized on an international basis. Government officials from all over the world met in Geneva in May 1981 to discuss the feasibility of an agreement establishing an international export guarantee facility. The purpose was to enable developing countries to offer credit terms in foreign currencies similar to those already offered to exporters from developed countries. The discussions, sponsored by the United Nations Conference on Trade and Development (UNCTAD), are being viewed with some concern by the developed world, which not only stands to suffer market erosion from such a scheme but which would also be the main source of the funds needed to set up and maintain it.

Export incentives are further intensified by the increasing development of export processing zones (EPZs). A London *Economist* Intelligence Unit Report lists and analyses the zones in considerable detail. A distinction is

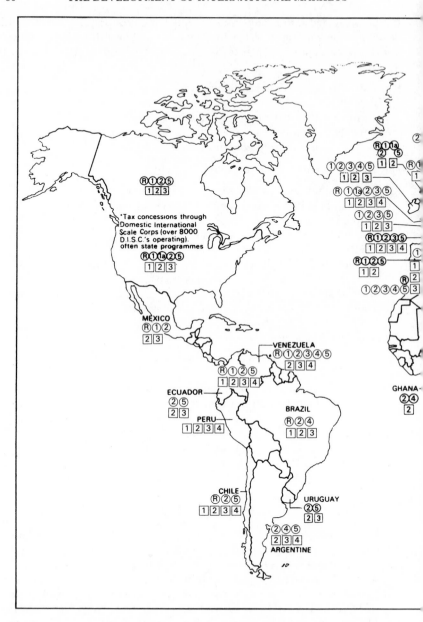

Figure 2.1. Map showing world export and investment incentives.
○: investment incentives (®: "regionalized" incentives);
□: export incentives (see pp. 28–29).

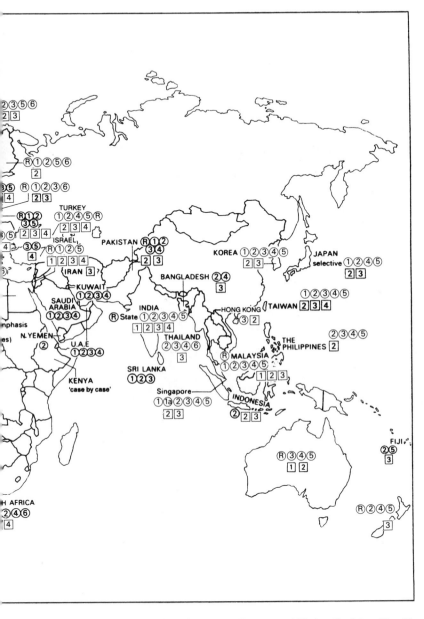

Business International Corporation's, *Investing, Licensing and Trading Conditions Abroad* is a useful source of more detailed information on these matters.

Figure 2.2. Maps showing the percentage of equity participation that an overseas investor is allowed to hold. Shaded areas indicate freedom of remittance of profits (the heavier the shading the greater the freedom)

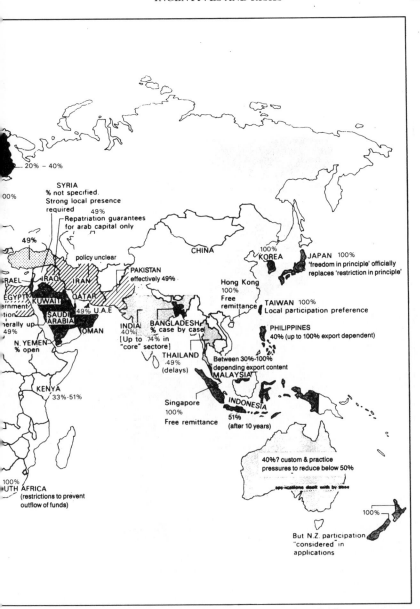

20% – 40%

SYRIA
% not specified.
Strong local presence
required   49%
          Repatriation guarantees
          for arab capital only

49%

policy unclear

CHINA

100%
KOREA

JAPAN 100%
'freedom in principle' officially
replaces 'restriction in principle'

PAKISTAN
effectively 49%

Hong Kong
100%
Free
remittance   TAIWAN 100%
               Local participation preference

RAEL

IRAQ   IRAN

EGYPT
KUWAIT
SAUDI   49% U.A.E
ARABIA
OMAN

QATAR

INDIA
40%
[Up to 74% in
"core" sectore]

BANGLADESH
% case by case

PHILIPPINES
40% (up to 100% export dependent)

ernment
tion
erally up
49%

N. YEMEN
% open

THAILAND
.49%
(delays)

Between 30%-100%
depending export content
MALAYSIA

KENYA
33%-51%

Singapore
100%
Free remittance

INDONESIA
51%
(after 10 years)

100%
UTH AFRICA
(restrictions to prevent
outflow of funds)

40%? custom & practice
pressures to reduce below 50%

100%
But N.Z. participation
"considered" in
applications

Business International Corporation's, *Investing, Licensing and Trading Conditions Abroad* is a
useful source of more detailed information on these matters.

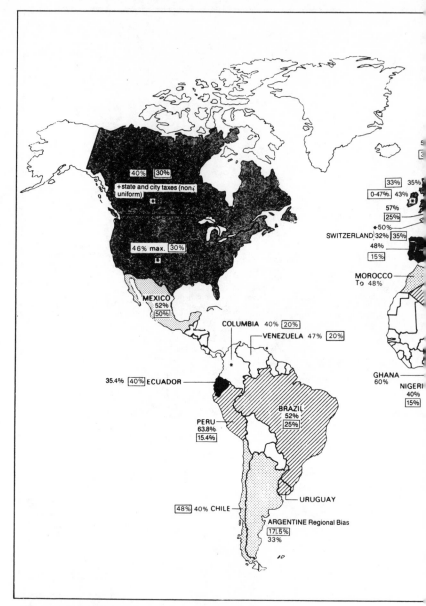

Figure 2.3. Maps showing (approximate) applicable percentage rate of corporation tax, and ([%]) application of withholding tax to externalized dividends. ★ indicates strong, protective patent and licensing systems. The shading indicates the degree of setting-up support (or lack of hindrance): the darker the shading, the greater the support.

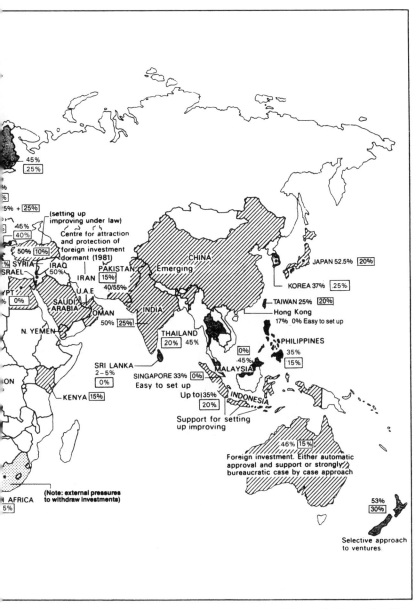

45%
25%

%
%

5% + 25%
                    (setting up
45%   improving under law)
40%   Centre for attraction
                    and protection of
50% 10%   foreign investment
% SYRIA IRAQ   dormant (1981)
SRAEL   PAKISTAN   CHINA
          50%   Emerging   JAPAN 52.5% 20%
         IRAN
PT   U.A.E 40/55%   KOREA 37% 25%
% 0%   SAUDI
         ARABIA   TAIWAN 25% 20%
         OMAN   INDIA   Hong Kong
N. YEMEN   50% 25%   17% 0% Easy to set up
                  THAILAND
                  20% 45%   PHILIPPINES
         SRI LANKA   0%   35%
ON   2–5%   -45%   15%
         0%   SINGAPORE 33% 0% MALAYSIA
              Easy to set up
KENYA 15%   Up to 35%   INDONESIA
               20%
              Support for setting
              up improving

                              46% 15%
                    Foreign investment. Either automatic
                    approval and support or strongly
                    bureaucratic case by case approach

         (Note: external pressures
AFRICA   to withdraw investments)   53%
5%   30%

                                         Selective approach
                                         to ventures.

Business International Corporation's *Investing, Licensing and Trading Conditions Abroad* is a
useful source of more detailed information on these matters.

MEDITERRANEAN & MIDDLE EAST

Cyprus	Syria
Larnaca	Adhra
Egypt	Latakia
Cairo·	Tartus
Alexandria	Aleppo
Suez	Deraa
Port Said	Damascus (2)
Red Sea Zone	
Jordan	
Aqaba	
Zarqa	
Jordanian/Syrian Frontier Zone	
Queen Alia International Zone	

CARIBBEAN & CENTRAL AMERICA

Dominican Republic	Costa Rica
La Romana	Moin
San Pedro de Macosis	Santa Rosa
Herrera	**El Salvador**
San Cristobel	San Bartolo
Barahona	**Guatemala**
Puerto plato	Santo Tomas
Santiago	**Honduras**
Haina	Puerto Cortes
Jamaica	**Mexico**
Kingston	Border Zones (USA frontier area)
Puerto Rico	**Nicaragua**
Mayagöez	Las Mercedes
	Panama
	Colon

SOUTH AMERICA

Brazil
Manaus
Chile
Iquique
Punta Arenas
Colombia
Barrcenquilla
Santa Marta
Cartagena
Manuel Carvajal
Buenaventura

Figure 2.4. Export Processing Zones

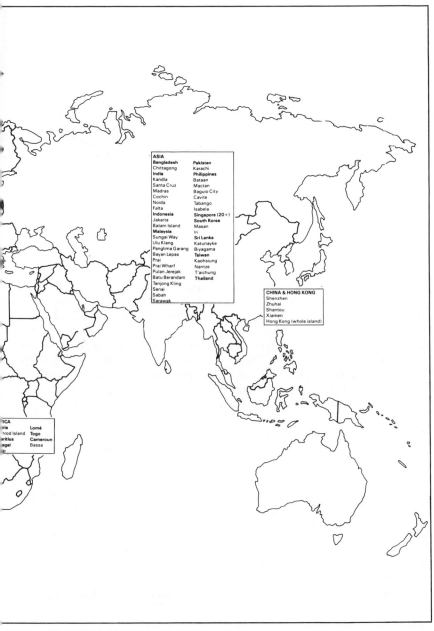

ASIA

Bangladesh	**Pakistan**
Chittagong	Karachi
India	**Philippines**
Kandla	Bataan
Santa Cruz	Mactan
Madras	Baguio City
Cochin	Cavite
Noida	Tabango
Falta	Isabela
Indonesia	**Singapore** (20+)
Jakarta	**South Korea**
Batam Island	Masan
Malaysia	Iri
Sungai Way	**Sri Lanka**
Ulu Klang	Katunayke
Panglima Garang	Biyagama
Bayan Lepas	**Taiwan**
Prai	Kaohsiung
Prai Wharf	Nantze
Pulan Jerejak	T'aichung
Batu Berandam	**Thailand**
Tanjong Kling	
Senai	
Sabah	
Sarawak	

CHINA & HONG KONG
Shenzhen
Zhuhai
Shantou
Xiamen
Hong Kong (whole island)

PICA
ria   Lomé
nrod Island Togo
aritius   Cameroun
egal   Bassa

Source: Based on information from Jean Currie, *Special Report No. 64: Investment: the growing role of export processing zones* (1979) and *Export Processing Zones in the 1980s: custom free manufacturing* (1985), The Economist Intelligence Unit, London W.1.

drawn between commercial free trade zones, of which 344 are recorded world-wide, and zones where manufacture takes place under duty-free conditions. While EPZs are not unknown in developed countries, they occur mainly in the South. In 1984, seventy-nine significant activity centres were noted and are shown in the map in Figure 2.4; the growth pattern of EPZs is examined in detail in Table 2.1.

To put EPZ activity in context, it is estimated that by mid-1984 approximately 500,000 people were employed in the Asian zones, 150,000 in the Central American zones, and, say, 100,000 in the Caribbean zones. EPZs have tended to concentrate on electronic and textile and clothing manufactures, which represent 30 per cent and 20 per cent of manufacturing activity world-wide, respectively.

Originally, there was a strong emphasis in setting up EPZs to stimulate exports, but some countries have tended to change their approach to attract high-technology industries to their area. From a strategic point of view the importance of EPZ activity in developing a skilled workforce with nearby supporting services should not be overlooked. It is difficult to maintain any argument concerning manufacturing or commercial inadequacy, if across a theoretical 'frontier' nationals from the same country are making high-technology components for the world market.

The extent of these exporting incentives draws attention to the degree to which world exports are 'subsidized'. Exporting in the future, it can readily be assumed, will become an increasingly competitive field unless the potential of the world's currently undeveloped markets can give rise to opportunities faster than the 'Newly Industrializing Countries' can swallow them up. The moment any new manufacturer loses his first overseas order he will turn to his government for treatment comparable to that offered to his competitors by their governments. 'Stalemate', although not inevitable, is certainly a strong possibility.

This situation underlines the need for the most careful consideration of forward strategies: to see to what extent there is a need to integrate overseas manufacturing into a company's business activity to make full use of product, process, and technological life-cycles.

These theories are dealt with in greater detail in Chapter 4. Summarized, these international cycles propose: the extension of a product's valuable life by overseas manufacturing; the manufacture of components in different international locations to optimize the overall cost of production; and the offsetting of R & D costs from the initial stage by planned use of international markets for revenue returns.

Acknowledgement has already been given to the imperfections involved in portraying such a variety of information in such a simplified form, but, overall, the information in this Chapter provides data that allow the following conclusions to be drawn:

1. That there is a positive movement on the part of the developed countries to encourage private investors to set up overseas.
2. That export incentives have reached a significantly high and sophisti-

Table 2.1. Overview of Growth in Export Processing Zones (EPZs) 1979–1984

Location	No. of Zones by 1979	Estimated No. of Industrial Projects*	No. of Zones by 1984	Estimated No. of Projects*
Asia				
Bangladesh	–	–	1	N.A.
China	–	–	4	3000
Hong Kong (Zones only)	–	–	2	40
India	2	72	6	203
Indonesia	–	–	2	18 (plus incorporated)
Malaysia	10	63	10	85
Pakistan	–	–	1	43
Philippines	3	N.A.	6	64
Singapore	general	N.A.	general	1500
South Korea	2	100	2	186 (1059 nationally)
Sri Lanka	1	46	2	193
Taiwan	3	267	3	263 (capital investment and exports up say 100%)
Thailand	–	–	1	8
Mediterranean and Middle East				
Cyprus	–	–	1	1
Dubai	–	–	1	N.A.
Jordan	1	N.A.	3	N.A.
Syria	5	N.A.	7	N.A.
Tunisia	–	–	National (14)	N.A.
Africa				
Liberia	1	N.A.	1	N.A.
Mauritius	National	89	National	156
Senegal	1	5	1	N.A.
Caribbean and Central America				
All Countries	15	43	15	129
Mexico (Mainly USA border zones)	7	500	7	531 (many closures and new set ups)
South America				
Brazil	1	4+	1	200+
Chile	1	N.A.	2	N.A.
Columbia	7	28	6	56+

* Project information is not always directly comparable as some zones include applications as well as established operations; some zones also incorporate existing businesses or have the authority to allow start-ups in other agreed locations.

Source: Special Report No. 64: Investment: the growing role of export processing zones (1979) and *Export Processing Zones in the 1980s: custom free manufacturing* (1985), The Economist Intelligence Unit, London W.1.

cated level of development and that exporting will become increasingly competitive.

3. That investors can enjoy considerable financial incentives when setting up overseas. Incentive levels are frequently governed by location criteria.

4. That the inducements offered reflect political as well as economic needs by generally requiring that some of the equity of new businesses is in local hands and that to this extent joint ventures are mandatory.

5. That the most liberal countries are those that are already developed.

6. That, generally, governments find difficulties in maintaining complete freedom for the repatriation of profits.

7. That withholding tax is a common feature, but that tax treaties already strongly evident in the developed world are becoming more widespread. There still remains, however, a strong incentive carefully to channel funds and profits to harvest tax benefits.

8. That the general level of corporate taxation throughout the world is high, and the effect on an inefficient business when a tax holiday ceases could be considerable.

9. That there is not a strong respect for patents in the underdeveloped world, and recompense for technological input is more readily obtained through a negotiated share of the profits from a successful business.

From the outset a view can therefore be taken that the general backcloth, explored in Chapter 1, when examined in greater detail shows that there is a strong contest well under way to redress the balance between North and South by influencing business decision-taking and through the use of a wide range of incentives.

INTERNATIONAL RISK

A general assessment was made earlier on that the institutions, working practices, and environment in the developed world had sufficient similarity between them to give a ready confidence when setting up businesses within these countries. This cannot be said of third world developing countries and therefore the risks have to be carefully considered at an early stage. International risk analysis is becoming a well-trodden area and more and more texts appear on the subject.

Before examining the main trains of thought it is appropriate to tabulate what the businessman is afraid of in general terms. This is shown clearly in Tables 2.2 and 2.3, where the varying degrees of intervention affecting foreign investments and the effect of political motivations on business operations are considered.

To a large extent, the view which emerges from the Tables represents the interventionist perspective of risk. The alternative view is essentially one which gives more credence to the contention that instability is the main causal factor for political risks likely to affect the business environment. Naturally, these opposing views are not mutually exclusive, and it is worth

Table 2.2. Ways a Host Country May Deal with Foreign Investors: Intensifying Degrees of Intervention

Non-Discriminatory actions	Discriminatory Actions	Discriminatory Sanctions	Dispossession
Require the hiring of nationals for management posts	Authorize only joint-ventures (in which the foreign firm owns a minority interest)	Disguised expropriation (compel the firm to reinvest profits in a given sector)	Expropriation
Negotiate the price of transfer in order to improve the taxation basis in the host-country	Levy special taxes or duties on public services	Levy taxes or duties meant to prevent the making of a profit	Nationalization
Require exporting companies to sell on the home market at a price equal to the break-even point in order to subsidize local consumption or encourage local investment	Bureaucratic hurdles and red-tape	Demand huge compensation for past inequities	Socialization (generalized nationalization)
Ask the investor to build some social or economic facilities and equipment	Encourage a boycott against the products or the personnel of the company		
Demand the use of a given percentage of locally made components			
Make the local currency temporarily non-convertible			

Source: A. Chevalier and G. Hirsch, 'The Assessment of the Political Risk in the Investment Decision', *Journal of the Operational Research Society*, 32/7 (1981), pp. 599–610. Reproduced courtesy of Pergamon Press Ltd.

Table 2.3. National Political Motivations and Functional Domains of the Company

Political Motivations	Management	Finance	Marketing	Production
(A) National Interest	Reduction of unemployment Training of managers Technical training	Inflow of permanent national capital Improvement of trade balance and balance of payments Increase in public income	Meeting of demand Decrease in imports	Creation of an efficient base of production Creation of commercial relations (customers, suppliers, etc.)
(B) National Sovereignty	Quotas imposed on some categories of foreign personnel Presence of nationals on the board of directors	Increasing participation of local capital Control over investment policy	Development of and control of the destination of exports	Generation of self-sufficiency Promotions of continuous operations
(C) National Identity	Progressive elimination of foreign personnel	Control over local borrowings Reinvestment of all local profits Discriminatory practices	Creation of local markets and products	Development of a nationally owned production capacity Gearing of production to local needs

Source: A. Chevalier and G. Hirsch, 'The Assessment of the Political Risk in the Investment Decision', *Journal of the Operational Research Society*, 32/7 (1981), pp. 599–610. Reproduced courtesy of Pergamon Press Ltd.

considering that the moderate strengthening of the interventionist approach is a reasonable expression of political will, and in so far as it is protective towards local nationals and their businesses, to that extent, it may be considered a stabilizing influence.

A difficulty that has to be taken into account when endorsing the instability approach is that not all political disruption is bad for business profits. Business lore has it that war is often good for production and that the threat of political change can have a consolidating effect on business communities which have investments to protect.

It is probably because of the recognition of the inevitability of government intervention in business, and the wide variety of results that can occur from instability, which accounts for researchers finding that while businessmen quickly recognize risks in overseas operations, they tend not to treat them as matters of paramount importance. Clearly, if business people were to hold such adverse views, the easiest answer would be complete avoidance of the country concerned, but this is not generally consistent with the traditional view of taking risks in search of profit.

There is consequently a growing strength of business opinion which is moving towards the view that generalized political studies are of limited value because of their frequent superficiality. It is also further argued that the risks of expropriation and severe forms of government action are becoming less likely to affect businesses, it is therefore more appropriate to keep a constant check upon indigenization processes and imminent changes in local regulations rather than constantly to evaluate and conjecture on the political climate.

Such thinking is apparent in the responses to the Conference Board's questionnaire which formed the basis of Report 794 concerned with the assessment of the political environment. To quote directly from the summary:

> Corporate awareness of the relevance and importance of political information is growing; there is an awareness, however, that regulatory and administrative problems overseas may be much more important to businesses than the more visible and dramatic aspects of politics.
>
> Today, as in the past, corporate executives worry about political stability and military coups; about civil violence and mob rule. Questions are asked by corporate leaders about many of the countries in which they have invested and where they may contemplate investing still more, or perhaps pulling out. Many multinationals have discovered that cataclysmic changes—the Cubas, Chiles and Irans—are only the tip of the iceberg. Beneath the surface less dramatic changes are taking place in the day to day political and administrative policies and practices of national governments. More often than not it is these changes that affect the viability of overseas enterprises.
>
> It is predictable that government scrutiny of proposed and existing foreign direct investments will increase, that trade-offs demanded in the form of value added, export capacity, local sourcing, equity sharing and so on will be vastly greater than before and that most governments themselves, as regulators or as direct participants in enterprise, will be the key factor that affects foreign business ventures in their countries.

An improved capacity to assess the overseas political environment may provide a distinct competitive advantage in indicating their host country leaders are prepared to offer new incentives, to bargain among chosen objectives or otherwise enhance business projects.

Source: Stephen Blank, with John Basek, Stephen J. Kobrin, Joseph LaPalombara 'Assessing the Political Environment: an Emerging Function in International Companies', *Conference Board Report* 794.

This appraisal throws a very generous light on the activity which should be required of support staff, local managers, and joint venture partners. Such an appraisal devalues global assessments and veiled hints from 'well-known sources', association chit chat, and paraphrases of bankers' broadsheets, and shows why special country supplements, even by papers and journals of high repute, so often fail to serve real business interests. Significantly, too few journalists know and write about real basic business considerations that affect the 'bottom line'.

Corporate international managers are often engulfed in a plethora of overseas information which is largely irrelevant to their daily tasks. Where such information is specifically produced for them on a regular basis by their colleagues, it often becomes a major source of irritation and it is seldom read.

What business people require is the analysis and simple portrayal on a regular basis of events which are most likely to affect profits.

The persuasive view that is beginning to emerge more strongly, and which is consistent with the very real problems of finding and harnessing new business opportunities, concerns the ways and means of working with international risk and of coping with uncertainty.

Actions for coping with uncertainty tend to concentrate into four broad areas:

- business control techniques;
- developing flexibility;
- financial structuring;
- conditioning the local environment.

Where researchers like Briance Mascarenhas and Alan C. Shapiro have analysed actions rather than theories, they have found evidence of very positive attitudes and inventiveness in the above areas.

With regard to business control techniques, one can perhaps start with the general recognition that the benefits to a host country of a new venture tend to be highest at the beginning. In overall terms, a policy of avoiding intervention by creating high visibility attractions is therefore an important element of strategy. Clearly, a business which portrays itself as a contributor to the local economy is going to have a stronger negotiating position than one that appears to treat the venture purely as a 'milk cow'. The way in which Hindustan Lever developed a strategy to circumvent the Indian Government's requirement of equity dilution is sometimes quoted as a good example of successful bargaining between investor and government. The essence of Hindustan Lever's approach was to incorporate products that were given high priority for manufacture by the government and generally to feed into the business increasingly higher levels of technology. The development of local R & D facilities which tackled local problems by reducing the raw materials import bills further increased the company's attractiveness. There was also a consistent policy of boosting foreign exchange earnings through exports. These were tripled in five years to US $62m, thus ensuring further favourable government attention.

In a broad sense, therefore, creating visible dependence raises the cost to the host government of taking action against a particular business.

Other legitimate strategies for increasing control and influence can incorporate the following:

- Integrating the business backwards to control supply sources.
- Integrating the business forward to control markets.
- Long-term contracts for supply and sales.
- Cartels to buy raw materials at advantageous prices.
- Developing external financial shareholders.
- Multi-location policies.
- Establishing a single globe trademark, which cannot legally be duplicated.
- Developing operating/production distribution R & D policies, which require strong support from an overseas plant.

Additional policies which have been suggested, which some may consider more questionable, incorporate:

- Developing customer influence through PR.
- Government lobbying.
- 'Selected' payments.

Strategies for increasing flexibility include:

- Use of more general-purpose equipment to enable product modifications more easily.
- Ensuring a wide distribution of sales.
- Developing a project through licensing, franchising, or subcontracting rather than investment.
- Decentralized decision-taking to improve speed of reaction at local level.
- Inserting break clauses in agreements, and reducing and increasing equity clauses in joint venture agreements.
- Maintaining a sound monitoring system (as advocated in the Conference Board Report (see above).

Equally, on the financial side there are actions which can be taken, depending upon one's view of the severity of the uncertainty which has to be encountered. From the accountant's point of view it is often better to plan against the worst case of expropriation as this sets a bench-mark against which lesser risks can then be put into context. The main policies in the financial armoury are:

Table 2.4. Methods Used by Ten Companies for Coping with Uncertainty in International Business

Company	Type of Project	Political Uncertainty	Foreign Exchange Uncertainty	Input Uncertainty	Production Uncertainty	Output Uncertainty
1. Airline	Set up of branch in Kuwait	Operation is internationally integrated. (C) Leased ground-handling equipment. (F) Reciprocal government agreements. (C)	Payment accepted in hard currencies only. (A)	Ability to adjust frequency of flights. (F)	Availability of back-up-aircraft. (F) Rescheduling capability of other flights. (F) Ability to transfer passengers to other airlines or accommodate them in a hotel. (F)	Leasing permits firm to terminate or step up operation quickly. (F)
2. Clothing	Entry into the Mexican market	Little commitment of resources. (F)	Money market hedging capability. (F)	Sub-contracted inputs. (F) Used multiple tailors. (F)	Initially tested tailors' capability (F) Used simple labour-intensive technology. (F)	Undertook a testmarket to check if market existed. (F) Ability to produce many different styles using same tailors. (F)
3. Food Processor (i)	Set up of a dairy plant in Saudi Arabia	Dehydrated compounds imported from firm's plant in Europe. (C)	Payment in hard currency. (A)	Use inventories (F)	On-site expatriate personnel to maintain and run plants. (C)	Prediction of demand for diary products using demographic factors. (P)
4. Food Processor (ii)	Set up of a pineapple plantation in Kenya.	Integrated export markets. (C) Duplicate planta-tions in other countries. (F)	Money market hedging capability. (F)	Developed its own strain of higher yielding and more resistant pineapple seeds. (C)	Existence of plantations in other countries to offset bad crop in one area. (F)	Captive export distribution network downstream. (C).

Industry	Project						
(continued from previous page)		capacity. (F)	capability. (F)	specification. (C)			
6. Pharmaceutical firm	Set up of a pharmaceutical plant in Colombia	Insurance. (I)	Money market hedging capability. (F)	Ability to process multiple inputs. (F)	Uses general-purpose machinery. (F)	Ability to make different drugs from same production facilities. (F)	price. (F) Ability to sell different products with existing facilities (F)
7. Mining and Mineral Processor	Smelter in Ghana	Insurance. (I) Integrated upstream and downstream. (C) Substantial prediction efforts. (P)	Metal priced in hard currency on world market. (A) Forward contracts. (C)	Integrated upstream. (C)	Duplicate production lines. (F)	Integrated export markets. (C)	
8. Petroleum drilling and production	Oil exploration and production in Indonesia	Insurance. (I) Contracts. (C) Integrated downstream. (C) Substantial prediction efforts. (P)	Petroleum priced in hard currency. (A) Use of forward contracts. (C)	Geological investigation before making substantial commitment required for oil production. (P)	Maintains emergency funds to buy oil in spot market if necessary. (F)	Internationally integrated downstream. (C) Contracts. (C)	
9. Construction	Construction of a bridge in Jamaica	Used old equipment to reduce commitment. (F)	Payment guaranteed in hard currency by EX-IM Bank. (A)	Used parent country workers as much as possible. (C)	Covered by a cost-plus agreement. (A)	Bids and contracts. (C)	
10. Automotive parts	Set up of a plant in Venezuela	Insurance. (I) Internationally integrated upstream and downstream. (C)	Money market hedging capability. (F)	Copes with labour shortage by training workers to perform multiple functions. (F)	Duplicate production lines. (F)	Integrated downstream. (C) Sells products to multiple countries. (F)	

Notation: A=Avoidance   C=Control   F=Flexibility   I=Insurance   P=Prediction

Source: Briance Mascarenhas, 'Coping with Uncertainty in International Business', *Journal of International Business Studies* (Autumn 1982).

- Short pay-back periods.
- Adjusting project cash flows and shortening discount rates.
- Maintaining a financial cushion of liquid assets.
- Insurance: most risks are insurable but the problem is that only assets are usually protected and not the present value of future cash flows.

Exchange rates clearly have an important role to play and buying forward reduces uncertainty. Exchange rate predictions are a difficult enough task for economists: the imposition of a further assessment concerning exchange rates movements in relation to political risk might be considered as raising a half-science to a fully fledged art. The facts are clear in so far as it is accepted that non-trivial information concerning political news and government actions can lead to capital inflows and outflows, causing exchange rate appreciation or depreciation. A practical analysis by Cosset and De La Rinderie convincingly shows exchange rate movements against unanticipated news, with movements being more exaggerated towards bad news than towards good news. Repetition of an in depth study of this nature for any prospective investment area is probably out of the question, but it would be wise to examine exchange rates over a period of time and assess the intensity of fluctuations. Furthermore, it would be wise to look at the media in a developing country and to make a judgement with regard to the accessibility of economic information. In terms of exchange rate fluctuation, it is clearly the unanticipated nature of information which is most likely to cause difficulty.

The above synopsis would tend to suggest that there are many ways and means of coping with political risk and uncertainty; by and large the suggestions are positive ones. Should it be that in a deteriorating situation that desperation begins to creep in, then there are some fairly obvious 'Beggar-thy-neighbour Policies' that can be applied. Areas of cost saving, for example, could include the reduction of maintenance and marketing costs, eliminating R & D, and the cessation of local training. And in the worst cases a bridge to the future could be provided by changing to management agreements, know-how and licence agreements, or any other support agreement which will bring recognizable benefits. It must be stated, however, that the generality of opinion is an optimistic one and is based on the general understanding that in the developing world there are few countries which would take the full risk of acting in a way which would give long-term discouragement to future investors. It is not uncommon to hear the pithy advice of 'Sweat it Out' or 'Ride it Out' in business discussions concerning worst-case situations. Table 2.4 shows how ten companies adapted their strategies and policies to cope with uncertainty around the world.

CONCLUSION

The details of incentives and policies which are relevant to business people have been examined, and the appraisal of political risk and uncertainty reviewed, with practical ways suggested of coping with possible problems. And while some real problems have been identified, it is felt that, overall, positive attitudes prevail. As a generality, the facts are supportive of international business development and underwrite the attempts made in subsequent Chapters to determine the optimum routes to profit overseas.

References

1 Jean Currie, *Special Report No. 64: Investment: the growing role of export processing zones* (1979) and *Export Processing Zones in the 1930s: custom free manufacturing* (1985), The Economist Intelligence Unit, London W.1.

2 Asayehgn Desta, 'Assessing Political Risks in Less Developed Countries', *Journal of International Business Strategy* (Spring 1985).

3 S. Robock, 'Political Risk Identification and Assessment', *Columbia Journal of World Business* (July/August 1971).

4 Douglas Nigh, 'The Effects of Political Events on United States Direct Foreign Investment', *Journal of International Business Studies*, 16/1 (1985).

5 Thomas W. Shreeve, 'Be Prepared for Political Changes Abroad, *Harvard Business Review* (July/Aug. 1984).

6 Stephen Blank (with John Basek, Stephen J. Kobrin, and Joseph La Palombara), 'Assessing the Political Environment: An Emerging Function in International Companies', Conference Board Report 794 (1980).

7 Briance Mascarenhas, 'Coping with Uncertainty in International Business', *Journal of International Business Studies* (Autumn 1982).

8 Dennis J. Encamation and Sushil Vachani, 'Foreign Ownership when Hosts Change The Rules', *Harvard Business Review* (Sept./Oct. 1985).

9 Jean Claude Cosset and Bruno Doutraux de la Rianderie, 'Political Risk and Foreign Exchange Rates: An Efficient Market Approach', *Journal of International Business Studies*, 16/3 (1985).

3

Problems and Advantages of Expansion Internationally

Chapters 1 and 2 have set a scene that testifies to a struggle to achieve a new balance in world business activity and relationships and which poses questions concerning future aims and strategies that cannot sensibly be ignored. Taking account of the wider issues will offer no easy options for many businesses. Some will already hear the thundering of the hooves, some will just see a cloud of dust in the distance and wonder at the cause, for others it is already too late—they can make their products no longer and are already trampled under foot. Will there be a straightforward nut, nail, screw, or bolt made in Europe in the year 2000? How many customers will automotive manufacturers have at the turn of the century? Are televisions and videotape players and recorders growth industries for Europe and America?

When looking at wider issues it is also necessary to evaluate international business techniques and it is important to look at the organizations and people that must implement them.

The major decisions to be taken start from the very fundamental standpoint of how wide a view must be taken of future market-places to ensure scope for business growth. A single step forward from the United Kingdom to France, or from Germany to America, for example, is often the subject of intense internal debate and difficulties. Working in the relatively cosy atmosphere of the cohesive North can still send shivers down the spines of some boards and their accountants, and even more so the half-way house of an EPZ or a third world country. Yet, a quick glance at the unit trust pages of any newspaper shows how quickly thousands of people are prepared to make the theoretical leap in order to benefit from the development of overseas businesses.

To pick a few unit trust names at random readily shows an attack to sustain public attention for the global business world; there are the specific trusts for Europe with sub-packaging for the United Kingdom, Holland, Germany, France, and Scandinavia, as well as heavy representation for

Asia, Australasia, Japan, Hong Kong, and Singapore, plus the more provocative consumerism of, say, Marco Polo, Tiger, and Sunrise Trusts.

Alongside the basic judgement of how wide a market participation is required are of course the finer value-judgements of how fast, and to what level, resource commitments can be justified and tolerated. The simple solutions of more exports will no longer suffice, since in the Northern markets the growing intensity of competitive defence strategies will necessitate that would-be expansionists will require more than a man and a dog to sustain customer attention, let alone customer allegiance overseas. Every alternative business strategy, however, takes the business person further and deeper and increases the need for research and new methods of control to achieve market and financial goals in different, and frequently alien, environments. In the vernacular, one often knows little about Poms, Froggies, Krauts, etc. until one has to deal with and motivate the lower echelons of an overseas organization; waiters, taxi-drivers, and beach attendants are far removed from salesmen, secretaries, and order clerks. The former are after your custom, the latter may question your presence.

Organization structures and people skills will come under pressure; conflicts will arise throughout organizations and as the reality of any changed emphasis permeates the business, and the newer vision and aspirations of an emerging team of internationally orientated employees bubbles to the top, most employees will see more threats than opportunities. Few businesses have either the luck or the judgement necessary to burst on to the world scene; for most, mundane evolution rather than revolution will be the order of the day.

The much-studied multinational, so often the villain of the piece in the third world, and the university professors' well-trodden research path and therefore guiding-light, clearly still struggles with the international proposition overall.

It is to be hoped that lesser companies will be able to respond more vigorously as a result of using their sharper entrepreneurial skills as a springboard. Most companies widening their horizons will arrive in new market-places as relatively weak players and without the comfort of any previous segment domination or niche attraction. The need for co-operation between people of different cultures, training, and experience will give rise to many stories, some good, some bad. The value of partner judgements, long-term relationships, and co-operation without the power and authority of equity rights will give rise to a new branch of management science, of which today's papers on joint ventures are but the tip of the iceberg.

Alternative business growth techniques have in general been well defined and growth vector analysis along with its closely associated derivatives, such as the directional policy matrix and product sector portfolio analysis, have strong adherents, appear in many standard text books and are usually the basis of consultants' discussion and planning techniques. John Daniels quite rightly asks 'Why haven't strategic and international business objectives been brought more closely together in business literature?' He concludes, and circumstantial evidence appears to support the argument, that international options are simply not a natural part of the strategic decision-taking process. Research further indicates that this still seems to be the case even when companies already have a strong international presence.

There is a case to be made that business growth remains a difficult subject for many boardrooms. The search for new products and their development, and in general the ways and means of generating innovation probably cover as many pages as any other business subject in recent management papers.

The search for new market-places is equally difficult and perhaps the restatement and painful truism is that 'creativity' and use of the broader brush when dealing with business opportunities are some of management's rustier skills. Implementation of the new and the innovative takes a long time. The marketing man with his '4 Ps' ('Product', 'Price', 'Place' (i.e. distribution), and 'Promotion') and a pencil and paper can often be there in a flash, particularly if his research work has been good, but the designer and the production team have to slave for much longer, moreover, resources often limit the amount of change that can be generated. Consequently, the genuinely new suffers—generally, the company is better at 'dancing on the sixpence' that it knows best.

Having stated the vector analysis options, such as those set out in Table 3.1, for example, Daniels was able to continue his argument in a very lively way to show how international opportunities could be associated with each matrix decision. The point is conceded that there is nothing new or

Table 3.1. Growth Vector Matrix

Market Options	Product Alternatives		
	Present Products	Improved Products	New Products
Existing Market	1 Gain market share by price reductions and/or brand identification	2 Gain sales by differentiating product features from competitors	3 Replace or add products which can be sold through existing channels of distribution
Expanded Market	4 Increase product usage through promotion, price reductions, new distribution, and/or new product uses	5 Add product variations to appeal to different consumer segments	6 Add related products through vertical or horizontal integration to sell through new distributors
New Market	7 Expand into new geographic area	8 Make product variations to appeal to new geographic area	9 Diversify simultaneously by geography and product

Source: J. D. Daniels, 'Combining Strategic and International Business Approaches through Growth Vector Analysis', Management International Review, 3 (1983).

revolutionary in the choices, but simply what is on offer is the merging of two thought-processes. Table 3.2 shows this process in detail.

As always, filling in the boxes is the easy bit; accumulating the background knowledge and skill to choose the correct box is quite another matter. The value of the exercise at this stage is to cover the ground and to see that the range of opportunities is not overlooked.

The point has already been made that international development is not usually a comfortable process because of the reduced confidence that arises from the lack of previous market strengths and practical understanding. Many companies will therefore feel that they are 'starting again' when entering new overseas markets. The reactions at this stage can range from indignation to pioneering idealism, or from hope to fear. Briance Mascarenhas found another way of stating the problem:

> The concentration of the leaders in the domestic market reflects their commitment to it and may result in an invincible domestic presence which may signal an inflexibility in expanding internationally. Even if international expansion becomes strategically imperative later, a dominant firm may not have the advangtages overseas that it possesses in the domestic market. Some advantages such as reputation and economies of scale may not readily spill over into international markets

Therefore, the overseas export opportunity may be a great equalizer. Appendix I to this Chapter has been incorporated to allow this argument to be pursued further by evaluating an analysis of international strategies pursued by non dominant firms. Mascarenhas does an excellent job by pointing up two fundamentals very clearly:

1. International strategies are open to all.

and

2. International strategies allow non dominant firms to develop competitive advantages against larger firms without necessarily meeting them head on.

Such arguments need to be carefully evaluated. It is generally accepted that Theodore Levitt made the globalization of markets an issue in 1983, although he acknowledges Robert Buzzel's 1968 article 'Can you Standardize Multinational Marketing?' as a landmark paper.

Levitt's potent opening statements and several well-chosen examples further on are very appealing and they brim with the sort of logic to which most people can relate. The single power-line with one television set at the end of it will surely bring the remoter regions into the world of marketing and emancipate the potential consumer. Coca Cola, Pepsi Cola, branded burgers, branded jeans, films, videotapes, and international music all testify to the potential for globalization and a drift towards harmonization. Reference to Japanese successes, particularly with their hi-fi products which have swamped Northern high streets, also show how effectively globalization can bite on the hardware side as well.

Table 3.2. International Business and Growth Strategies

	Present Products	Improved Products	New Products
Existing Markets	Reduce costs via international purchasing, know how, or buy back/compensation trading. Improve image/product by acquiring rights or trade marks of better brand or through association (i.e. J.V.).	Product diversification through licence, world research for improved benefits. Product quality improvement from process license, new sourcing of components or raw materials.	Expand customer profile distribution or license for/from overseas companies. Replace existing products as above or by J.V. (home base) or J.V. overseas and buyback. Consider EPZs.
Expanding Markets	Promote more effectively through researching higher usage rates overseas-show how/market development agreements. Cross boarder staff posting/ Foreign business exchange/ International associations.	Segment market with product variants from international license, research overseas trends to widen development horizons.	Extend product line horizontally as above or vertically by integrating with international supply routes.
New Markets	Expand into new markets geographically;- Export alone Export with Agents etc. Joint Venture License Merger/investment Countertrade	Translate products (see page 178) to improve appeal to wider market spectrum. Consider global strategies. Reorientate technology gained but not exploited overseas.	Diversification into unrelated products in wider markets. Global application own R & D, shared R & D. Identify key business stregths (e.g. profitable service) and apply know how to new area J. V. Management Contracts or acquisition.

Source: Adapted from J. D. Daniels, 'Combining Strategic and International Business Approaches through Growth Vector Analysis', *Management International Review,* 3 (1983).

Levitt was very conscious, however, in his original paper that the customization of the product, and the use of the other 3 Ps to sell it, remained a necessity, thereby modifying the global concept more correctly as a search for sales opportunities in similar market segments across the globe to pull out products of low-cost homogenized technology. (As well as the 4 Ps detailed above, some argue that there is a 5th P, namely 'People'). The process continues through low-cost products eroding local preferences. Inevitably, the argument leads to cracks in the marketing concept as most people know it, and that Ford (any colour as long as it is black) was right all along.

Levitt's concluding paragraphs are important:

The purpose of business is to get and keep a customer. Or, to use Peter Drucker's more refined construction, to *create* and keep a customer. A company must be wedded to the ideal of innovation—offering better or more preferred products in such combinations of ways, means, places, and at such prices that prospects *prefer* doing business with the company rather than with others.

Preferences are constantly shaped and reshaped. Within our global commonality enormous variety constantly asserts itself and thrives, as can be seen within the world's single largest domestic market, the United States. But in the process of world homogenization, modern markets expand to reach cost-reducing global proportions. With better and cheaper communication and transport, even small local market segments hitherto protected from distant competitors now feel the pressure of their presence. Nobody is safe from global reach and the irresistible economies of scale.

Two vectors shape the world—technology and globalization. The first helps determine human preferences; the second, economic realities. Regardless of how much preferences evolve and diverge, they also gradually converge and form markets where economies of scale lead to reduction of costs and prices.

The modern global corporation contrasts powerfully with the aging multinational corporation. Instead of adapting to superficial and even entrenched differences within and between nations, it will seek sensibly to force suitably standardized products and practices on the entire globe. They are exactly what the world will take, if they come also with low prices, high quality, and blessed reliability.

The importance of the conclusion lies in the acknowledgement of gradual process and the acceptance of time, as well as the skill and determination that is required to influence the convergence. This is not the same as saying that globalization is here in a form that makes it a prerequisite for any potential new entrant to today's international markets. Certainly, it is a powerful way of thinking about the future, but it does not preclude its application through research to the entry of one or two new overseas markets.

Probably much damage has been done by polarizing the debate on globalization as a straight contest between current and revolutionary market theories.

Restated, it is fair to argue that purchasers sum up product quality, price, and delivery and if it is found that in combination a product offer is made that optimizes these advantages, then commonization and globalization will be seen to emerge. Logically, therefore, if one were, for example, to keep cutting the price of British cheese and German sausage, and they could be made readily available, then even, say, Italian people would begin to sink their preferences and eat them. But would they? Where the optimization of the product offer cannot overcome the local preference then customization and adaptation will still be necessary. Most marketing will continue to segment and highlight product differences so the globalization process will never be an even one—a little like marketing 'snakes and ladders'. A balanced view is clearly necessary, but the price of putting one's head in the sand can be high as perhaps, say, Black and Decker might testify following their fight with Makita over cheap hand tools: top management saw the signs but the fringes were very reluctant to move.

Certainly, Levitt has set the marketing world alight, but possibly arguments have reached a point where we should be warned not to let the sparks from the grinding of the axes set alight to the cotton wool which is being pulled over our eyes. For those readers who like to savour the battle between two gurus, an article from the *Financial Times*, which is also useful in showing how the lazy adaptation of the globalization concept can cause problems, is reprinted in Appendix II at the end of this chapter.

Gunther Von Buskem of Henkel K. G. introduced a very pertinent point concerning the effects on company structure that have to be taken into account when globalization is implemented. He usefully highlighted the tensions arising in the issue of competence between regional and national company teams or partners and associates. One might assume that competence is a euphemism for vested interest and all the other people factors that are inherent in any business development.

Equally, the point has also been made that control, once globalization has been achieved, can be traumatic in terms of analysing and responding to market changes. The information has to be summed from the world market and the implications for long-term planning methods and organization structure are considerable. To set up and to maintain suitable departments is clearly a very costly process, if a reasonable degree of accuracy is to be achieved.

Some interesting analysis has been carried out by Sandra M. Huszach, Richard J. Fox and Ellen Day to identify markets susceptible to the global approach and to ascertain if there are products with similar acceptance rates, and the characteristics of such products. It comes perhaps as no surprise when reading the results to see that similar countries are clustered in the north, but even then it is necessary to give them eight separate groupings. Products susceptible to this limited globalization tended to be non-durable, sensory, or personal. The analysis emphasizes, therefore, that 'going global' is a concept which needs careful thought; it is clearly not a ball which someone just passes so that companies can simply run with it and score tries or touchdowns in a world series.

Halliburton and Hunerberg (Figure 3.1), reviewing the arguments after four years' duration in 1987, may be forgiven for stating the obvious with regard to the potential for globalization by comparing standardization and

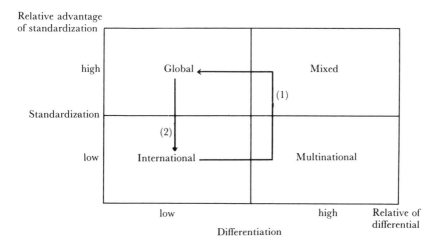

Figure 3.1. Relative Advantages of Standardization and Differentiation

Source: See Fig. 3.2.

differentiation in matrix form. Further, these researchers bring both relief and diplomacy to the confusion by suggesting that the main question is not 'whether?' but rather, 'How much?'. Therefore standardization and differentiation should be seen as a continuum rather than as conflicting opposites. With this in mind, the bud bursts into bloom in Figure 3.2 where in a 'no-nonsense' way some of the options for advertising to various age groups are clearly stated: other parts of the market mix need a similar treatment, and therefore how much standardization/differentiation is required becomes a matter of sounder judgement.

Through the plethora of papers and comment a certain amount of confidence can be gained that services have a quicker potential for globalization than manufacturing. It is clearly easier to see a global role for services where machines are carriers of methodology and, if necessary, the input of facts just changes to suit local requirements.

The general tendencies that support the globalization of services are thought to be:

- Service companies following home-based clients to international locations, particularly those prone to later withdrawal following the termination of licensing, management, or know-how agreements.
- Socio-economic changes creating ageing populations, the absorption of more women at work, and thereby the creation of health, home, and urban services.
- The general reduction in the protection of services as being evidenced in the European Economic Community.
- The transfer of labour-intensive industries to the third world.

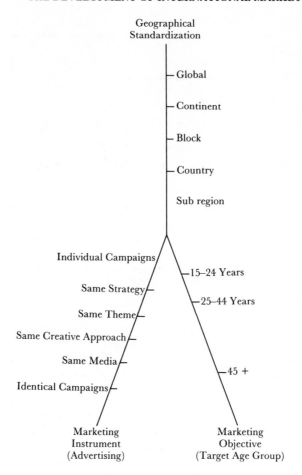

Figure 3.2. An Example of Differentiation for Advertising for target Age groups—but with a degree of standardization.

Source: (Figs. 3.1 and 3.2) 'The Globalization dispute in Marketing', C. Halliburton and R. Hünerburgh, *European Management Journal, 5/4 (1987).*

Aubrey Wilson, whose research check-list will be referred to later, in his normal methodical way, categorized as follows, services capable of globalization with reference to their hardware content:

People-based services with minimum product involvement with global markets:

Consultancy	Financial instruments
Accountancy	Employment agencies
Advertising agencies	Market research
Architecture	Entertainment

Services with a product dominance:

Fast foods	Car hire
Personal care	Telecommunications
Construction	Equipment leasing
Freight transportation	

Services with a balanced product/service situation:

Couriers	Computer services
Contract R & D	Information services
Surveying (some branches)	Training

Source 'Selected Excerpts from the Economist Conference Unit, Summer 1985', *European Management* Journal, 4 (1986).

One of the interesting features of services is that they are non-proprietary and therefore the perception of their quality and value is interwoven with personal relationships which give them very wide market-entry criteria. Such markets are clearly highly competitive and the commodity is highly perishable, often being no better than the judgement made on last service provided for the last client. Therefore, the opportunities for new competitors to gain entry may be considered as being ever present.

There seems to be an almost natural assumption that global means big. It is true that it sounds big and certainly researchers all rush to 'study' multinationals and to magic them into 'Globals'. Further, there is no shortage of people who get worked up at the idea of global power, sufficiently so that it passes into common currency by the provision of television programmes (fact and fiction). It is important to remember that no one has argued that to be global you have to be big. To introduce a personal example, the present author's earlier book about joint ventures had the good fortune to find readers in most countries throughout the world. Writing in mid-England even I was apparently global.

What should be abundantly clear from the continuing debate over the globalization of markets is that there are trends in industry and commerce that are shrinking the world and that the underlying dynamics of change are meaningful and powerful. The extent to which we perceive this to be true underlines the point made earlier that the international option is not just an interesting opportunity to spread a company's wings, to enjoy a little diversification and growth, or perhaps to enjoy a little extra 'cream' from the added volume. It may well be an essential ingredient for survival if today's comfortable home market is the subject of imminent attack.

Before considering the methods available for internationalizing business it is useful to look at organizational structure and its relationship to the overall strategy.

STRUCTURE AND STRATEGY

Strategy options have been broadly covered and the general need for internationalization has been made clear. What is now required is some consideration of appropriate organization structures and the people who are to staff them. The conventional wisdom is that strategy leads to structure, but such a relationship is not without its problems. If for no other reason than the fact that considerable time-lags are often found between strategy determination and organization change; periods of many years have often been noted. Further, organization structure tends to be fashion-driven from time to time and therefore weakly connected with existing company strategies, albeit that the structure matches perceived general goals in a period of specific economic conditions.

It is not surprising, therefore, that there are some schools of thought where the process is reversed and the claim is made that strategy follows structure. That is to say that given the right people the ideas flow and the strategy emerges. Within the general process of determining to internation-alize a company the case for putting the structure first and the detailed strategy second is not totally untenable. There are three main ideas that support such a suggestion:

1. In the internationalization process different cultures will have to work together (either formally or informally) and it is wrong to assume that this will be trouble free.
2. The international route contains risks, uncertainties, and unknowns which will not necessarily sit readily on the shoulders of staff principally schooled in domestic markets.
3. The physical side, particularly physical distribution and its associated paperwork, is often complex and invariably different. These areas usually have disproportionately higher costs and commercial penalties than home trade orders when mistakes occur.

Whatever the international strategy the above considerations all require provision to be made in organization structures to handle them effectively from the outset.

The impact of different cultures on an organization are going to create severe strains. The subject can be a long one and is not without generous measures of subjectivity. A shortcut can be taken however by looking at Hostedes's view of the main aspects of cultural differences which focus on areas that relate to most business people's experiences. The key areas for consideration are:

- Individualism—often a function of wealth.
- Masculinity—the deep-seated traditions of the roles of males and females in society.
- Power Distance—the acceptance or otherwise of equality.
- Uncertainty Avoidance—the strength of concern about order and security.

With such a broad spectrum of difference on fundamental attitudes it is easy to see how areas such as power-sharing, decision-taking, problem-solving, and reconciling status to responsibility can cause difficulty when it is necessary to get management ideas and commands to penetrate an organization with an international dimension.

As with so many business situations, recognizing the problem is part of the solution and it is clear that organizations will need to find some formula to get cultural empathy into both functional and line management. There is nothing soft or emotional in such a task since the objective of the exercise is not simply 'understanding foreigners', it is much more about making sure that contributions to, as well as responsibility for, the business plan and its associated budgets and action plans, are both understood and handled effectively. It is often tempting to believe that the problems follow the North/South divide; this, however, is often far from the case. The American/European divide can be greater than language suggests, and inter-European, Asian, and Arab differences can have similarities to iceberg tips.

It follows, therefore, that the international dimension requires consideration at a higher level than perhaps either initial values or volumes merit. If such support has wide international experience and languages then that is so much additional advantage, but even so this is not necessary if the staff concerned have the ability to recognize and understand their own culture and its differences from other cultures. The CEO's (Chief Executive Officer's) role will be crucial in determining a climate in which cultural differences can be examined and worked out.

Having stressed the differences, the next important clue to success is to stock the organization at crucial levels which interface with overseas activity with staff who are confident in dealing with the world's markets and their peoples. Once again, quite apart from any specific skills, it is rather a question of mental attitude and commercial maturity. In the most obvious of examples, and one of the most frequently forgotten, one cannot have a switchboard which speaks nineteen languages, but it is possible to have staff who respond to overseas calls helpfully and positively, rather than collapsing in confusion—or even worse, in a fit of giggles—at the first onslaught of a torrent of strange words.

Almost certainly, prejudice and antagonism will be found lurking in many corners of the organization; the ravages of history have guaranteed that. It is often impractical and certainly irrational to sack the people concerned, who might hitherto have performed well, but what can be done is to ensure that each department has its number of first-rate personnel who both understand the nature of world business and encourage others to gain such an understanding.

With regard to the overall structure, one notes the general tendency to endorse the pyramid structure which tends to ensure that the decision-takers are as far away from the action as possible. This may be satisfactory for a well-oiled domestic operation but it will not serve an international organization. Further, it is not unusual to find long management lines leading to an export department and longer ones still terminating in a shipping cul-de-sac.

However, if a decision is taken to change the structure then how should it be done? The traditional forms of international organization can be reduced to three main types, all of which are open to criticism and difficulties, namely:

1. The International Division or Department.
2. The International Product Structure—much favoured by globalists.
3. Matrix Management—with responsibility shared between central and national management.

The characteristics of each style is clear enough but the effectiveness of any chosen route is contentious.

The International Division (ID) solution abounds with political problems; usually the ID starts off with a high level of authority and power, but, over time, product groups, who have the wherewithal for overseas trade, win it back. It would seem that product support cannot be provided when the market is at its zenith, or that when there is an abundance of capacity, markets have just gone off the boil. The whole question as to who pays for the ID, whether or not it should make profits out of in-house suppliers, or, worse, whether it should have the right to develop markets using third party (and frequently competitive) suppliers is usually the subject of increasingly long memorandums and of bitter recrimination. The solution is, however, not a bad one in principle and the development of international expertise for complex markets and trading methods (e.g. China or countertrade deals) is sensible. IDs, however, come in many shapes and sizes, and appear to have a tendency to 'fly high and live high' as well as to lack an understanding of what they often see as a needlessly pedestrian way of life on the asset-based product line. It is possible to suggest sensible formulas whereby the joint determination of overseas business plans leads to relationships based on objectives rather than objections. Such plans could be described as strategy briefs and be drafted along the lines of the document printed as Appendix III at the end of this Chapter. The relevant simplicity of this approach should be clear and it will be noted that the salient points concern people and their joint commitment. However the ID is funded, its management will benefit from the knowledge that the resources will be spent on a known cause and that if success ensues there is an open commitment from all concerned to take, rather than squander or remain indifferent to, the opportunity. The only true profits that can be generated are those accruing outside the company, therefore a little imagination from the accountants to credit back an allocation of those profits which arise from a strategy brief to the participating parties might be more meaningful than allowing both sides to go for their own profits, which may well kill the business.

International Product structures have been fashionable since the early 1980s largely because they fit snugly into Strategic Business Unit (SBU) concepts, which place the maximum pressure for the profit optimization of distinct business areas. For control and motivation the SBU has a proven record in tough economic conditions. When related to international business the product-orientated structure often yields immediate gains, but, as is so often the case, immediate benefits sometimes cost dear in the long run. The generally accepted advantages and disadvantages of this type of structure are:

Advantages

- cost effectiveness on an international basis;
- improved communication;
- global strategic focus;
- management control and accountability;
- job satisfaction and reduction of internal politics.

Disadvantages

- sub-optimization of total overseas resource;
- possibility of confusion of aims in markets;
- optimum cost effectiveness vulnerability (e.g. single sourcing);
- lack of understanding in overseas markets, particularly if home-base activity predominates;
- fragmentation of international expertise and lack of scope for individual development;
- the difficulty of finding management with sufficiently broad experience to run international SBUs.

Rather akin to the International Division there are solutions which can tackle the downside problems, CEOs can insist on an element of international trade in business plans and monitor real progress through action plans. If overseas plans are accorded the correct importance and a conflict occurs due to pressures in the domestic market then a 'subsidy' can be allocated from the centre. Of course, any self-respecting SBU manager and his accountant will try to screw the most out of the centre, if, however, there is a sound aim and a tangible hope of success then this is a small price to pay to achieve the company's international focus.

The CEO can also have a human resource plan to ensure that each overseas product grouping has its input of international experience, to balance up the more parochial views. One large group had 'export supremos' nominated in every SBU—2 years later most SBU managers could not recall the appointments they had made.

The matrix approach of shared responsibility has a long proven history of custom and practice application. It certainly appears to work well, particularly in larger companies where the level of decision and appraisal is a little distant from the day-to-day operations, thereby ensuring a balanced view of the company's long-term aims. Generally, such structures need there to be sufficient control and power at the centre to ensure that 'decisions stay sold'.

The people problems involved in the matrix approach are well demonstrated by the research carried out by Wiechmann and Pringle who analysed the friction areas between headquarters and foreign operations. An extract from their *Havard Business Review* article 'Problems that Plague Multinational Marketeers' is reprinted as Tables 3.3 and 3.4. The concern so adequately expressed in this analysis cannot just be put to one side if another solution is chosen. Matrix management becomes inevitable for many international business situations, particularly with joint ventures. The breeding-grounds for discontent in matrix management are clear and the control of such structures also requires a confident and committed management with the time to handle the 'people problems'.

None of the solutions determines beyond doubt that provision has been made for handling international logistics correctly. All the structures described are susceptible to using a central organization which can optimize and co-ordinate the movement of goods, but that still leaves in doubt the effectiveness of administration of contracts often with high values and potentially high commercial penalties (either technical through the understanding of contracts and letters of credit or trade-related through linkage to future market potential). Pulling orders through the system with due attention to specification, delivery, documentation, and contract terms is best co-ordinated as close to the production base as possible and overseen at a senior level of management. The overseer needs to have the clout for making things happen and the understanding to see the wider aspects of the contract. There are many classic case histories concerning initial contracts and sample orders to open up a new market and the like which have failed to get management attention, become lost in the system, and, as such, 'door openers' for competitors. Equally, production staff have made well intentioned changes for expediency, without understanding the implications; 'if only' someone had made the need clear they could probably have made a more necessary change and not put the contract in jeopardy. It is very rare indeed for the blame for an international problem to lie at a low level, management should be aware of the non-standard or unusual requests that are being put into a routine system, and it is their responsibility to assist and monitor, to adjust priorities, and to take the responsibility for seeing that the overseas customer gets what he ordered. The goods will take longer to deliver, rectification will be costly, and mistakes prove what many buyers thought they knew in the first place, that they should not risk their own reputations through making purchases from distant suppliers.

It is clear that there are a series of structure options for the international company but each has advantages and disadvantages. The main issue, however, is that no structure will survive the course on its own: the attitude of the CEO, the careful placement of understanding staff, and the responsibility for overseas trade at a high level are prerequisites. Further, the organization needs to plan to deliver at the same time as it learns to sell. Empathy needs to rank higher than international skills, although the latter should not be devalued, and the inevitable politics between home and overseas operations need to be kept in check. Managers will be happier if

Table 3.3. Key Problems Identified by Headquarters Executives

	Rank (out of 182)	Score (%)
Lack of qualified international personnel		
Getting qualified international personnel is difficult	1	73
It is difficult to find qualified local managers for the subsidiaries	1	73
The company can't find enough capable people who are willing to move to different countries	15	60
There isn't enough manpower at headquarters to make the necessary visits to local operations	22	57
Lack of strategic thinking and long-range planning at the subsidiary level		
Subsidiary managers are preoccupied with purely operational problems and don't think enough about long-range strategy	3	71
Subsidiary managers don't do a good job of analysing and forecasting their business	5	65
There is too much emphasis in the subsidiary on short-term financial performance. This is an obstacle to the development of long-term marketing strategies	13	61
Lack of marketing expertise at the subsidiary level		
The company lacks marketing competence at the subsidiary level	4	69
The subsidiaries don't give their advertising agencies proper direction	8	63
The company doesn't understand consumers in the countries where it operates	8	63
Many subsidiaries don't gather enough marketing intelligence	17	59
The subsidiary does a poor job of defining targets for its product marketing	20	58
Too little relevant communication between headquarters and the subsidiaries		
The subsidiaries don't inform headquarters about their problems until the last minute	5	65
The subsidiaries do not get enough consulting service from headquarters	13	61
There is a communications gap between headquarters and the subsidiaries	31	51
The subsidiaries provide headquarters with too little feedback	33	50
Insufficient utilization of multinational marketing experience		
The company is a national company with international business; there is too much focus on domestic operations	25	56
Subsidiary managers don't benefit from marketing experience available at headquarters and vice versa	28	53
The company does not take advantage of its experience with product introduction in one country for use in other countries	36	49
The company lacks central co-ordination of its marketing efforts	45	46
Restricted headquarters control of the subsidiaries		
The headquarters staff is too small to exercise proper control of the subsidiaries	8	63
Subsidiary managers resist direction from headquarters	17	59
Subsidiaries have profit responsibility and therefore resist any restraint on their decision-making authority	38	48

Source: Ulrich Wiechmann and Lewis G. Pringle, 'Problems that Plague Multinational Marketers', *Harvard Business Review* (July/Aug. 1979). Reprinted by permission of Harvard Business Review. Copyright © 1979 by the President and Fellows of Harvard College; all rights reserved.

Table 3.4. Key Problems Identified by Subsidiary Executives

	Rank (out of 182)	Score (%)
Excessive headquarters control procedures		
Reaching a decision takes too long because we must get approval from headquarters	2	58
There is too much bureacracy in the organization	5	55
Too much paperwork has to be sent to headquarters	6	54
Headquarters staff and subsidiary management differ about which problems are important	17	46
Headquarters tries to control its subsidiaries too tightly	22	45
Excessive financial and marketing constraints		
The emphasis on short-term financial performance is an obstacle to the development of long-term marketing strategies for local markets	1	65
The subsidiary must increase sales to meet corporate profit objectives even though it operates with many marketing constraints imposed by headquarters	7	50
Headquarters expects a profit return each year without investing more money in the local company	10	49
Insufficient participation of subsidiaries in product decisions		
The subsidiary is too dependent on headquarters for new product development	13	47
Headquarters is unresponsive to the subsidiary's requests for product modifications	22	45
New products are developed centrally and are not geared to the specific needs of the local market	22	45
Domestic operations have priority in product and resource allocation; subsidiaries rank second	31	43
Insensitivity of headquarters to local market differences		
Headquarters management feels that what works in one market should also work in other markets	2	58
Headquarters makes decisions without thorough knowledge of marketing conditions in the subsidiary's country	12	48
Marketing strategies developed at headquarters don't reflect the fact that the subsidiary's position may be significantly different in its market	13	47
The attempt to standardize marketing programmes across borders neglects the fact that our company has different market shares and market acceptance in each country	27	44
Shortage of useful information from headquarters		
The company doesn't have a good training programme for its international managers	7	50
New product information doesn't come from headquarters often enough	22	45
The company has an inadequate procedure for sharing information among its subsidiaries	27	44
There is very little cross-fertilization with respect to ideas and problem solving among functional groups within the company	27	44
Lack of multinational orientation at headquarters		
Headquarters is too home-country orientated	17	46
Headquarters managers are not truly multinational personnel	17	46

Source: Ulrich Wiechmann and Lewis G. Pringle, 'Problems that Plague Multinational Marketers', *Harvard Business Review* (July/Aug. 1979). Reprinted by permission of Harvard Business Review.

they get a due reward for their department's efforts and a little imagination from the accounts department can prevent the anomalous search for two false profits. International trade is governed by a different set of rules and contracts and it is better to start incorporating INCO terms, for example, rather than trying to argue with a crane-driver as to which side of the ship's rail to put the goods to retain possession: specialists' time and commitment will also be integral parts of the international style.

To digress before summing up: if the question of structure before strategy (or vice versa), together with the lack of any real consensus of opinion as to the appropriateness or otherwise of International Divisions and product or matrix structures, leaves lingering doubts in this area, a glance into the crystal ball may do no harm.

For such an exercise Peter Drucker's 'Coming of the New Organization', published in the *Havard Business Review* at the turn of 1988, is a reasonable starting-point. The suggestion may seem a little premature for some, as Drucker's article has not yet had time to mature to the usual 'seminal' status.

The essence of the 'New Organization' is that it will be knowledge-based and largely staffed by specialists.

> The specialists will largely direct and control their own performance through feedback from colleagues, customers and headquarters . . . it will be an information-based organization . . . as a company takes the first tentative steps from data to information, its decision processes, management structure and even the way its work gets done begins to be transformed.

For an international organization with an enormous span of control and a high requirement for the analysis of world-wide information on both products and markets in order to ensure the optimization of world profits, the ideas begin to hold attraction. The management of international organizations also fits snugly into the next suppositions made. The availability of information, as opposed to data, generates policy decisions and processes that allow for the disbanding of the staff and middle management echelons that used to churn the paper, and the remaining knowledge-specialists can move closer to the sharp end. Here they will become market-orientated task forces and work in 'synchrony with' rather than 'in sequence to' specialists from other disciplines. The examples chosen to divine the possible shape of organizations to come make the point well. An orchestra plays a good tune to one CEO because it knows the score and needs no middle management, as it were. Equally, the British administration of the Indian Subcontinent was undertaken for many years by no more than a thousand people, most of them under thirty years of age. What emerges, therefore, is the need for clear and unequivocal direction, with tempo and interpretation coming from the centre, and specialists, with full responsibility, responding to the information they receive. A CEO intent on achieving results across borders will therefore set the aims, and seek to achieve them through the use of multidisciplined specialist teams by ensuring that information flows to them that allows good decisions to be taken with regard to finance, product cost, and sales-volume/price-benefits to his overall organization. By today's standards the loss of control may well appear considerable; it has to be compensated for by the quality of decision-taking and by the sense of responsibility at the sharp end. Such organiza-tions will lend themselves readily to local adaptation and, however dimly viewed, would appear at one and the same time to incorporate many of the personal attributes that are sought of management today, as well as avoiding the conflicts inherent in today's product or matrix structures.

Such an approach would appear to offer solutions to the problems found by Bartlett and Ghoshal when they assessed international organizations and found that the real need to cope with the complexities of international business life was to optimize efficiency, responsiveness, and learning simultaneously. A regional, national, or project (SBU-style) task force of multicultured specialists should make inroads into this problem.

As always, people hold the key to success and attention is now being paid to the skills and attitudes required to be a transnational manager. The idea of a manager without national ties is perhaps a difficult one, but it relies more on the attitude of mind rather than imitative culture behaviour patterns. It is more a question of understanding and responding to all of the parameters of international business than learning mid-Atlantic jargon; it should be within the scope of any professional specialist, providing his information base is fast and accurate. 'Transnational person' or, as Sanders prefers, 'Global Business Diplomats' (GBDs) will probably need to be more co-operative internally than their counterparts today, have a wide under-standing of the organization's international objectives, and feel comfortable in responding with speed and personal judgement to management informa-tion supplied 'neat'. Awareness of the nature of global competition and the ability to discern the implications of changes in competitors' strategies, not only locally but with reference to the organization's wider objectives, will be important. More contentiously, perhaps, GBDs will have to have know-ledge of and participate in the 'political realities and analysis' of the territories in which they operate.

The CVs and People Specifications begin to look onerous. Are GBDs born or made? Do GBDs develop and pursue a fundamental global business morality which perhaps can only be glimpsed today? There is at least tentative evidence in some areas to suggest that tomorrow's professionals will have to grapple with wider environmental issues (like those over aerosols and the ozone layer) and social issues (such as basic pay and conditions, already prescribed by others for South Africa for example). The people to learn from today's 'tips' how to cope with tomorrow's 'icebergs' will probably learn on the forges of international experience: they will learn faster if their managements encourage and reward open minds as well as professional skills.

An idea as to the possible shape of a future international organization is given in Figure 3.3: if it prompts the pencil to the fingers and it gets a new set of lines, it will have served a purpose.

Chapter 3 has covered a wide area, examining strategy and structure and

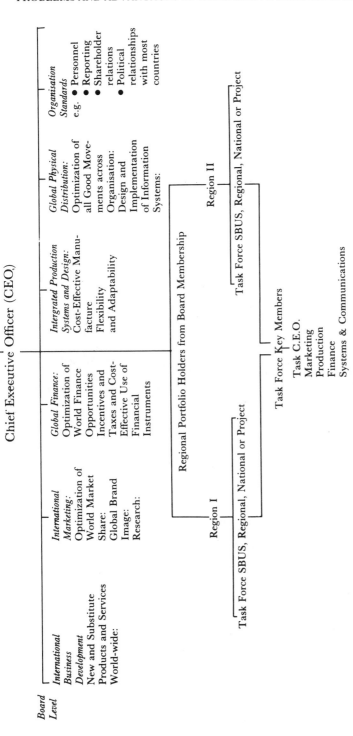

Figure 3.3. A Possible Future Organisation for an Internationally Orientated Information-Based Business

It is likely in order to retain international view points and understanding that the combination of portfolio holders for regions will change regularly and that Task Force Key Members will be cross posted within a planned career development pattern.

considering to some extent the people involved. In Chapter 4 it will be necessary to look more closely at the overseas opportunity by considering market research requirements. Furthermore, because in the majority of cases companies do not work alone overseas there is a requirement to look at Partner Selection, and it will be argued that there is a strong and vital connection between these two topics.

References

1 P. Kotler, *Marketing, Management, Analysis Planning and Control* (Prentice Hall: London, 1984.)
2 M. J. Baker, *Marketing Strategy and Management* (Macmillan: London, 1985).
3 J. D. Daniels, 'Combining Strategic and International Business Approaches through Growth Vector Analysis', *Management International Review*, 3 (1983).
4 Briance Mascarenhas, 'International Strategies of Non Dominant Firms', *Journal of International Business Studies* (Spring, 1986).
5 Theodore Levitt, 'The Globalization of Markets', *Havard Business Review* (May/ June 1983).
6 Robert D. Buzzel, 'Can you Standardize Multinational Marketing?' *Havard Business Review* (Nov./Dec. 1986).
7 G. Horstede, *Culture Consequences* (Saga: London, 1980).
8 David Ashton, 'Cultural Differences', *Management Education and Development* 15 (1984).
9 P. G. P. Walters, 'International Marketing Policy: A Discussion on The Standardization Construct and its Relevance to Corporate Policy', *Journal of International Business Studies* (Summer 1986).
10 A. D. Chandler, *History of The American Enterprise: Strategy and Structure* (M.I.T. Press: New York, 1962).
11 J. D. Whitt, 'Motivating Managers in Subsidiaries in Developing Countries', *Managerial Planning* (1982).
12 P. Haspelagh and W. H. Davidson, 'Shaping the Global Product Organization', *Harvard Business Review* (July/Aug. 1982).
13 B. R. Scott, 'Stages of Corporate Development', Havard Business School (1971).
14 L. Donaldson, 'Strategy Structure and Performance', Australian School of Management (1984).
15 C. Halliburton and R. Hunerberg, 'The Globalisation Dispute in Marketing', *European Management Journal*, 5/4 (1987).
17 E. Trondsen and R. Edfelt, 'New Opportunities in Global Services', *Long Range Planning*, 20/5 (1987).
18 J. A. Quelch and E. J. Hoff, 'Customizing Global Marketing', *Havard Business Review* (May/June 1986).
19 J. Thackray, 'Much Ado About Global Marketing', *Management Today* (Apr. 1985).
20 S. M. Huszagh, R. J. Fox and E. Day, 'Global Marketing: An Empirical Investigation', *Columbia Journal of World Business* (Twentieth Anniversary Issue).
21 'Going Global', Selected Excerpts, *Economist* Conference Unit (Summer 1985).
22 W. R. Fannin and A. F. Rodriques, 'National or Global? Control versus Flexibility', *Long Range Planning*, 19/5 (1986).

23 C. A. Bartlett and S. Ghoshal, 'Tap Your Subsidiaries for Global Reach', *Havard Business Review* (Nov./Dec. 1986).

24 G. J. Davies, 'The International Logistics Concept', *International Journal of Physical Distribution and Materials Management* (1983).

25 Lord Layton, Selling Abroad: The Distribution Factor, OCL Lecture (London, 1985).

26 G. Davies and C. Freebury, 'The Management of Documentation By British Exporters', *International Journal of Physical Distribution and Materials Management* (1986).

27 M. Rowe, The International Sales Contract: Central to Trade Negotiations, *International Trade Forum* (July/Sept. 1987).

28 L. Kelly, A. Whatley, R. Northley, 'Assessing the Effects of Culture on Management Attitudes: A Three-Culture Test', *Journal of International Business Studies*, 19/2 (1987).

29 Peter F. Drucher, 'The Coming of the Now Organization', *Havard Business Review* (Jan./Feb. 1988).

30 N. Chankim and B. A. Maubogue, 'Becoming an Effective Global Competitor', *Journal of International Business Strategy* (Jan./Feb. 1987).

31 Theresa Domzal, Lynette Unger, 'Emerging Positioning Strategies in Global Marketing', *Journal of Consumer Marketing*, 4/4 (1987).

32 Joel A. Bleche and Lowell L. Bryan, 'The Globalization of Financial Markets', *McKinsey Quarterly* (Winter 1988).

33 Hideki Yoshirara, 'Internationalization at the Top', *Management Japan*, 20/2 (1987).

34 Mitsuyo Hanada, 'Management Themes in the Age of Globalization', *Management Japan*, 2/2 (1987).

35 P. Saunders, 'Global Managers for Global Corporations', *Journal of Management Development*, 71 (1987).

36 Christopher Bartlett and Sumatra Ghoshal, 'Managing Across Borders: New Organizational Responses', *Sloan Management Review* (Autumn 1987).

APPENDIX I[a]

Strategies of Non Dominant Firms

Table 1 Illustrative Examples of Non Dominant Firms Reducing Direct Competition by International Strategies

Industry	Dominant Firm(s)	Non Dominant Firm	International Strategy Chosen	Reason for Strategy	Source of Information
1. Automobile	General Motors	Ford	Larger international presence outside US where General Motors was not established. Concentration in major similar countries where it was possible to maintain control: for example, in 1980, 99% and 85% of Ford's motor vehicles were, respectively, produced and sold in nine countries.	General Motors was dominant in domestic US market and first to introduce a full product line.	1
2. Farm Equipment	International Harvester, John Deere	Massey-Harris	Aggressive international expansion to major markets where larger competitors were not established and where conditions did not require the latest in technology and high quality.	Massey-Harris's products were considered of lower quality and technologically inferior compared to those of International Harvester and John Deere; smaller size and less vertical integration relative to industry leaders did not permit firm to compete effectively on a low-cost basis in North America.	2

Industry	Dominant Firm(s)	Non Dominant Firm	International Strategy Chosen	Reason for Strategy	Source of Information
3. Nuclear power engineering	Quadrex	Impell	Heavy emphasis on international expansion to developed countries with nuclear power programmes.	Firm was confronted with a larger US competitor and a slowdown of the US nuclear energy industry because of tighter government regulations after the 'Three-Mile Island' accident. Foreign countries, however, have maintained their nuclear power programmes.	3
4. Computer Data Entry Equipment	IBM	Computer Machinery Corp.	Entered European market before larger competitors could enter with similar products. Perceived developing countries' markets difficult to penetrate.	Established itself overseas because it could not guarantee a continuing stream of innovations and because it wanted to pre-empt the European market with its few existing innovations before larger firms moved in.	4
5. Electronics	Parlex	Advanced Circuit Technology	Set up licensing and joint venture arrangements with local firms in order to be close to customers and to conserve scarce resources. Concentration in major industrial markets where market potential for electronics products was large.	Other firms were domestically orientated; international expansion viewed as an uncrowded avenue for growth. Firm had a narrow product line and a proprietary product but was uncertain about its future product development potential. Firm tried to maximize its geographical coverage before competitors sprang up.	5

[a] Briance Mascarenhas, 'International Strategies of Non Dominant Firms', *Journal of International Business Studies* (Spring 1986).

Table 1 *cont.*

Industry	Dominant Firm(s)	Non Dominant Firm	International Strategy Chosen	Reason for Strategy	Source of Information
6. Viral Diagnostic Products	MA Bioproducts Flow Laboratories	Bioassay	Joint Ventures in major industrial countries.	Domestic competitors had a strong hold over local market. Firm was privately held and had limited financial resources but executives felt international joint ventures permitted expansion into foreign markets with little resource commitment without substantially diluting domestic efforts. Top executives were able to negotiate effectively with the bureaucratic government agencies involved in providing health care services overseas.	6
7. Automobile	Toyota	Nissan	Larger use of overseas production and joint ventures to enter otherwise closed markets in developed countries. Tailored cars to local demands.	Avoid low-cost competition from Toyota in Japan and overseas through its exports; Toyo Kogyo and Honda surpassed firm in technological innovations.	7
8. Chemicals	Dupont, Dow Chemical	Monsanto	Heavy emphasis on specialty chemicals in developed countries outside US where local firms existed. Developing country markets were distant and too small to achieve scale economies.	In contrast to competition in specialty chemicals, competition in bulk chemicals in developed countries is usually intense because of the well-known technology and the presence of many local and international competitors.	8

Industry	Dominant Firm(s)	Non Dominant Firm	International Strategy Chosen	Reason for Strategy	Source of Information
9. Consumer Electronics	Matsushita	Sony	Relatively greater use of R & D and aggressive international expansion to major developed markets.	It is difficult for Sony to compete with Matsushita in Japan. Matsushita quickly copies Sony's innovations and has a more efficient manufacturing capability. Matsushita also has a strong hold over the traditional, fragmented distribution system in Japan. Japan has 60,000–70,000 stores specializing in electronic goods out of which 40,000 sell Matsushita products, and 26,500 stores sell nothing else. Sony has only 3,000 stores selling mainly Sony products. Traditional retail outlets are reluctant to switch suppliers and direct distribution by Sony is difficult.	9
10. Robotics	Matsushita Electric Industrial Fanuc, Hitachi, Kawasaki Heavy Industries, and Yaskawa Electric Manufacturing	Dainichi Kiko Co.	Early expansion to major industrial foreign markets using technological licensing and market arrangements with local firms to offset its limited resources. Larger competitors were selling stand-alone robots to large customers who, in turn, would develop their own manufacturing system. In contrast, firms focused on smaller customers with an application/user orientation, developing a manufacturing system for these firms that did not have an in-house design capability.	Firm was small, privately held, and lacking financial technological, and marketing resources. Employees were young and not taken seriously by potential Japanese customers. Domestic market pressures were severe, characterized by larger firms, overcrowding (200 competitors), and price-cutting. Top executives and employees were ambitious and opportunistic.	10

Table 1 *cont.*

Industry	Dominant Firm(s)	Non Dominant Firm	International Strategy Chosen	Reason for Strategy	Source of Information
11. Vibration Monitoring Instrumentation	Bentley-Nevada	Metrix Instrument Company	Firm focused on speciality products designing user-friendly equipment that incorporated electronic circuitry presence in major industrial markets.	Dominant firm had olver 50% of domestic market but was a slow innovator. Some European competitors also present industry equipment generally sold in major industrialized countries to contractors who utilized it in plant construction the world over. Felt overseas markets were easier to penetrate than domestic market.	11
12. Gas Chromatography	Perkin-Elmer Corp.	Antek Instruments	Firm had some patents and decided to concentrate initially in advanced countries through an effective marketing programme involving careful selection of agents and promotion that would be sufficient to win customers who were not loyal to competitors.	Although largest competitor had strong reputation and brand name recognition in domestic market, executives discovered that customer knowledge of and loyalty to competitor were not great overseas.	12
13. Photocopiers	Xerox, Sharpe, Ricoh	Clark Copy	Joint venture with the People's Republic of China	Unique firm skills in negotiating with a command economy, willingness to provide China with hard currency earnings, to transfer technology, and to provide desired top-management personal development. Large firms had operations in Japan, China's	13

Industry	Dominant Firm(s)	Non Dominant Firm	International Strategy Chosen	Reason for Strategy	Source of Information
14. Telecom-munications	A.T.T.	I.T.T.	Acquired under-capitalized and inefficient state-owned telephone companies overseas when governments were unable to finance them further.	Founder was charismatic and able to strike deals with heads of state. A.T.T. was dominant in domestic market but international expansion was constrained by attention diverted to litigation problems with domestic local authorities by Justice Department's concern about its further growth, and by US consumers who did not want to cross-subsidize its marginally profitable international activities. Therefore, A.T.T. sold its international manufacturing facilities to I.T.T. in a market segmenting arrangement.	14
15. Plastics	Shell International Chemical Co.	Sunde Plastics Industries (AS) (Norway)	Use of licensing to make quick, extensive international push. Specializes in design and set-up of small-scale plants costing less than $2 million. Heavy emphasis on developing countries where markets are small and insulated, and where import-substitution pressures are strong. Willing to use local contractors and local materials in constructing plants. Lower-quality product was acceptable in these countries.	Being small, firm could not compete head on with industry giants with large plants in developed countries. Potential customers for Sunde products in Western countries were owned by larger competitors. Firms developed a technology and market-entry method appropriate for developing countries with small markets and high uncertainty.	15

Table 1 *cont.*

Industry	Dominant Firm(s)	Non Dominant Firm	International Strategy Chosen	Reason for Strategy	Source of Information
16. Household Appliances	Zanussi, Indesit	Merloni	Firm pursued an intense technological licensing and export policy to European and particularly to Middle Eastern markets. Specialized in low-priced/cost products obtained through simple designs, more efficient materials, and low labour costs. Strategy led to high growth and higher gross margins than other Italian competitors.	Firm as a late entrant, entrepreneurial facing two larger Italian competitors: Zanussi, which had the high quality position, and Indesit, which had the low-cost position. Major competitors also existed in other European countries, where market saturation, excess capacity, and price-cutting existed. Consumers in non-Italian European countries had a negative image of Italian-made appliances. Yugoslavian and Spanish competitors were penetrating low-price end of European market.	16
17. Automotive Tires	Goodyear Firestone General Tire, Goodrich Uniroyal	Two-ply Manufactures	Concentration in European countries to pre-empt markets before local firms and US competitors could establish themselves. Extensive use of joint ventures, managed to sell to OEM manufacturers in Europe and experienced rapid growth with the rise of European auto production. Firm experienced joint venture problems in developing countries of Mexico and Ivory Coast.	Larger firms in domestic market had a strong hold over new OEM sales. In US, firm was relegated to selling to replacement market segment through automotive chains, gas stations, and private labelling. Firm had managers with international experience and took advantage of Marshall Plan incentives for investing in Europe.	17

Industry	Dominant Firm(s)	Non Dominant Firm	International Strategy Chosen	Reason for Strategy	Source of Information
18. Aluminium	Alcoa, Reynolds	Kaiser Aluminium	Formed joint venture in Argentina, Brazil, India, Ghana and Jamaica to tap richer deposits of bauxite.	Firm was a late entrant, obtaining entry because of antitrust divestiture decrees requiring larger firms to sell some of their plants. High quality bauxite ores in US, however, were already taken.	18
19. Steel	US Steel	Bethlehem Steel	Moved overseas to secure sources of raw material	Firm was a late starter; larger, more experienced firms had already secured the best raw material source in US so had to look overseas.	19
20. Canning	American Can Continental Can	Crown, Cork, and Seal	Set up plants in many developed and developing countries where competitors were not present. Specialization in containers for 'hard-to-hold' objects. Tailored equipment and product design to different country needs, unbundling permitted market entry in some markets.	Buyer-supplier pressure and intense competition from larger firms in US market.	20

Table 1 *cont.*

Industry	Dominant Firm(s)	Non Dominant Firm	International Strategy Chosen	Reason for Strategy	Source of Information
21. Courier Delivery Service	Federal Express Airborne, UPS, Purolator	DHL Worldwide Courier Express	Quick and reliable international delivery of mail and packages, particularly to countries plagued by communication problems where there is a demand for an alternative delivery channel.	Most competitors were concentrating on domestic market. Firm is privately held and developed a strategy to fit its limited financial resources. Costly company-owned planes were not necessary for international delivery because landing rights were often not granted. Delivery was made through commercial flights with courier carrying excess baggage which ensures greater control and quicker unloading than unaccompanied regular airline cargo, and avoids public holiday delays. Difficult for competitors to enter overseas markets now because of DHL's pre-emptive deals with national postal authorities.	21
25. Consumer Products	Procter & Gamble	Colgate-Palmolive	Largest in production and marketing of products outside US. Quickly introduces overseas the idea that its domestic competitors pioneer in US. For example, after Procter & Gamble introduced fluoride toothpaste in US, Colgate was first to introduce it in the UK. Colgate quickly copied in Mexico the idea pioneered by Procter & Gamble in the US of creating and supporting soap	Colgate's R & D was not very successful relative to competitors; often only came up with 'me-too' products in the US. Embarked on an aggressive international market development strategy instead, quickly utilizing ideas overseas that its competitors were first to introduce in the US.	25

1. O'Donnel and Andresky [1982]; Tamorkin [1979]; interviews with company executives.
2. Cook; p. 1 [1981].
3. Interviews with company executives; Wiegner [1982].
4. Sweeney [1970].
5. Interviews with company executives.
6. Interviews with company executives.
7. Stokes [1983].
8. Interviews with company executives.
9. Smith [1983]; *The Economist* [1982].
10. Nef, 1984.
11. Interviews with company executives.
12. Interviews with company executives.
13. *International Management* [1983].
14. Interviews with company executives; Sobel (1982).
15. Hill [1981].
16. Barre (1983).
17. Wells (1971).
18. Interviews with executives.
19. Interviews with company executives.
20. Christensen *et al.* [1982]; interviews with company executives.
21. Interviews with company executives; 'An International Courier Takes on Federal Express' (1983).
25. Interviews with company executives; Terpstra [1983, p. 279, p. 438], Byrne [1982].

APPENDIX II[a]

The Overselling of World Brands

Ted Levitt is disarmingly unrepentant. Having thrown the worlds of marketing and advertising into turmoil with his latest blockbuster article, 'The Globalisation of Markets,'* he admits that it contains a good deal of exaggeration:

- that 'the world's needs and desires have been irrevocably homogenised' (they actually haven't);
- that 'everything gets more and more like everything else' (it actually doesn't);
- and that national and multinational companies that do not 'go global' have little chance of survival (they may actually have a greater chance, though they will have to be nimble-footed).

Levitt who, for almost a quarter of a century has combined his professorship at the Harvard Business School with a more glamorous role as America's leading marketing sage, also concedes that the article failed to make a quite basic and crucial distinction between products and brands; that, just because the same product is sold in different countries, its branding, positioning, promotion and selling need not be identical. They *may* be, as Levitt advocates, but the decision is not automatic. (See Monday's feature on page 16, 'Why new products are going global'.)

'All I'm really trying to do is to stress the need for companies to examine the growing *similarities* between consumer preferences, as well as the *differences* which still persist,' Levitt explains. 'Of *course* I'm exaggerating.'

If you're trying to change human behaviour, you don't present people with convoluted or judiciously balanced arguments, he maintains. 'When it comes to implementing the ideas in my article, I assume that the reader is someone of commonsense and prudence.'

The trouble is that quite a lot of Levitt's readers, both of the original article a year ago in the Harvard Business Review, and of the longer version in his new book, 'The Marketing Imagination', appear to be taking him literally. Hence the controversy which is now raging in the advertising world, and the near-outraged response from Levitt's friend and challenger for the title of global marketing guru, Professor Philip Kotler of Northwestern University.

'He's setting marketing back,' Kotler complains. 'He wants to bend consumer demand to suit the product, rather than vice versa.'

Having spent the last two decades persuading companies to put market considerations first and the product second—to shift from a sales to a marketing-led approach, in other words—Levitt is now bent on 'going back to sales'. Kotler argues. He is concerned that Levitt's message 'is going to rejustify the approach which got international companies into such trouble in the past'.

Rather than anticipating the narrowing range of products which Levitt appears to predict, Kotler maintains that 'the reverse is occurring. Many new lifestyles are emerging and new, differentiated markets are opening up. Companies need a *wide* range of products, and a *wide* range of messages to the consumer, not the reverse.'

Kotler's criticism is not softened by Levitt's clarification of his article's rather unclear stance on market segmentation versus homogenization. 'Globalisation does not mean the end of market segments', Levitt now argues more emphatically than in

---

[a] Reprinted from an article by Christopher Lorenz, *Financial Times*.

the original, but 'it means that they expand to worldwide proportions' (he cites, for example, the widespread availability on both sides of the Atlantic of pitta bread, lasagna and Chinese food).

To which Kotler replies that only a very small proportion of the world's products will be able to be branded globally ('between 4 and 8 per cent'). One might add, on Kotler's side of the argument, that most of the segments which Levitt cites are supplied by regional, national or even local companies, not by global giants, and that their status (and therefore their positioning) varies from country to country; most Britons would laugh, for example, as the way that one of their most down-market foods, Scotch eggs—boiled eggs encased in sausage meat—are being promoted in New England as prime delicacies.

If one allows for the admitted overstatement of Levitt's article, for his subsequent clarifications, and for his jibe that 'Kotler's only looking at the present, not the future,' the difference between the two men becomes largely one of degree. But this still leaves, as a major cause for concern, the remarkable speed with which an extreme interpretation of Levitt's manifesto has caught the imagination of advertising agencies and their clients.

There has been plenty of evidence of this in the past few months and weeks. First Saatchi and Saatchi, the fast-growing upstart of the international advertising world, set the bandwagon in motion by positioning itself—in double-page newspaper ads on both sides of the Atlantic—as the agency which can help clients seize what it calls 'the opportunity for world brands'. Like Levitt's article, it seemed to assume—wrongly—that standardized, global products should automatically be marketed (i.e. positioned, promoted, advertised and sold) in a standardized fashion.

Then, at the end of last month, a more established international agency BBDO, nailed its colours to the same mast by calling clients and other outsiders to a seminar on global marketing at which it was claimed that over a fifth of the combined population of France, Britain and West Germany now constituted four new 'global constituencies'. (Underlining the argument that the new communicating technologies are a key influence behind this growing 'homogenisation', Levitt himself took part in the seminar via direct satellite transmission from the US.)

BBDO's overstated expressions of conversion to the 'global' cause, and McCann Erickson's clumsy—and fence-sitting—response to Saatchi (filling three pages of 'Advertising Age', the leading US trade paper), illustrate the dilemma which confronts agencies which have handled global campaigns for years but which have been left floundering by Saatchi's preemptive strike. They are all now faced with the unenviable task of demonstrating their global expertise while preserving their reputation for sophisticated understanding of the overwhelmingly predominant need for market-by-market differentiation.

* *Harvard Business Review* Repr. No. 83308. Fuller version in 'The Marketing Imagination'. Free Press ($16.75, US); Collier Macmillan (£14.25, Europe).

APPENDIX III

Strategy Brief for International Expansion

Co-operation between SBU (Home) and ID (International)

SBU (Home) is a specialist company with skills in manufacturing 'x' machines *and* extensive knowledge in both financing and operating 'y' businesses.

The company's export sales have essentially been limited to Europe with the exception of one small, but successful, distributor in the Middle East.

The servicing of equipment is considered crucial to the success of any operation and SBU (Home) are concerned that sales in developing countries could require a level of practical commitment from them which they would not be able to finance during the early stages of any market development, thereby putting their reputation at risk. Equally, experience suggests that potential distributors do not appreciate the intricacies involved in establishing such businesses and would therefore require a level of commercial assistance beyond SBU (Home)'s current ability.

SBU (Home) has, however, developed a working relationship with ID (Int.) which it is felt allows them to investigate ways and means of achieving overseas development while keeping commercial risks to a minimum.

Main Objectives
1. SBU (Home)'s main objective outside Europe is to secure a viable market presence in the main geographical regions upon which future activity can be based. As SBU (Home)'s only valid experience is in the Gulf region it has been decided that activity will initially be confined to that area while effective methods of working are proven.

Therefore:

2. In the smaller Middle Eastern States SBU (Home) wishes to develop its business around a main distributor in a way which will enable it to retain commercial and policy control but at the same time keep support costs within specified limits.

And:

3. In the larger territory of Saudi Arabia, to identify a suitable partner and establish a main distributorship for the whole territory.

Subsequently:

4. From this knowledge of Middle East operations to determine which order of priority to give to other potential areas of development world-wide.

Methods of Working
In view of the limited nature of SBU (Home)'s immediate objectives and the requirement to integrate new activity into the company's day-to-day business, it has been decided that a project team comprising SBU (Home)'s Contract Director, Export Sales Manager, and ID (Int.)'s Development Director will be set up. In broad outline, the field-work and overseas negotiations will be undertaken by ID (Int.) and all UK business development aspects will be undertaken by SBU (Home).

It is the nature of this arrangement that there is to be a complete interchange of information within the project team and a constant co-ordination of thought and effort.

Responsibilities
The outline responsibilities and planned timing to implement the main objectives are tabled in the Action Plans attached to this Strategy Brief. SBU (Home)'s main responsibilities are:

1. To evaluate and respond to formal recommendations of the Project Team within 8 weeks.
2. To maintain an export support system and accord sensible priority treatment to new overseas distributors.
3. To make available training aids and literature to support the operations at their own cost.
4. To provide training facilities for newly appointed distributors.
5. To provide ID (Int.) with copies of all correspondence and quotations relevant to the project area.

ID (International)'s responsibilities are:

1. To make available adequate time during overseas territorial visits to undertake project work.
2. To report back in writing after overseas visits and to be available for all project discussions when reasonably required to do so.
3. Wherever necessary, to co-ordinate Head Office effort to support SBU (Home) (e.g. Legal, Tax, and Finance Departments).
4. To ensure that SBU (Home) staff are introduced to any new contacts and that all relevant contact information is made available to SBU (Home).
5. To pursue the best interests of SBU (Home) and to support decisions of the Project Team in the field.

Costs
ID (Int.) will not seek reimbursement for any of its services: it is understood, however, that SBU (Home) will co-operate with ID (Int.) to ensure that uneconomic overseas visits (i.e. short single-product/single-territory visits) do not occur. SBU (Home) will cover all its own direct and indirect costs. Should it become necessary for ID (Int.) to incur costs on behalf of SBU (Home) these will be reimbursed to ID (Int.), always provided that such costs are identified, invoiced, and agreed *in advance*.

Nominated Contacts in SBU (Home) are:
Overall policy: ——— ——— (Managing Director)
Project Team: ——— ——— (Director and Commercial Manager)
            ——— ——— (Director and Contracts Manager)

Note: Detailed action plans with timing agreed by the project team are required to make the strategy brief work.

4

Research and Overseas Partner Selection

The relationship between the two subjects is a very close one because in basic terms one is talking about the detail of the market that is going to be developed, and the person or organization that is going to be responsible for achieving planned objectives on the ground. The term 'partner' will be used throughout this Chapter to denote the selected presence in a foreign country. Generally, more specific names are used such as agent or distributor and often the partner title is used for associates in a joint venture (i.e. joint venture partner (JVP)). The choice of partner in the overall context is, however, not simply a whim because it does have a value in denoting a willingness to work together without either side, of necessity, having authority one over the other. It will be argued later that this remains true even when there is majority holding in a joint venture—the facts of life are that if one party is constantly overruled, co-operation ceases.

The relationship between research and its application is fundamental. It can be argued that if the basic proposition is to develop a market, the proposer has no right to waste other people's time and money unless the basis of a valid opportunity is proven. Equally, a prospective partner who will not set aside the time, resource, and effort to assist in developing a valid proposition into a cogent task-orientated market plan is not worthy of further consideration either.

So often it would appear that the emphasis is on linkage with partners of obviously perceived quality, but limited communication skills cause the basic questions about what the partner is capable of contributing and achieving to be inadequately evaluated. As a result, the expectations of both sides rarely match and a weakening and erosion of association often take place. Such associations are often characterized by constant delays, lack of support, and suspicion. It is certainly not unknown for large groups to audit their overseas agents only to find that the large majority are either dissatisfied or defunct, suggesting that a true commonality of purpose never existed.

Many companies would be better off selecting and making the effort to develop smaller or less-obvious partners who would grow into the market, rather than simply slotting in with the obvious and never bringing the power of local skills and knowledge to the market plan. Developing any market requires sustained effort: if nothing else one should expect that a partner who spends his life thinking about his market-place has some valid thoughts to contribute in excess of those that the principal might have garnered in his part-time assessments.

RESEARCH

All research is going to take time and cost money with the only alternative being to act on hunch or gut feeling. The latter appoach often turns out to take considerably more time and frequently incurs losses in the long run. The reasons why this should be so stem from the fact that one is not simply trying to assess if there is an opportunity but also to determine how an opportunity can be developed on a profitable long-term basis. Once again the linkage between partners and research resurfaces since if there is no long-term profit for partners then they lose interest and rightly so. After all, who wants to be a busy fool? Therefore it is not simply a question of getting started but rather the problem of planning to keep going. The questions of market size are only of relative importance compared with the setting of objectives and the planning of both time and resource to achieve them. In the end it is the implementation of specific plans by named people that brings researched markets to life. In this sense it is not only partners and research that are linked, but equally an overall link is forged between the wish and fulfilment of strategy.

A broad issue that may require consideration is whether to buy research or to carry out one's own. Given that the basic dangers of time wasting and reinventing the wheel can be overcome by obtaining readily published data, there is a strong case for personal involvement. In domestic markets relationships between companies and customers can be well organized, proximity gives confidence, and there are generally enough 'reference points' for all parties to back their judgements. Market researchers are working in their own medium and project control can usually be as tight as one wishes to make it. The moment research moves overseas, however, a new set of dimensions are added, and picking up the answer from a third party can cut out an important part of the overall understanding and learning curves. Equally, the communication chain gets longer as consultants themselves subcontract work overseas to other companies or subsidiary offices. Clearly, in such circumstances the potential for misunderstandings and 'watering down' becomes greater. Some will also consider that the responsibility for results will have been weakened.

In some countries research can present particular problems as a result of cultural differences, with respondents lacking familiarity with research techniques. Straighforward problems concerning language and the lack of accurate up-to-date basic data also occur. It is suggested that the weaker the research conditions the greater the validity in using company personnel becomes.

Frank Dale, writing in the *Industrial Mareting Digest*, puts forward a very acceptable no-nonsense approach for awarding research contracts and running research projects:

- Select from three (or so) competitive quotes.
- Note that the speed of response and that the quality of the proposal is indicative (of what is to come).
- Heavily word-processed proposals are both obvious and insulting.
- Visit the consultants' office and meet the research team.
- Do not place too much value on related experience—it often makes consultants lazy.
- Demand a list of recent clients and contact them.

and on running a consultant-based project:

- Meet the research team frequently.
- Trust the appointed consultants.
- Ensure your own confidentiality.
- Do not change direction half way through the project.
- Treat consultants' work seriously, and use normal people–relation techniques to get the best out of them.

In overseas research work it is particularly important to meet local researchers to ensure that their understanding is clear.

The main judgements throughout, and not just at the end of research work, and which applies equally to both in-house and consultancy work are:

- Is the level of knowledge increasing?
- Is the interpretation valid in helping key judgements to be made?
- Is the information coming through of management significance (as opposed to statistical interest)?

If confirmation is coming through strongly in the above-mentioned areas then perhaps it does not matter over-much to the company whether an in-house or a consultancy team is coming up with the answers. It could, however, be more significant in a new market where the lack of personal interest and involvement, which can be accompanied by a comparable lack of detailed knowledge and understanding, might become long-term defects. Prospective customers and partners, who may well be important links in the research study, can sometimes draw adverse conclusions from an early lack of personal involvement. When negotiations do start in earnest there is of course a perceptible difference between real knowledge gathered 'on the hoof', and gleanings from a nicely bound report which, while it may say it all, nevertheless does so second-hand.

If it is felt that the assessment is a little too 'black and white', a valid point has, however, been made concerning commitment and the building of confidence; moreover the point concerning empathy made in Chapter 3 has been echoed. If the basic points concerning attitude to the market have been fully assessed then clearly a number of compromise solutions are possible.

THE PURPOSE AND METHOD OF RESEARCH

The overall purpose of research in a practical sense is to define the optimum method of entry into an international market and to assess the level of 'Product Translation' that is necessary to achieve long-term profitability and market share. Further, the means of physical supply and distribution have to be assessed, and 'trade offs' calculated. A decision also has to be taken with regard to partner selection. If a positive long-term presence is to be achieved it is important to remember that the depth of research suggested above is as important for setting up agency or distribution arrangements as it is for establishing a joint venture or the like. The point has already been made that markets which do not have long-term profit life in them do not maintain interest.

With regard to method, adjustments have to be made for international work.

The first important feature is to ensure that there is a written company commitment and brief to investigate and, if appropriate, to negotiate market entry within broad parameters. This requisite ensures not only that the cost of research is not wasted, but, more importantly, it ensures that any general discussions that may have taken place on strategy come down to a firm commitment to act. All those issues which are natural to most companies in the internationalizing process (such as the fears of the unions and the production and financial departments, for example) should all be resolved in principle at a stage prior to research. No one should be asked to put a foot on a boat or a plane or cash a travellers' cheque unless there is a written brief of company commitment. Obtaining such a brief should also ensure that a thought-out case of activity has been presented.

To have made such a case it will have been necessary to focus on the relevant macro data, some of which will undoubtedly have been used in defining general areas of interest, perhaps through risk analysis or the assessment of levels of investment incentives (see Chapter 2).

Additionally, information will have been required which is specific to the industry in question. Most business activity has between three to five key factors which determine its existence, such as the number of people in specific groups, or the numbers of buildings, main products, transactions, or movements, etc. In a practical way, at this stage the knowledge can be expanded and brought to life by ensuring that the maximum information is gleaned from market participants such as overseas businessmen visiting the home territory and, equally importantly, from expatriates who have recently worked full-time in the proposed market. Seminars, embassy junkets, inward missions, and the like may not be everyone's idea of deep research but they do provide useful lists of people who can be contacted and who are usually willing to offer their opinions; there is always something in being asked for advice that seems to bring the best out of people.

All of this activity can constitute what is often more formally known as the desk research programme. Developed in an imaginative way it can provide an informative and useful background, as well as many short cuts for those who are going to carry out the field research work. To set off with a list of known names and contacts and up-to-date background notes can be a godsend and far superior to a list culled solely from directories—often where the size of print is in inverse proportion to the importance of the companies concerned!

For a full discussion on research methods and processes, reference should be made to a more detailed work on the subject such as Aubry Wilson's 'Assessment of Industrial Markets', which is particularly thorough. Wilson's check-list of questions, as presented by the British Overseas Trade Board—which for many may be an 'eye-opener' in its scope—has been included as Appendix I at the end of this chapter.

Some recourse to statistical method is usually required and Richard Levin's *Statistics for Management* is thorough but perhaps a little too heavy for a handbook; slimmer and good on the subject of sampling is A. H. R. Delens, *Principles of Market Research* (Crosby & Lockwood & Son Ltd., 1964 reprint).

Whatever selection of information is considered appropriate, the international research brief is going to concentrate on four key areas:

(1) The market and the best route to it.
(2) Product orientation and technical considerations.
(3) Financial and legal issues.
(4) Partner considerations.

Setting out an acceptable brief together with a valid questionnaire is, however, often the starting-point for another set of problems in international market research. Therefore an early view needs to be taken of the breadth and depth of research that is required. While clearly no firm rules on time allocation can exist it is not unusual to set aside six to eight weeks and to split that time into two equal parts.

While this time span may appear to be considerable and costly, the task of getting around and tracking people down can cut aggressively into any pre-planned schedule. Further, those who have had experience of European or North American field research will have worked with respondents who know and appreciate the reseach routine, and who will have given succinct answers to straight questions which facilitate resonably quick assessment.

In developing countries, however, different rules may apply. As expatriates are often short of time and beset with a host of problems, their availability cannot always be taken as read; nevertheless, there is often a strong spirit of camaraderie and a genuine desire to help. The problem of bias should be looked at since there is no reason for respondents to be worried about your return on assets. The thought of local availability for any product can often be sufficient cause to give encouragement. The local respondent will not necessarily have been subjected to research techniques to any great extent. His style of discussion does not always lend itself to direct questions and answers. Moreover, in a direct response sequence he may have the annoying habit of responding 'what do you think?' and, frequently, he is out of touch with the time-consuming techniques that may not be in his opinion directly related to the rapid growth of business.

In order to achieve contact with the correct sample of respondents, it is not an unreasonable task to contact four local people a day during the first research period, as well as fitting in expatriates at easier times and venues. In the third world in particular, Beaty's words will ring true: 'The researcher's attitude should reflect the dictum, "understand before being understood".'

The first two or three days in a territory are often best spent on straightforward physical research, walking around areas of basic industrial interest, and getting a feel for the business environment, for the product or service. This prevents researchers appearing as complete novices and asking inept questions.

On balance, the most universally acceptable style of questioning is the semi-structured interview. That is to say, keeping the questionnaire well out of sight, but nevertheless firmly guiding the conversation and agreeing that notes will be taken. The semi-structured interview is more acceptable to local people and certainly prevents 'drying-up' and the embarrassment that can be caused when the answer to a direct question is not readily available.

Other advice concerning research in the third world would be to seek to be as casual as possible, to ensure that there is no mixture of levels of authority in interviews, or mixture of language with joint respondents, and, perhaps above all else, to ensure that any comments cannot be traced back to an individual.

The golden rule is to write up notes as the research develops, whatever the cost in midnight oil. The day after is too late; there are too many other problems and intrusions, and too many new ideas that come with the tomorrow. In concentrated research the mind is clearly focused and everything may seem quite clear at the time but the speed with which that clarity fades the moment one returns home to a laden desk is nothing short of alarming. Consequently, pressures and problems that come in the first two or three weeks will make a break imperative if intellectual integrity is to be maintained. A break will also give an indispensable opportunity to move away from the minutiae of any problems and to assess, evaluate, and prepare for the next important phase of action, which in most cases will involve partner selection.

Amongst all the major considerations, one working practice is certainly worth following world-wide: the researcher should keep detailed notes of how to get to various offices, and retain all business cards, etc. so that he will have begun to form an invaluable database for future operations.

From the foregoing it will have become clear that it is not only the interpretation of language that is important, equally important is the wider interpretation of the different market-place where, for example, from the outset culture can exercise an important influence on understanding. Therefore the validity of working with a local partner once sufficient basic information has been gained begins to gain currency. The problem that cannot be avoided, however, is that the first meeting with a prospective partner is also the first stage of the negotiating process. Therefore, before taking matters further forward it is useful to examine criteria concerning partner identification and selection.

PARTNER SELECTION

After the selection of a territory for development the choice of a working partner has to be considered as the most important single consideration. The key to partner selection is to see the activity as part of the research process as it is only in this way that identification, evaluation, and negotiation can be amalgamated to achieve a mutually agreeable long-term arrangement. Simply to link up with a recommended name or to capitalize on a supposed opportunity is unlikely to produce the required result.

It is important to remember that in a chosen market the selection of a partner will indicate, to a company's potential customers and competitors, the quality of expertise, local knowledge, and commitment that is going to be brought to bear. Appearing as the 47th agency on the left of one of the traditional outlets is hardly likely to comfort customers or put the fear of God into competitors! A mistake in this area is, of course, an open testimony of commercial ineptness, which not only has its own problems, but which is likely to make negotiations for a subsequent change very difficult to handle. The financial downside in an agency arrangement might not be too damaging, although the loss of opportunities might prove irksome, and clearly the stakes are higher in more permanent arrangements such as joint ventures.

It has already been argued that partners and principals should spend time together in joint research to improve the quality of knowledge; but the subject is again reiterated because the future of any relationship has to be a task- and work-orientated one. It can only benefit from both sides proving one to the other that they can work together, that they can communicate, and that there are no cultural or personality issues that will constitute a barrier in the future. On the positive side, if the parties can move to a point where they share common ground on the ways and means of developing a market the relationship will be off to a better start than most. In any co-operative situation there is a fundamental need to know what each partner can contribute because this reflects the expectations of the partners and the costs of participation which are essential ingredients to any negotiation. The process should also signify whether the sum total of skills and resources is adequate for the task in hand. It is difficult to deny the principles although it is clearly easy to fall into the temptation of taking short cuts on what may be considered simple market entry situations such as the agency arrangement. It should not be forgotten, however, that any form of market entry is a market test which, if successful, can lead to a more committed presence. The time to decide on the critical issues of personality, working styles, and basic market judgements and assumptions is before an operation commences—not half way through the piece, when the recriminations have already begun to flow.

From a negotiating point of view it is both comforting and good practice to know that there is a choice of partners to deal with initially. It should also be noted that there is a growing body of agency law developing around the world which is generally protective of the incumbent and aimed at penalizing the caprices of principles. Provision for compensation on the termination of agreement emphasizes the importance of giving professional and thoughtful consideration to partner selection. It is important to know the state of agency and kindred laws, as well as the environment that is prompting their drafting, before contemplating the negotiating of any formal contract. Once again, the commitment that arises from joint research is of help in filtering out partners who may have a more tactical negotiation in mind and a 'shield' to hide behind.

Within the selection process there are three main areas of consideration:

(1) Conceptual matching—which type of partner best matches the principal's style of operation?
(2) The proposed partner's business effectiveness.
(3) The proposed partner's likely effectiveness with the product in question.

Conceptual matching is important since it draws out at an early stage who best suits the style and aspirations of the incoming company. An organization may feel more comfortable dealing with a company of its own size and market status, albeit in relative terms. Alternatively, a smaller organization may be preferred with a view to supporting the 'lean and hungry' and allowing the retention of a more dominant role. Some principals, perhaps prior to investing in assets, prefer partners to have strong connections at government level, while others may feel that a clear management structure and succession planning, and a task force approach enables them to install and develop longer-term strategies. With some products the prime concern could be with technical appraisal, or ethical considerations.

Mistakes in this area are generally identified by companies feeling uncomfortable with the support that they are getting. There will be arguments about business purpose and the pace of development and unease about access to and supervision of the customer base. Evaluation of a partner's business position may be judged by reference to points similar to those set out in Appendix II at the end of this chapter. Likely effectiveness with the product in question may be judged by consideration of the points set out in Appendix III at the end of this chapter.

It has been acknowledged previously that failed selections occur in generous abundance and while no foolproof method has been identified the ideas of researching, evaluating, and working with partners prior to final selection, as well having a shared set of facts and assumptions that constitute the backbone of the market plan, are sound enough concepts. However demanding on one's reserves of skill and time, this process should be sufficient to prevent a perfunctory jumping into bed in haste, to be followed by regret at leisure. Most considerations of partner selections draw upon metaphors concerning engagement and marriage as well as associated activities; such ideas generally feature at some stage in negotiation and generate ad lib comments. Such ideas may be at one and the same time trite but meaningful in passing a message. It is recommended, however, before reaching any firm conclusion that at least a cursory view is taken of the way in which the other side treat their womenfolk! Once again it is underlined that even a simple word can be obscured by cultural differences. By definition, the general programme of activity outlined requires the principal to be active on the ground in his chosen market-place from the start. No consideration has been given, nor indeed should be given, to setting up any arrangement by letter or to falling for a good presentation in one's own offices. It is to be hoped that such sins no longer feature so prominently in the shrinking world, or if they do they belong to the congenitally lazy rather than the ill-informed. Such phrases as 'Let's give them a try' and 'Anything we sell there is better than a kick in the pants', are but two well-known business death wishes. Failed and ineffective partners are signposts of a principal's ineffectiveness and such associations will be of little interest to final customers who did not realize that they were buying a 'Marginal Blessing' from an indifferent distant management.

The combination of market research improved by local knowledge and a soundly selected partner will enable the principal to put the final touches to his territorial plan (alternatively market plan, business plan, or feasibility study.) As such, a firm view will have emerged as to how the market should be developed over a series of finite phases.

Therefore, through a funnelling-down process a point has been reached where the overall strategy has been married to a structure, people have been allowed the time and resources fully to research an overseas opportunity and to decide what type of local help they need. In the broadest sense, a level of market involvement will have been determined which, for ease of reference, one might fit into Vern Terpstras general international activity modes:

- Active exporting.
- Licensing.
- Overseas marketing.
- Foreign production.

These broad categories can be broken down into more detail by adapting a Figure first published in 1970 by Reijo Luostarinen showing the flow of various levels of international involvement. The adapted Figure 4.1 is a very good way of gaining a quick summary of the levels of complexity and

Basic Business Environment Considerations Governing International Partner Selection

Overall Company Position	Present Strengths	Customer Perceptions	Financial Stimulus	Knowledge of International Locations
Financial Returns	Size and Competitive Position	Product Presentation	Home Control and Export Incentives	Economic Environment
Market Position	Technological Advantages	Distribution Service	Overseas Control and Incentives	Political Environment
Resource Allocation	Economic Advantages	Price	Predicted Home Economic Environment	Legal Considerations
Control Criteria	Management Skills	Promotion and Packaging		Cultural Considerations
Experience of Key Executives	Stage in Product Life Cycle			Post Experience

Preferred International Position

Low Commitments — Medium Commitments — High Commitments

Low Commitments

Passive Exporting
1. Use of Trading Houses Import/Export Agencies
2. Export Management Companies
3. Factors
4. Sale of Parts/Accessories to Other Exporters (piggy back)

Medium Commitments

Positive International Participation
1. International Agents
2. International Distributors
3. International Marketing Offices
4. Franchises
5. Counter Trade
6. Commercial Joint Ventures
7. Controlled Importing

High Commitments

International Production and 'Symbotic' Activity

Short term
Local Assembly
Licensing and Buyback
Turnkey Projects
Management Contracts

Long term
Joint Ventures
Acquisitions
Set up New Plants

Possible Benefits Sought:

	Low Commitments (Passive Exporting)	Medium Commitments (Positive International Participation)	High Commitments (International Production)
Key Commitment Requirements			
Reduce Costs		×	×
Reduce Supply Problems		×	×
Restrictive Industry			×
Improve Product Awareness		×	×
Improve Sales to New Areas			×
Reposition Product in Life Cycle		×	×
Clear Strategy and Policies		×	×
Research	× (to ensure future not prejudiced)	×	×
Organisation Structure			×
Senior Management Involvement and Control			
Finanical Involvement			×

Source: Based on Reijo Luostarinen, 'Foreign Operations of the Firm', Helsinki School of Economics (1970) and J. D. Daniels, 'Combining Strategic and International Business Approaches Through Growth Vector Analysis', *Management International Review*, 3 (1983).

Figure 4.2. Positive Relationships Between International Product Life Cycle (IPLC) and International Commitment

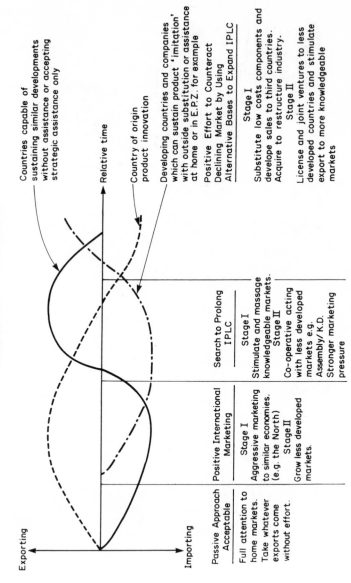

Source: Extended and adapted from S. Onkvisit and J. J. Shaw, 'An Examination of the International Product Life Cycle and its Application within Marketing', *Columbia Journal of World Business* (Autumn 1983). The importance of the presentation also lies in understanding *the potential* for international strategies to disrupt and benefit from the promotion of alternative IPLCs for specific products and markets.

commitment in international trade and to a degree it can be restated by reference to the international product life cycle shown in Figure 4.2.

To progress further it is now necessary to consider in greater detail the various methods of entry to foreign markets and such considerations will form the main content of the following chapters.

References

1 John Walmsley, *Handbook of International Joint Ventures* (Graham and Trotman: London, 1982).
2 R. J. Wooding, 'Choosing a Distributor in a Third World Country', *International Management* (Nov. 1983).
3 P. W. Beamish, 'Joint Ventures in LDCs: Partner Selection and Performance', *MIR* 27 (1987).
4 'Distribution', *Industrial Marketing Digest* (2nd Quarter 1980).
5 David T Beaty, 'Helping Business Graduates Capture Third World Research Data', *Business Graduate* (1985).
6 E. L. Cussler, 'How to do Basic Research', *Chemical Engineering* (Feb. 1981).
7 G. P. Moschis and T. Stanley, 'What Managers Should Know about Market Research', *Business* (July/Sept. 1984).
8 R. Paul, 'How to get There from Here', *Sales and Marketing Management*, Special Report (Antar extract ZC50).
9 P. Dale, 'Choosing and Using Your Industrial Market Research Consultant', *Industrial Marketing Digest* (Antar extract LP73).
10 Ger van der Most, 'Industrial Research Should Go', *European Research* (July 1984).
11 J. F. Laman Trip, 'International Research Needs', *European Research* (July 1985).
12 Philip Barnard, 'Conducting and Coordinating Multi-Country Quantitative Studies across Europe', Paper to the American Marketing Association (Oct. 1983).
13 S. T. Cavusgil, 'Qualitative Insights into Company Experiences in International Research', *Journal of Business and Industrial Marketing*, 2/3 (1987).
14 A. J. Williamson, 'Field Research', *Journal of International Marketing and Marketing Research* (Antar extract ZH65).
15 S. Hawkins, 'How to Understand Your Partner's Cultural Baggage', *International Management* (Sept. 1983).
16 C. L. Ratza, 'The Strategic Marketing Process: A Practical Framework for Analytic Market Planning and Analysis', *Managerial Planning* (Mar./Apr. 1983).
17 R. L. Cook and J. R. Burley, 'A Framework for Evaluating International Physical Distribution Strategies', *International Journal of Physical Distribution and Marketing Management* (Antar extract GH56).
18 S. Onkvisit and J. J. Shaw, 'An Examination of the International Product Life-Cycle and its Appreciation within Marketing', *Columbia Journal of World Business* (Autumn 1983).
19 J. D. Daniels, 'Combining Strategic and International Business Approaches Through Growth Vector Analysis', *Management International Review*, 3 (1983).
20 P. Varadarajan and D. Rajaratnam, 'Symobiotic Marketing Revisited', *Journal of Marketing*, 50 (Jan. 1986) 7–12.
21 M. J. Thanas, 'International Product Life-Cycles and the International Automobile Industry', *European Journal of Marketing*, 15/3 (1982).

22 V. Terpstra, *International Marketing* (3rd edn. Dryden Press: London, 1983).
23 J. D. Goodnow, 'Developments in International Mode of Entry Analysis', *International Marketing Review* (Autumn 1985).
24 'New World in the Making: World Economic Power is shifting towards the Pacific Region', *Financial Times*, 30 June 1988.

APPENDIX I[a]

Industrial Marketing Researcher's Check-List

Market Size

1. What is the size of the total market for the product?
2. How durable is the market?
3. What is domestic consumption (volume or value)?
4. What proportion or amount (volume and/or value) is met from domestic production?
5. What proportion or amount (volume and/or value) is met from imported sources?
6. What are the main export markets from (a) domestic productin (b) re-exported imports?
7. What factors limit the size of the total market?
8. What are the sizes of the various market strata?
      by geographical regions;
      by size of user;
      by industry;
      by type, quality, design or price of product;
      by type of distributor.
9. What is the size of the total market for a substitute product?
10. What are the export possibilities?

Market Structure

1. Who are the main domestic suppliers to the market?
2. Which countries are the main source of imports?
3. Which importing firms are the most important?
4. What is the export performance of main competitors?
5. Which are their main markets?
6. What are the geographical variations in the domestic market?
7. What are the seasonal/cyclical variations in the domestic market?
8. What factors currently favour the emergence of new competitors?
9. What factors are currently likely to lead to the reduction of competitors?
10. Which are the main user industries?
11. Which are the subsidiary user industries?
12. Is in-feeding significant in the user industries?
13. Do reciprocal trading practices exist?

Market Trends

1. How does the market size compare with
      10 years ago;
      5 years ago;
      last year?
2. How does product demand differ from
      10 years ago;

[a] Reprinted from Wilson, *The Assessment of Industrial Markets*, courtesy of Aubrey Wilson Associates, London.

    5 years ago;
    last year?
3. What trends are revealed indicating a shift in demand over the last
    10 years;
    5 years;
    last year?
4. In what ways are market changes likely to manifest themselves?
5. What changes are occurring in the user industries likely to induce a change in demand?
6. What changes are occurring in the non-user industries likely to induce a new demand?
7. What changes are occurring in the firm's products and processes likely to induce a change in demand?
8. What changes are occurring in the economy likely to affect demand for the firm's products?
    levels of employment;
    levels of income;
    level of industrial investment;
    level of industrial profits;
    industrial dividends;
    rates of corporate taxation;
    wholesale prices;
    level of industrial production;
    consumers' expenditure;
    personal savings;
    rates of personal taxation;
    retail prices;
    population trends;
    rates of interest;
    credit restrictions;
    hire-purchase debt;
    export trends;
    import trends;
    balance of payments
9. What trends are likely to attract new entrants into the industry in the future?
10. What trends are likely to reduce the numbers of competitors in the future?
11. Are changes in materials or production methods likely to reduce the need for the product?

Market Share

1. What share of the market does the firm command?
2. What are the main competitors' shares?
3. What is the firm's share of the market when broken down?
    by industries;
    by size of firms;
    geographically.
4. What are the main competitor's shares?
    by industries;
    by size of firms;
    geographically.
5. What share of the market is held by imported products?

6. What factors support the market of imported products?
7. What percentage of business is from:
   old customers;
   new customers?
8. How concentrated or dispersed are sales?

The Firm

1. What is the reputation of the firm within the user industries?
2. What is the reputation of the firm's products within these industries?
3. What is the firm's 'image'?
4. What are the firm's individual 'brand images'?
5. Is the name and reputation of the firm established?
6. Do the firm's suppliers form potential markets for its products?
7. Does the firm absorb any of its own products?
8. What services are provided by the firm?
9. How do these relate to market requirements?
10. What guarantees are offered?
11. How advisable is it to brand own products with private brands?
12. What are the critical factors for success (e.g. distributive network 'approvals', local participation, etc.)?

Marketing Methods

1. What marketing tools are currently used and how do they compare with the firm's current choice of tools?
2. How does budget percentage in each of the following media compare with competitors'?
   newspapers;
   journals;
   outdoor;
   direct mail;
   exhibitions;
   education campaigns;
   catalogues and brochures;
   public relations campaigns;
   point of sale;
   films;
   sampling;
   others
3. What reasons can be ascribed for any differences?
4. What other tools should be considered?
5. What criteria will be used for rejection or acceptance?
6. What methods of evaluation of total marketing and of individual tools exist?
7. How often is an evaluation of effectiveness made?
8. What is the history of the firm's marketing expenditure in value, and per unit sold?
9. What is the cost of marketing?
   annually;
   per enquiry;
   per order;
   per salesman;
   by media.

10. What is the marketing expenditure broken down by?
    method;
    media;
    seasonally;
    geographically;
    industry;
    application.
11. How does the firm's marketing history and performance compare with competitors'?
12. What is the copy strategy used on the firm's products during the last 5 years?
13. What are the major changes and causes of change in copy strategy which have occurred in the last 5 years?
14. To what type of advertising and other media are users and potential users most exposed?
15. In what way does competitive advertising differ from the firm's?
    other media;
    frequency;
    space;
    copy;
    strategy.
16. What is the audience (in numbers) for specific methods?

Personal Selling

1. What are the usual personal selling methods adopted for the product?
2. What is the history of the firm's personal selling methods?
3. What is the user industry structure, organization, and geographical division for the sale of the product?
4. How does this compare with the firm's usual structure, organization, and geographical division for the sale of the product?
5. What is the sales history of the product in value and volume?
6. How specialized is selling among competitors?
7. If the product is seasonal, can fluctuations be evened out by balancing sales of varying types of products or by buying inducements?
8. What aids do salesmen need?
    advertising support;
    technical advice;
    marketing data;
    catalogues;
    drawings;
    samples;
    educational slides or film demonstrations;
    offers of credit;
    offers of HP facilities.
9. How effectively are tenders handled?
10. What proportion of inquiries are converted to sales?
11. How does this compare with
    5 years ago;
    last year.
12. What is the image of the firm's salesmen?
13. How are salesmen motivated and how does this compare with competitors?
14. Do salesmen concentrate on benefits or features?

15. Is the call reporting form adequate for providing information on customer needs, reactions, and reasons for lost business, etc.?
16. Could the sales reporting form be adapted to provide market information?
17. Is there a reporting back system to individual salesmen on best and total sales performance?
18. Are salesmen technically qualified?
19. What proportion of total calls are committed to existing customers?
20. How many calls are for new business?
21. How many initial approaches are required, on average, to begin a meaningful dialogue?
22. What is the average number of calls required to secure one order?
23. How many quotations are submitted, on average, in order to obtain one order?
24. What is the average order value for new business?
25. What is the average order value for repeat business?
26. What proportion of calls are made by appointments?
27. How many telephone canvass calls are made in a day?
28. How many telephone canvass calls are required, on average, to secure one appointment?
29. How many letters are sent to prospects each day?
30. What proportion of these are followed up by phone or by a visit?
31. What proportion of letters produce a response without follow-up?

Distribution Methods

1. Approximately how many distributors of the product are there in the market as a whole?
2. How effective are the distributive methods used?
3. How do they compare with competitors' distributive methods?
4. What alternatives exist?
5. What is the division of the firm's sales by:
    each type of distributor;
    size of distributor;
    geographical location of distributors;
    industrial concentration of distributors?
6. What percentage of total sales for each product is directly transacted with users?'
7. What is the history of the introduction of the product and the sequence of marketing steps which led to its present distribution?
8. What is the replenishment lead time?
9. What is the history of 'out-of-stock' situations?
10. What stocks are normally held at the plant?
    average;
    seasonal.
11. What stocks are normally in the distributive pipeline?
12. How far do distributors handle service, maintenance, spares, etc.?
13. How far do distributors handle competitors' service, maintenance, spares, etc.?
14. How technically competent are distributors?
15. Are franchise and exclusive dealing arrangements prevalent?
16. Are the distributive outlets the most efficient available?
17. How effective are distributors' selling efforts?
18. What aids do competitors give to distributors?

19. How do the firm's aids to distributors compare with those offered by competitors?
20. To what extent do distributors concentrate on the product group?
21. To what extent are distributors verticalized?
22. What other types of product do they handle?
23. What types of customer/industry do they supply to (e.g. across all industries, only to small customers?
24. Do distributors influence the *make* of products purchased by the end user?
25. Is the role of the distributor increasing, decreasing or remaining constant in importance in the market under review?
26. Do distributors compete for customers with their suppliers? If so, to what degree?
27. What is the size of discounts offered to distributors?
    By the firm and by competitors?

Shipment and Packaging

 1. How is the package shipped?
 2. How do the firm's physical transport methods compare with competitors'?
    cost;
    speed;
    liability to damage;
    liability to pilferage.
 3. What are the comparative shipping costs and times using alternative methods?
 4. Would standard crate dimensions affect cost of shipment?
 5. Is the package destroyed, returned, or reused?
 6. Is the package used to hold contents until empty or is it immediately emptied?
 7. Should the package have a dispensing device?
 8. What is the average amount of contents used on each occasion?
 9. Is other material subsequently stored in the package?
10. At what distance must the package be identified?
11. How is identification of contents achieved?
12. How is the package handled in the stockroom, on the factory floor, and elsewhere?
13. How long is a package held in stock?
14. What stock protection measures are necessary?
15. How are empties stored?
16. What protective measures are required against damage in transit and storage by vermin, moisture, temperature, pilferage?
17. How is the package handled in storage and shipment?
18. What is the history of delayed deliveries?
19. Are customers informed when the product is despatched and by what route or carrier?
20. How far are late deliveries caused by delayed despatches and how far by slow transport methods or handling?
21. Are customers made aware of delays caused by carriers?

Profit

1. What is the profit history of the product?
2. What is the unit profit history?
3. What is known about profits of other manufacturers in the same field?

4. What contribution to profits of other products does the product make?
5. What non-profit advantages does the firm derive?
6. What changes in profits have changes in marketing strategy achieved in the last 5 years?

Costs and Pricing

1. What is the cost history and structure of the firm's product?
2. What information is obtainable on competitors' cost structures?
3. Does the firm have any advantages in production costs over the competitors?
4. Does the firm have any advantages in marketing costs over the competitors?
5. Is a standard cost system in use for projecting profits?
6. Does the firm have any advantages in procurement costs over the competitors?
7. How do R & D expenditure and results compare with competitors?
8. How is the quoted price for an order calculated (e.g. individually standard list prices and discounts individually for large orders)?
9. What discount structure does the firm and its competitors operate—e.g. bulk, seasonal, type of customer (e.g. OEM, contractor, wholesaler, end user), retrospective, other?
10. What has been the annual average change in price of the firm's and competitors' products/services over the last 5 years?
11. What percentage of the overall price change over the last 5 years has been due to product/service modifications?
12. When was the firm's and competitors' last price change?
13. What were the reasons?
14. How does the firm's price compare with competitors'? What accounts for this similarity/difference?
15. Do any of the products/services under review act as 'loss leaders' to the total range? If so, which?
16. Are variances from list price controlled by the appropriate managers?
17. Are special pricing arrangements, promotional prices and 'deals' reported as variance from list prices?
18. Are prices compared country to country?
19. Are competitive pricing analyses and rationales available explaining differences?
20. Are there historical records on product pricing including percent increases and decreases?

The Product

1. What are the major and subsidiary uses for the firm's product?
2. How do the major uses for the firm's product compare with the major uses for competitors' products?
3. What is the width of the firm's range?
4. What is the depth of the firm's range?
5. Under what conditions are the firm's products used?
6. Is the product incorporated into any other products and is it identifiable when incorporated?
7. What is the extent of these additional uses?
8. What is the idealized 'profile' for a product of the type being marketed?
9. How far does the firm's product accord with the users' idealized conception of the product?

10. What are the products' unique qualities?
11. What are the product's 'plusses'?
12. What are its weaknesses?
13. How does the product differ from
    10 years ago;
    5 years ago;
    last year?
14. What changes have been made in the product since its introduction?
15. What were the reasons for changes?
16. What technical changes have occurred in the processes in which the product is used?
17. Have ranges been extended or reduced since they were introduced?
18. What were the reasons for range changes?
19. What support do your other products/services give the main product (e.g. extends range, production and procurement advantages, sells to same buyers)?
20. What is the reputation of the firm's product in its principal applications?
21. What changes in materials, products, processes or end-use products are likely to limit or increase demand for the firm's product?
22. How do proposed modifications in product or product range measure up to market demand and trends?
23. What is the percentage of the firm's and competitors' sales broken down by quality range?
    high;
    medium;
    low.
24. What is the image of the product?
25. What is the quality spread?
    great;
    small.
26. How far beyond the buyer is the product known in the user firm and how far is it associated with the supplier's name?
27. How far can special orders be handled or undertaken?
28. How strong are patents?
29. Can raw material purchases be bulked?
30. What standards exist for the product, and does the product conform to them?
31. What new standards are likely to be adopted?
32. What guarantees are offered and what is guarantee claim record?
33. Is it possible to achieve a high 'break cost'?

Services

1. What design services are required?
    physical planning;
    pre-sale service and advice;
    prototype fabrication;
    equipment design and checking;
    facilities advice;
    packaging advice.
2. What pre-start-up services are required?
    assembly;
    installation;
    engineering and inspection and testing.

3. What negotiation services are required?
   resolving complaints;
   warranty adjustments including exchange of product;
   liaison between customers and production department.
4. What education services are required?
   guidance on application use and adaptation of products to customers' needs;
   on-site demonstration, instructions, training and in-plant lectures;
   handling and safety advice;
   library service;
   technical literature;
   general industrial advice.
5. What visiting services are required?
   general and specific purpose visits to customer's plants;
   customer visits to service and production departments.
6. What maintenance and repair services are required?
   periodic testing and adjustment;
   cleaning and repairing;
   rehabilitation and reconditioning.
   Is loan equipment required?
7. What product adaptation services are required?
   modifications;
   applications research.
8. What emergency assistance is required?
9. What standby facilities for emergency and peak load periods are required?

Marketing Research

1. How does marketing research expenditure compare with competitors?
2. What marketing research has been accomplished in home and export markets?
3. How effective has it been?
4. How efficient are the firm's information sources?
5. How comprehensive are the firm's statistical data?
6. Which methods of marketing research have been found to be most effective?
7. What experimentation in marketing research is taking place?
8. In what circumstances is the use of independent agencies preferred to the firm's own research?
9. What methods exist for obtaining product intelligence?

Overseas Markets

1. Have all possible overseas markets been evaluated (screening)?
2. What criteria will be used to decide on the attractiveness of a market?
3. What official assistance is available for (a) provision of information on individual markets (b) finance for research (c) market entry (d) market consolidation?
4. Can earnings be remitted to the exporting country?
5. How narrowly based is the economy and what are trading conditions for principal exports?
6. What is the local taxation position on:
   products;
   profits;
   labour;
   turnover?

7. What is the import duty for each of the main exporting countries?
8. Do quotas or licensing arrangements exist?
9. Are local producers protected?
10. Do specific countries and/or firms have official or unofficial preferences in seeking supplying countries?
11. What are local charges?
     dock dues;
     landing charges;
     clearance charges;
     weighing and measuring;
     shipping agents;
     local transport.
12. What production under licence from foreign competitors is taking place?
13. What development schemes are taking place or are planned which will affect demand for the product and business conditions in general?
14. What physical conditions call for product and packaging modifications?
15. What type of sales organization will be required for the territory (e.g. own salesmen, distributor, agent trading company, joint venture, etc.)?
16. What criteria will be used to select and evaluate the sales organization appointed?
17. How will distributors/agents, etc., be remunerated?
18. What form of contract will be used (exclusivity, provision of services, minimum stock levels, extent of marketing effort, etc.)?
19. What contribution will the firm make (sales visits, sales aids, exhibitions, advertising, point of sale, etc.)?

New Products

1. What industries will use the new product?
2. Has the product a potential market among institutional and government users?
3. Will the new product round out the firm's lines?
4. How will the new full line compare with those of competitors?
5. Will the new product fill idle time of plant and equipment?
6. Will the new product contribute to long-term growth and security of the business?
7. Will the new product contribute to a lessening of the effects of business cycles?
8. Will the new product put excess capital to work?
9. Will the new product be accepted because it satisfies some need and sells at a price prospective buyers will pay?
10. Will the new product have to penetrate an already developed field?
11. Does the new product offer some important competitive advantages in a developed field?
12. Will the new product, even without competitive superiority, penetrate a developed field by virtue of the firm's reputation or other factors?
13. Will marketing agreements, franchises, etc. in any way limit production, sales, or the use of the product?
14. Is there any element in pricing policy or trade practice which may be a violation of law or accepted trade practice?
15. Are buyers of the new product accustomed to purchasing ahead of need or do they order for immediate delivery?
16. What is the structure of the raw and processed material and equipment supply industries for the manufacture of the new product?

17. How secure are material and components supplies?
18. What stocks of material and components are necessary and usual?
19. What substitutes are available?
20. How deep seated are existing loyalties and how receptive are buyers to new products?
21. What are user preferences in relation to distributive channels and methods for the products of the new product type?
22. What standards (official or unofficial) exist or are likely to be adopted?
23. Can 'top out' signs be identified?
24. Are there any influences or specifiers involved in purchase decision (e.g. consultants, contractors, etc.)?

Competitive Climate

1. Which firms make competitive products?
2. What are their respective market shares?
3. How firmly entrenched are competitors?
4. What specific advantages do the main competitors have?
    geographical;
    industrial;
    size;
    related products;
    commercial and industrial associations and liaisons;
    protection—official and unofficial;
    tied-in distributor network;
    image;
    approvals.
5. What is the reputation of the leading competitors?
6. What methods of distribution are used?
7. Are franchises used?
8. What is their sales structure?
9. What sales promotion techniques are used?
10. What services do competitors offer?
11. What are the usual credit and discount practices?
12. What guarantees are offered?
13. What is the firm's and competitors' policy in relation to the use of technical and non-technical salesmen?
14. What is the sales history of the firm's and competitors' technical and non-technical salesmen?
15. What is the extent of competitors' product research and development?
16. What is the quality of personnel and management?.
17. What is the manufacturing potential of principal competitors?
18. What are competitors' appropriations for advertising and sales promotion generally?
19. Are changes in materials or methods likely to increase present competitors' sales?
20. What proportion of competitors' output is sold for export?
21. Which are their principal export markets?
22. What is the extent of competitors' marketing research?
23. What is the image of competitive firms?
24. Have competitive firms built in a 'break cost' element?

25. Do competitors offer loan equipment?
26. What is the extent of manufacturing for private brands?

Competitive Prices

1. How does gross price compare with strictly comparable products?
2. How does net price compare with strictly comparable products?
3. How does gross price compare with substitute products?
4. How does net price compare with substitute products?
5. How does the firm's discount structure compare with competitors'?
6. What hidden discounts are offered by competitors?
7. What other 'off-setting against price' factors exist?
8. What is the price history of the most popular unit of sale?
9. What is the price history of the least popular unit of sale?
10. How do distributor margins allowed compare with those granted by competitors?
11. How do distributors' profits actually obtained compare with those obtained on competitors' products?
12. What are the reasons for fluctuations in price?
13. Is price used as part of competitors' marketing strategy?
14. How do spares/service/installation/maintenance/technical advistory charges compare with those of competitors?
15. Is price fixing practised?
16. How sensitive is the market to price changes?

Competitive Processes

1. Do processes not incorporating or using the product offer significant cost advantages?
2. Do processes not incorporating or using the product offer significant production advantages?
3. What technological developments are occurring or being explored which may lead to product obsolescence in particular processes?
4. What technological developments are occurring or being explored which may lead to new demands for the product in new processes using or incorporating them?
5. What is the reputation and record of success of processes not using the product?
6. What is the reptutation and record of success of processes using the product?
7. What is the reputation of the firm's product in its principal applications?

Competitive Products

1. How do competitive products closely similar in characteristics compare?
2. How do competitive products, dissimilar but substitutable for the firm's product, compare?
3. What are competitive products' 'plusses'?
4. What additional products in competitors' ranges give them sales advantages?
5. What sales advantages does availability of products in depth give competitors?
6. To what extent do unrelated products or processes compete with the new products?
7. How far do competitors' products accord with the idealized 'profile' for the product?
8. What is the reputation of competing products?

9. How does the product compare on:
    price;
    quality;
    performance;
    finish, design;
    length of service;
    packaging or methods of packing;
    guarantees;
    other characteristics.
10. What are bases of the purchasing decision in relation to competitive products?
    price;
    technical specification;
    other physical characteristics;
    delivery and services;
    packaging or packing method;
    supporting services provided;
    company's reputation and guarantees;
    brand or product reputation;
    reciprocal trade agreements;
    company affiliations;
    personal relationships;
    approvals.
11. What stocks are normally held?
    at the plant?;
    by distributors;
    by users.
12. What is the history and cause of sales fluctuations over the last few years?
13. What is the history of firm or brand leadership over the last few years and what were the reasons for changes?
14. Under what manufacturing conditions are competitive products used?
15. How far beyond the buyer are competitive products known in the user firms and how far are they associated with competitors by name?
16. What users do the products have other than those promoted?
17. To what extent are these uses practised?
18. What changes have competitors made in their products since their introduction?
19. What were the reasons for changes in products?
20. Have ranges been extended or reduced since they were introduced?
21. What were the reasons for range changes?
22. How strong are patents?
23. How closely do competitors' products conform to official and unofficial standards?

Demand

1. What is the demand history for the product?
2. How well is demand met by current suppliers?
3. What are the limitations to demand?
    technical characteristics;
    availability of purchasing power;
    availability of products;
    substitutions;

    obsolescence;

    fashion;

    se asonal or physical factors;

    price;

    availability of services.

4. How do the firm's products fit within acceptable style/quality price range?
5. Are the product characteristics acceptable to the majority of purchasers?
6. How does demand vary between the various strata of the market?

    industrial;

    geographical;

    by size of firm;

    in specific uses.

7. What conditions in the end-user markets are affecting demand?
8. How many potential users are there of the product in terms of:

    industries;

    firms;

    geographical areas;

    in specific uses;

    by specific benefits?

9. What is the average rate of consumption?

    by industry;

    by size of firm;

    by process;

    by season;

    in specific uses.

10. What factors affect consumption rate?
11. What characteristics identify the largest customers?
12. What characteristics identify the smallest customers?
13. How stable would demand be in time of depression?
14. How stable would demand be in time of war?
15. What requirements are there for hire or lease facilities and loan equipment?

User Attitudes and Behaviour

1. What are the decision-forming factors in purchasing, broken down by:

    industry;

    size of firm;

    geographical areas;

    job function of buyers;

    seaon?

2. What subjective factors are important in buying decisions?
3. Who comprise the decison-making unit in customer firms?
4. What is the usual status and job common to buyers of the firm's and competitive products?
5. How far is buying a function of a committee?
6. What is the usual method of negoitating orders and contracts?
7. What inter-personal factors exist affecting sales by the firm and by competitors?
8. What preferences exist among users for specific methods of selling and sales promotion?
9. What is the frequency or periodicity of purchase?
10. What is the extent of user knowledge of the firm's products?
11. What is the extent of user knowledge of identical competitive products

12. What is the extent of user knowledge of competitive substitute products?
13. What is the extent of misuses of the product?
14. How does the user judge the end of the useful life of the product?
15. How do decisions concerning the end of the useful life of the product vary between industries and firms?
16. Are the criteria for judging the end of the useful life of the firm's products the same as those applied to competitors' products?
17. Does buying responsibility change at discrete points, which may alter the product's acceptability within an industrial firm?
18. What size of orders should be expected, broken down by:
    industry;
    size of firm;
    geographical location;
    job definition and status of buyers?
19. What are the history of and the reasons for lost orders?
20. What are the history of and reasons for cancelled orders?
21. How postponable is purchasing?
22. What commercial conditions are required?
23. What requirements exist for products to be supplied under 'own brand'?
24. Have user preference distributions been studied?
25. What is the total number of firms or installations which could feasibly utilize the products/services?
26. Do users buy direct or through other channels (e.g. distributors, contractors)?
27. What lead times do users generally require?
28. Are there any technical or commercial links between competitors and customers which influence the market?

Governmental Factors

1. What is the current tax structure on:
   the product;
   the end products?
2. What is the history of taxation of the product and end products?
3. What is the import duty?
4. What restrictions on imports exist?
5. What restrictions are imposed on credit terms?
6. What would be the effect of tax changes on demand?
7. What is the position in relation to protection, subsidies, and support prices?
8. What is the government attitude to price agreements and restrictive practices?
9. What legislation exists on safety, quality control, and weights and measures?
10. What is the extent of government participation in purchasing?
11. What is the role of international agencies?
12. What governmental aid schemes exist—e.g. subsidies, protection, loans, credit, holidays, etc.?

Image

1. What is the industry image reference?
2. How does the firm's image compare with industry image?
3. How far does the industry image affect the firm's and its competitors' image?
4. To what extent is the industry image compared with the image of other industries?
5. How do the competitive firms' images compare?

6. What is the product or service image of the firm and its competitors?
7. What is the image of the firm and competitive supporting services?
8. What is the image of the firm's and competitors' personnel—sales, administrative, technical, service?
9. What is the image of the firm's and competitors' premises?
10. How do the images vary between different classifications of customer?
    regular;
    sporadic;
    single transactions;
    discontinued customers;
    failed quotations;
    no contact.
11. How far are the images uncovered based on:
    direct experience;
    known by reputation;
    heard of by name?
12. What is the 'mirror' image?
13. What is the 'wish' image?
14. Has the 'optimum' image been identified—
15. Is there any image variation within the DMUs?
16. What factors are influencing image perception?

Marketing Systems Audit
1. Are sales and margins of specific product and product group units reported regularly?
2. Do sales/margins reports go to the correct managers?
3. Are product line contribution reports produced regularly?
4. Do managers receive:
    price reviews;
    cost analysis;
    promotions analysis;
    product additions;
    product deletions;
    product line item count growth?
5. Are annual sales contracts reviewed regularly to determine the impace of cost changes?
6. Are receivables monitored by marketing management?
7. Are credits/returns corrected and detailed on sales and margin reports?
8. Are credits and returns monitored according to product and product lines? Reason? Authorized by management?
9. Is there a formalized credit rating system?
10. Is the credit rating of customers periodically reviewed?
11. Are detailed inventory reports available to appropriate marketing management?
12. Is inventory analysed in terms of on-going, obsolete, and related to short-term forecast sales?
13. Is there a formal marketing plan, by product line?
14. Do all relevant managers have copies of marketing plans?
15. Is the marketing plan regularly used by managers?
16. Does the senior marketing manager regularly review progress against plan with responsible manager?
17. Are objectives reviewed as to their relevance on the year's progress?

APPENDIX II

Analysis of Prospective Partners

Examples of Critieria that May be Used to Judge a Prospective Partner's Effectiveness by Assessing Existing Business Ventures and Commercial Attitudes

1. *Finance*
   (i) Financial history and overall financial standing (all the usual ratios).
   (ii) Possible reasons for successful business areas.
   (iii) Possible reasons for unsuccessful business areas.

2. *Organization*
   (i) Structure of organization.
   (ii) Quality and turnover of senior managers.
   (iii) Workforce conditions/labour relations.
   (iv) Information and reporting systems, evidence of planning.
   (v) Effective owner's working relationship with business.

3. *Market*
   (i) Reputation in market-place and with competitors.
   (ii) Evidence of research/interest in service and quality.
   (iii) Sales methods, quality of sales force.
   (iv) Evidence of handling weakening market conditions.
   (v) Results of new businesses started.

4. *Production*
   (i) Conditi ons of existing premises/works.
   (ii) Production efficiencies/layouts.
   (iii) Capital investment and improvements.
   (iv) Quality control procedures.
   (v) Evidence of research (internal/external), introduction of new technology.
   (vi) Relationship with main suppliers.

5. *Institutional*
   (i) Government and business contacts (influence).
   (ii) Successful negotiations with banks, licensing authorities, etc.
   (iii) Main contacts with non-national organizations and companies.
   (iv) Geographical influence.

6. *Possible Negotiating Attitudes*
   (i) Flexible/hardline.
   (ii) Reasonably open/close and secretive.
   (iii) Short-term or long-term orientated.
   (iv) 'Wheeler/dealer' or objective negotiator.
   (v) Positive quick decision taking or tentative.
   (vi) Negotiating experience and strength of team support.

These suggestions only form an outline sketch of the type of information which can be used to grade partners and cover areas where there is a reasonable change of forming a view by appraisal of published information and by sensible observation and questioning.

APPENDIX III

Proposed Partner's Likely Effectiveness

1. Existing contact with required customer base?
2. Is there adequate territorial coverage?
3. Have the staff the knowledge and skill to sell or learn to sell the product?
4. Do facilities exist for promoting the product?
5. Are there adequate facilities for getting the product to the customer?
6. Is there provision for after-sales service and the handling of complaints?
7. Is there the management capacity to give full commitment to the product?
8. What are the skills and experience of the day-to-day staff?
9. What conflicts of interest might exist?
10. What are the prospective customers' views of the partner?
11. How did the partner handle joint research tasks?
12. If the partner succeeds in the first stage what further support does he need?
13. Are there any associates who could be useful at a later stage to develop the market?

5

Exporting and Agents

In many ways exporting appears the simplest of international trade propositions; it can be done directly, with the advantages that accrue with direct control, but frequently an agent is preferred, or, to conform with local law, has to be used. In Chapter 4 the point was made that whatever the mode of entry to a foreign market, where a partner is required benefit will accrue from combined research of principal and partner. The use of this approach in the export/agent field of activity is of considerable importance.

It is still fashionable to describe the physical distribution function as 'The Last Frontier' in business science, and it would be a brave person who would deny this. If it is the case then one would doubtless need to describe the export agent fraternity as the 'Lost Tribe'. This situation probably derives from the following generally recognizable factors which lead to inefficiency in this area.

PRINCIPALS:

- never have enough time and all too often embrace the 'Kiss and Run' deal;
- have too many markets at their disposal and do not select for growth;
- have an overrated idea of their status and having granted a right believe that everything else is up to the agent.

AGENTS:

- prefer to have as many opportunities on the go as possible;
- are more interested in short-term commission than long-term growth;
- overvalue 'big names' to put gloss on their product portfolios;
- believe that they have to fight for support therefore omit to carry out the more difficult market tasks.

Others may well like to extend the list but the evidence all points one way, neither side gets the best out of the other, highlighting the fact that there is a barrier to market development.

If one feels like putting this to the test then a therapeutic experience can be a renewal programme for an existing agency network. Any company thinking of revitalizing its international effort would be well advised to start here: that is to say, 'making the best of what we have got'.

The agency audit proposal set out in Appendix I at the end of this chapter is one possible way of bringing a 'kick of a mule' to one of business's weakest areas; it is, however, likely to expose two attitudes: *a state of shock in most overseas representatives asked to carry it out* and *resentment and suspicion from those who are asked to submit to it*. The agency audit brings into focus the market, the performance of both the agent *and* the principal, and the appropriateness of the established contact. It is stressed that the proposal is not a 'one-way street'; it is equally valid for an agent to notify a principal that all is not well and that he would like a mutual audit. In many ways it is better that he does this rather than switch off and let the business slowly die.

Principals should be aware from the outset that an audit will highlight for them new commitments and workloads. And it is wrong that an adverse audit should automatically lead to a 'night of the long knives'—good agents are not easy to find and it may be that the local agency fraternity will feel that the lack of support lay with the supplier and so not have any inclination to accept any opportunity now supposedly on offer. In practical terms an agent will usually have some remnants of a good relationship within the principal's company, for example, with the person who originally appointed him, or with a junior executive who has supported him against the odds, and whose goodwill can be brought into play to get the arrangement working along the right lines again. Many agents who know their markets well and have good personal relationships with the suppliers' customers will welcome an opportunity to revitalize the arrangements if they believe that the approach is well thought out, genuine, and that it has support at board level.

Previously the agent/principal relationship was described in terms of counterproductive attitudes on both sides: this area now needs more careful examination. One of the main problem areas arises from the principal's lack of clarity in his approach and in his understanding of the type of arrangement that he really wants. Agency arrangements offer a very broad range of possibilities; it is the principal's job to determine on behalf of his company how he prefers to develop the market-place for his product and to negotiate the appropriate arrangement. Clearly he will be aided in this task if he has local knowledge and a soundly based view of the quality of any partner and the level of trust and confidence that may be placed in him. In broad outline the choices develop around the following:

1. Choice of contract terms.
2. Choice of territory and products to be covered.
3. The type of agency arrangement.

4. Choice of methods of payment.
5. Reaction to local agency laws.
6. The contribution to be made by each side.

These basic decision areas cover wide fields of decision-taking and a lack of clarity in any of these areas will result sooner or later in an unsatisfactory arrangement arising.

1. Choice of contract terms

(*a*) Exclusive.
(*b*) Non exclusive.
(*c*) Sole.
(*d*) Retention of rights to act for the principal.

2. Choice of territory and products to be covered

(*a*) Confined areas (geographical or business sector).
(*b*) National.
(*c*) Sub-regional or regional.
(*d*) All products.
(*e*) Selected products.
(*f*) Products for all or some companies in a group.

3. The type of agency arrangement (main variants)

(*a*) Commission agent/salesman.
(*b*) Agency company with or without specialist facilities, e.g. stocking or servicing facilities.
(*c*) Distributor.
(*d*) Stockist.
(*e*) Trading company.
(*f*) Using buying houses or confirming houses.
(*g*) Export merchants.
(*h*) Export management agency.

4. Choice of methods of payment (who accepts the *del credere* risk)

(*a*) Agent acts as go-between for principal and customers and draws commission (usually when the invoice has been paid).
(*b*) Agents accepts all or part of financial risk and commission levels are adjusted upwards to reflect this.
(*c*) Agent/distributor/stockist buys and sells on his own account and make a turn on the deal.
(*d*) Agent receives fee, part fee, and commission, or fee and any combination of the arrangements shown in (*a*) (*b*) above.

All of the above arrangements require a clear definition of the terms of trade that apply to be meaningful and for the value of commission to be assessed correctly. Clearly the value of commission varies if it is based on:

ex-works, Free on Board (FOB), Cost, Freight, and Insurance (CIF), or Free delivered customer's works terms. It is worth remembering that many agents do not make fine calculations in these areas, often because quotations for transport take too long and include too many variables; they often prefer to add a simple percentage which may blunt the competitive edge of the supplier's product or lead to back pressure on his prices.

5. Reaction to local agency laws

The growth in agency law legislation has already been noted. As a generality, in the more advanced economies it is an area of trade that benefits from clarity and redressing the balance against some of the one-sided bargains that prevailed in the past. While similar values act as the catalyst elsewhere, they often have ideas concerning indigenization or have state utopian principles added on. The growing requirements for consumer and environmental protection can also have a moulding effect on the legislation.

6. The contribution to be made by each side

The various opportunities outlined above show why it is important for the principal to have a clear idea with regard to the two basic questions that set the overall style of an agreement: the amount of authority that is going to be granted (or the degree of exclusivity) and where and for what products it is going to be exercised. The decision will be a better one if it reflects the requirements of the market plan rather than negotiating 'at best'. Principals will usually start by retaining as many rights as possible and restrict both the territories and the commission. Agents prefer complete protection and wide rights together with as much remuneration as possible. Neither approach is necessarily correct. The most appropriate answer lies in what is sensible in the market place and what the value of the contribution of both sides is going to be.

All in all the focus then returns to a plan of market action, people's contribution to it, and their rightful expectation as to what they are entitled to receive for their efforts. Without getting delayed by the semantics involved in 'agent' and 'distributor' and similar titles, the main requirement is to see how products are to be channelled into the market-place. It is often easier to see the requirements when no local stocking takes place—when stocking takes place it is important not to confuse the intake of the stockist/distributor (filling the pipeline) with the flow of goods to the ultimate end-user (emptying the pipeline). From the supplier's point of view market development is only really taking place when end-users are 'consuming'.

Before attempting to assess contributions specifically it is useful to have a basic understanding of distribution economics. In international trading this is an area of trade-offs where the agent/distributor, and sometimes the customer, are taking over some of the activity that the supplier might normally expect to do, if, for example he elects to sell on the ex-works basis (the ultimate case for practical discussion). The cost of selling in the foreign market-place, the movement of goods, the financing of stock and its protection, as well as the adaptation of the product and its presentation, are being transferred elsewhere. This might be described as the 'zero' theoretical proposition as the most appropriate questions concern the determination as to the optimum way to reallocate costs in order that the goods may arrive in the market-place in the most competitive way in terms of price, product presentation, speed of delivery, choice, etc. Once the principal has been grasped as to the existence of the costs and their make-up the valid trade-offs arise from the discussion as to who can handle them best.

For international trade purposes it can be beneficial to view products as 'ex-production line', although goods are never quoted as such. The concept is useful, however, in allowing discussion on the supply of products in bulk form and allowing 'breaking down,' and perhaps some local modification and packaging. Often in this way expensive operations in a distant factory can be greatly reduced and greater accuracy achieved in small but valuable areas, such as putting language labels in the correct places, the correct way up.

In practice there are a wide variety of costs that are 'in abeyance' in international trade until principal and agent agree how best to allocate them. Figure 5.1 shows this situation in outline. The focus remains not so much on who pays (it is clear that someone has to) but rather on who can best contain the cost, thus prompting agents and principals to attack the market rather than attack one another. Restated, the process can be looked at in a different way, as set out in Figure 5.2.

The principles may appear obvious and self-evident but by common consent they remain a long way from the rituals which so often prescribe dealings with the 'lost tribe' described earlier on. The requirement for a fundamental change of approach from 'our agent' to 'our channel to overseas end-users' is an important one. The search for profit through the

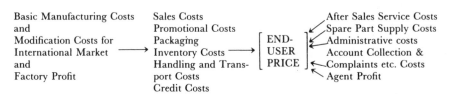

Figure 5.1. Costs 'in Abeyance' in International Trade until allocated by principals

Figure 5.2. How Best To Contain Cost

positive use of agency negotiation can stimulate new attitudes in international trading that puts more responsibility on the shoulders of the export sales team.

The other emphasis which arises from the contribution approach is a clear determination of what constitutes success. If principals act as suggested their agents will not be free-ranging representatives but rather executive allies who will help to bring pressure to bear in their respective markets. Given that the market has a finite size, principal and agent are to determine how to obtain an acceptable share of it. This will not be an act of faith but the result of answering such questions as: 'which types of business will buy, which are the attackable areas by sector or by region, what prices are to be charged, and how is the product to be presented, delivered, and serviced?' The particular answers to such questions are often better portrayed within the logic of a formal market plan, with suitable adjustments made for the international trade, largely concentrating on the contributions to be made by both sides. Such plans can be readily written, particularly by those who purvey them to the home trade, but it is wise to remember an important caveat, namely, that for the majority of suppliers export prices are lower than home trade prices, and a certain amount of ingenuity will be required to bring forward powerful strategies for an overseas market that are affordable for the volumes involved (albeit initially).

Some companies will already have well-tested and well-tried plan formats, but, one hopes, not obligatory strait-jackets. Generally, the decision-taker should be entitled to the research proposal, the research report, and a market plan that draws on the experience gathered. A possible outline for the documents concerned is given as Appendix II at the end of this Chapter. The research papers have been left until this stage so that the complete appraisal can be seen as one thought process and one decision-making request for the allocation of company resources on a logical basis. There is nothing sacrosanct in the formats as such. For illustration purposes a preference has been given to coming to conclusions first and proving and supporting them afterwards, largely because it seems that busy people like things that way. Providing a sound logical presentation emerges, clearly based on researched data, then each presenter should follow his own dictates and style. It is essentially a question of opinions based on facts. There are so many aids to presentation available, particularly through the use of word processors and computer graphics, that it is important to try and keep the presentation fresh and not to let the simple power of the written word become swamped by visual techniques.

A wide arc has been taken to emphasize the needs of the market-place in agency negotiation and to superimpose upon them international needs. The requirement for doing this was to ensure that principals had a clear idea of the potential and in consequence a good judgement of the role the chosen agent is to play. If there has been some form of joint market appraisal then negotiating positions will be more realistic than they might otherwise have been as the participants will know the size of the market opportunity and what support is going to be forthcoming to get a planned share of it. Equally, conflicts of interest (even perhaps in such simple matters as time management, style, and business ambitions) will have sent the potentially weak away and those who have stayed the course will have done so out of business interest. There can be no coercion, no direct control in the contract arrangement that has to be entered into—the limitations of both sides at this stage should be the general wish to maintain a strong long-term working relationship.

SECRET AGENTS

Before proceeding to contract terms a brief note might be called for concerning the use of bribery, in whatever way it might be described. Undoubtedly the issue is a moral one, but it is also of legal concern and negotiating consequence. The consensus advice is to recognize that it exists, and that it is worse in some parts of the world than others, although nowhere is immune; it is better not to participate unless (1) you do not mind paying a second or a third time, (2) you are prepared to put your company's reputation at risk, and (3) if caught, you have no objection to serving a prison sentence.

THE CONTRACT

Many trade organizations and quasi-official bodies have advice on contract formulation but in all probability it is to be assumed that provision will be made to have the assistance of a legal adviser, knowledgeable in the law of the land concerned, and sensibly aware of the wishes of the participating parties. The much-quoted adage that if the relationship is right then the agreement can be put in the drawer and then forgotten needs comment. The statement is probably true, but what those who tend to utter it forget is that getting to a good document is part of the asset of understanding on which good relationships are founded. If the future emphasis is to be on the market plan which is born of hard work and skill (and much frustration in the majority of cases), then the fewer the surprises on the way the better. A sound agreement is a thoughtful record of what is intended and as such greatly reduces surprises. Further, there is nothing wrong in getting it out of the desk and jointly bringing it up to date as times move on. Letters of agreement are a shorthand answer to a complex problem and offer an indication that neither side has the will, time, or inclination to take on the full task. Such letters are most meaningful if they own up to being a temporary arrangement. The most likely clauses in an agency agreement are:

- Statement of the parties to the agreement.
- The grant of rights and the exact nature of the grant.
- The nomination of products and territories.

- The agreed duration of the contract.
- The obligations of the principal (Statement on product prices and conditions of supply; Support activity; Limitations on the activities of other agents; Statement on retention of any market rights).
- The obligations of the agent (With regard to the products and the market/s; Price obligations and quantity/performance criteria; Prevention of competitive activity as far as allowed by local law; Secrecy and confidentiality; Assistance in any dispute; Limitations on exceeding territorial limits).
- The financial arrrangements (Commission overriders and rebates, etc.; Calculations and time and method of payment; Tax liabilities; Ancillary products and their special provisions).
- Expiry of contract; Termination clauses.
- Modification, amendment, and assignment provisions.
- Arbitration.
- Applicable law and language.

There is great scope for flexibility in the style of individual contracts although the syntax and form of legal writing often seems to work against it. If it appears that full provision cannot be made for the total intent of any joint market effort there is no reason why a marketing aid agreement may not be locked into the main agreement and signed concurrently. Any number of formulas are available for compensation under such agreements. Recognition by fee would be the simplest route and the extension of product range or territory might be useful inducements. The setting up of a joint company or local manufacturing could be logical extensions of successful market activity when certain levels of volume offtake have been achieved.

It is to be hoped that the agent and his potential role in exporting has by this review been somewhat upgraded from the generality of his 'Lost Tribe' status, and even those companies that have advanced and succesful policies in this area will have at least pause to ask if any further potential can be squeezed out. It is important to keep the agent and his development under constant review as he is the company's chosen route to the distant end-user. If the level of support appears at first sight to be too onerous it is important to remember that there are no set rules that have to be followed slavishly to the letter for success, it is the thought processes that are most important and the attitutes towards people. If overall principals elect to show greater selectivity in their choice of markets in order to set up and maintain their researched territories professionally, and agents set about refining their product portfolios, then some benefits will emerge.

References

1 Colin Mcmillan and Sydney Paulden, *Export Agents* (Gower Press: London, 1968).
2 'Exporting', *Business International* (1963) (Business International Corp., New York and Geneva).

3 H. W. Lane and D. G. Simpson, 'Bribery in International Business: Whose Problem is it?' *Journal of Business Ethics*, 3 (1984).

4 J. L. Graham, 'Foreign Corrupt Practices: A Managers' Guide', *Columbia Journal of World Business* (Autumn 1983).

5 Warren DeBord, 'Dealer Network Strategic Planning', *Journal of Business Strategy* (Antar extract ET37).

6 Theodore Levitt, 'After the Sale is Over', *Harvard Business Review* (Sept./Oct. 1983).

7 James Ward, 'Your Export Middleman Making a Wise Selection', *International Trade Forum* (Apr./June 1984).

8 Id., A Four-Step Approach to Selecting an Overseas Agent', *International Trade Forum* (Oct./Dec. 1984).

APPENDIX I

Agent Audit Considerations

Performance and Contract Analysis

1. *Internal Considerations*
   (i) Who appointed the agent?
   (ii) Who supports the agent and why?
   (iii) Who is against the agent and why?

2. *Contacts*
   (i) Is there a named contact in the agency?
   (ii) Does the agency have a named contact in the Company?

3. *Liaison*
   (i) When was the agent last visited and by whom?
   (ii) When did the agent last visit the UK?
   (iii) Has the agent ever received formal training?
   (iv) When was the last training session?

4. *Contract*
   (i) Is there a written contract? (the contract to be evaluated—see below)
   (ii) Is the contract valid?
      (*a*) In terms of time?
      (*b*) Is it between appropriate parties?
      (*c*) Is it in conflict with local agency regulations?
      (*d*) Do the original signatories still work for the respective companies concerned?

5. *Obligations*
   (i) What are the *exact* obligations of the agent?
   (ii) How is remuneration calculated?
   (iii) When are commission/expenses to be paid?

6. *Performance of Agent*

	1	2	Last 5 years 3	4	5
Enquiry values					
Order values					
Complaint values					
Commission paid					
Any other expenses paid					

7. *Business Objectives*
   (i) Have targets ever been set for sales?
   (ii) If targets set, what were they and were they achieved?
   (iii) Are there any minimum performance criteria in the contract?

8. *Market*
   (i) Does a viable market exist for the agency products?

(ii) What is the nature of the competition and what restrictions are there on trade, e.g.:
    (*a*) Market size and support information to indicate growth or decline?
    (*b*) Local manufacture?
    (*c*) Volume/price/quality considerations (cross-check raw material costs where significant to overall product cost)?
    (*d*) Nature of competition and *proof* of its activity and prices?
    (*e*) Duties, import licence, etc.?
    (*f*) Concentration/location of major customers?

9. *Agency Structure*
    (i) When was the agency founded? What are the locations of any branches? When were these branches opened?
    (ii) Which other agencies are held
        (*a*) Competing?
        (*b*) Non-competing?
    (iii) What new agencies have been opened up in the last two years?
    (iv) Which agencies have been discarded in the last two years?
    (v) Name, nationality, qualifications, training, languages and ages of owners/ senior staff:
        (*a*) Non-executive?
        (*b*) Executive?
    (vi) Number of salesmen employed and where located: how remunerated?
    (vii) Are there any sub agents/distributors or other special relationships which affect the sale/distribution of agency products?
    (viii) What is the agency total turnover—what is the turnover per employee?
    (ix) What is the turnover in agency products as a percentage of total turnover?
    (x) How much time is assessed as being given to agency products?
    (xi) What staff have any specific responsibilities for the products?
    (xii) How are the agent's activities split over various broad market sectors?

9a. *Competitive Agencies*
Which are the main competitive agencies? What significant plus points/minus points do these have over the appointed agent?

10. *Agent's Relationship with Company's Customers*
    (i) How are the company's customers identified and administered, e.g. are there separate files, card indexes, etc.?
    (ii) What evidence is there of regular contact with customers?
    (iii) Which new customers have been introduced in the last year?
    (iv) Which main customers show a decline in business?
    (v) Which customers have not been visisted in the last 12 months and why?
    (vi) Which parts of the territory are not visited regularly (say once every two months)?
    (vii) Are the correspondence files with the company up to date?

11. *Agent's Product Knowledge*
    (i) Does the agent have up-to-date brochures?
    (ii) Does the agent have literature, etc. to give to customers?
    (iii) If brochure is not in local language, if this is necessary, does the agent provide any aids to understanding?

   (iv) Has any specific product promotion taken place in the last 12 months? Is any planned in the next 12 months?
    (v) Does agent get regular knowledge of company activity, e.g. product development, production capability, design changes, new products, successful case stories from other territories?
   (vi) What other stong evidence is there that the agent understands the products, the customers, the nature of the market place?
  (vii) What product benefits does the agent stress to customers?
 (viii) What product benefits does the agent most value himself?
   (ix) How does the agent pass quotations to customers?
        (a) Are prices FOB or CIF—if FOB how does customer generally obtain and calculate delivered prices?
    (x) What interest does the agent take in ensuring payment?
   (xi) Does the agent have a system for handling complaints?

12. *Agent's Reputation*
    (i) What is the agent's reputation and status as viewed by authoriative and third parties: e.g. Banks, Embassies, Chambers of Commerce, Trade Associations?
   (ii) What outside business posts do the agent or his senior staff hold?
  (iii) How does the agent compare with competing agencies by:
        (a) Size?
        (b) Turnover?
        (c) Location?
        (d) Status?

13. *Future Potential*
Is it possible to agree with the agent a statement concerning the prospects of business for the company overall in the next 12 months, the likely value of orders, and the customers who will be the main purchasers? Where reservations are made with regard to price or quality, up-to-date supporting evidence of competitive activity must be given.

14. *Opinion*
Express an opinion based on the value of the market, the quality of the agent, and his potential long-term value to the company, whether it would be worth-while to:

    (i) Continue the agency, if so what should be done to make it more effective?
   (ia) Would it be useful to write a new up-to-date agreement? If so, what main points now need to be incorporated?
   (ii) Should the agency be discontinued? If so, how and when should this be done and should alternative arrangements be made?
  (iii) Should the agency be put on a trial basis with a clear understanding on both sides as to objectives during the trial period?
   (iv) By what *precise* criteria should the agent *and* the principle be judged during the trial period?

Contract Analysis

    1. Note any written amendments with dates.
    2. Who is the agreement between? Are the parties in the agreement still valid and are the people who have signed it entitled to do so—are the contracting parties truly representative of the actual parties carrying out the work?

3. What is the purpose of the agreement and specifically what has one party agreed to appoint the other party to do?
4. What is the main nature of the relationship:
    (a) Sole, exclusively/non-exclusively?
    (b) Acting for principal?
    (c) Purchasing for himself as principal?
    (d) Does the agent perform any other function, e.g. warehousing, stocking, distribution, servicing?
5. Territory
    (a) Is the territory clearly defined?
    (b) Is the territory logical in geographical terms?
    (c) Is the territory logical in political terms?
    (d) Is the territory within the scope/ability of the agent and his sales force?
6. Are the products covered by the agency agreement clearly identified?
    (a) Is the company's whole range of products covered or just part of the range?
    (b) What right has the principal reserved with regard to representation for future/new products?
7. Are there any agreed limitations to sales, e.g. house accounts?
8. (a) When did the contract come into force?
    (b) What is the term of the contract—when does it expire?
    (c) Do the time clauses in the contract give the agent sufficient incentive to make a real sales effort for the product?
9. Is it clear how orders not placed in the territory by the agent, but subsequently delivered into the territory, will be administered and accounted for?
10. Is the agent clearly limited from promoting sales outside the territory without written consent of principal?
11. Is the the agent prevented from selling competing products?
12. (a) Is the agent clearly bound to send orders immediately to the principal?
    (b) Does the principal reserve the right to accept or reject orders?
    (c) Is the principal bound to keep the agent informed with copy orders, invoices, and payment receipts?
    (d) What arrangements have been made, if any, for the agent to purchase products elsewhere if the principal cannot supply?
    (di) How much information is the principal entitled to concerning such transactions?
13. *Commission Payments*
    (a) Is the amount to be paid clear, is the method of calculation unequivocal, and is it based on net values, e.g. FOB?
    (b) Does the commission amount vary according to circumstances?
    (c) Is the commission based on payments received from customers?
    (d) How often is commission paid?
    (e) Are there any provisions for additional expenses—are these clear and are the sums of expenditure limited?
    (f) Does the agent have any security for checking his commission?
14. Are there any limitations on the actions that an agent may take on behalf of the principal, e.g. credits, discounts, warranties, claim settlements?
15. Has the principal reserved the right not to deal with certain customers—what are the circumstances in which this can be done?
16. Is there an arbitration provision?
17. (a) What law and language governs the contract?
    (b) If the contract is in dual language, is the prevailing text clearly defined?
18. (a) Can the contract be assigned?

    (b) What rights has the principal got concerning the assignment of contract in the event of any change of main personalities, etc.?

19. Are there any local laws and legislation concerning agency contracts with which the agreement might be in conflict?

20. For agents accepting the *del credere* risk, check for provisions on agreement of pricing policy in the market-place and verification of customer complaints, etc.

21. (a) For agents stocking, particularly on a consignment basis, check when the ownership of the stock changes hands and particularly who is responsible for the stock, and insuring and protecting it throughout its life.

    (b) Check what happens to the goods on termination.

APPENDIX II

The Market Research Proposal

1. Introduction and why the research is being carried out now.
     (a) Prime criteria which will be used to assess the market-place.
     (b) Project scope:
              Market size;
              Distribution channels;
              Product alignment;
              Competition and tariffs, incentives, etc.;
              Partner selection criteria.
2. Research objectives:
              Geography;
              Products;
              Market sectors;
              Sectors where partners will be sought.
3. Research methods:
     (a) Desk research—major sources and methods, limitations foreseen.
     (b) Field research—key questions and questionnaire (pilot tested); key respondents (official, commercial); partner selection criteria; short list.
4. Proposed report structure.
5. Timing and allocation of duties and experience for the job.

The Research Report

1. Title: 'on' 'of' 'in'.
2. Index.
3. Conclusions and Recommendations.
   What the opportunity is and how to get to it.
   (Fence-sitting not allowed.)
4. Discussion.
   Analysis of the research by, e.g.:
       current market;
       future market;
       Market structure;
       Customer requirements;
       Competition;
       Pros and cons of partners.
   Overall research carried out and methods.
5. Supporting material and appendices.
   including names and addresses of contacts and original research proposal.
   Support data-tables and graphs.

The Market Plan: International

(Based on the five 'P's: product, price, place/physical distribution, promotion, and people.)

1. Executive Summary: clear statement of overall issues asssuming the reader knows nothing, and clear statement of any assumptions that underwrite the plan.
2. Conclusions and recommendations: including who the chosen partner is.
3. Objectives.
4. Identified strengths and weaknesses in the market.
5. Essence of Strategy and the allocation of key roles.
6. Policies (only (a) set out in detail below).

   (a) People: detail of activity split between principal and agent. Support required by agent to set up, maintain, and develop market. Nominated contacts, liaison visits, plan review procedures. Contingency to cover any people failure.

   (b) Product: what needs doing for acceptance and promotion.

   (c) Price.

   (d) Physical Distribution, including service level criteria.

   (e) Promotion.
7. Detailed action plans of objectives, timing, and responsibility.

6

Countertrade

The simple expedient of paying for goods in 'coins of the realm' is not always the correct method for some purchasing agents, who prefer to complicate the situation by paying in kind. Such arrangements are usually lumped together under the one generic heading of 'countertrade'.

Traditionally, countertrade is linked to the supposed trading limitations of the state-dominated Eastern bloc countries. Examination, however, shows that countertrade is a growing phenomenon in international trade that has been, and is, applied by a large number of countries in a variety of forms. Further, a view is beginning to emerge that countertrade is not necessarily an evil impediment to world trade, but that on occasion by dealing with imperfections in world trade since it can stimulate business that would not otherwise take place. The incidence of countertrade activity is given in Figure 6.1.

For the intending exporter the likelihood of coming up against countertrade arrangements needs to be determined at an early stage, as price and cost structures will need to be adjusted to take into account such transactions. Equally, given that an organization is moving away from the traditional standpoint that all countertrade is inherently bad and to be avoided, an early view can be taken to decide if there are any products that might usefully be obtained in this way. This suggestion presupposes that a very close link will be forged between international trading departments and other company functions.

Before proceeding it is necessary to assess the full scope of countertrade activity. Typically, the following arrangements would qualify under the heading of countertrade, although it is more likely that various definitions will create overlaps or new subsections.

Barter
This is the most readily understood transaction, with classical precedents, whereby within one contract one product is exchanged for another without

Figure 6.1. Overview of Countertrade Activity

Country	High incidence	Medium use	Limited activity	Remarks
Eastern Europe	●			Trade often 'brokered' through Austria
Asia & Africa				
Algeria		●		
Bangladesh		●		
China	●			Mainly buyback
Ethiopia			●	
Ghana			●	
Indonesia	●			Public sector, long experience
India		●		Public sector
Korea			●	Growing interest
Libya		●		Usually oil based
Malaysia		●		State & well organised
Nigeria			●	
Pakistan			●	Growing interest
Philippines		●		Well established
Thailand			●	Limited
Tunisia			●	Declining
Uganda			●	Growing interest
Zambia			●	Growing interest
Zimbabwe			●	Intermittent
Middle East				
Egypt	●			
Iran		●		Usually oil based
Iraq			●	Usually oil based
Israel			●	State sector only
Jordan			●	
Qatar			●	Oil based
Saudi Arabia		●		Offset deals oil & defence
Syria		●		
Turkey			●	
South America				
Brazil	●			Highly organised
Cuba	●			Mainly with East Bloc
Equador	●			
Mexico				Growing interest
Nicaragua	●			Mainly staple products
Peru		●		Growing interest
Uruguay		●		State controlled
Venezuela			●	Public sector
Europe & Australasia				
Australia			●	Specifically defence
Austria			●	
Belgium			●	
Cyprus			●	State trade only
Finland			●	Specially defence
Greece			●	Public sector
Malta			●	

Country	High incidence	Medium use	Limited activity	Remarks
New Zealand			•	Public sector
Portugal			•	Public sector
Spain			•	Growing interest.

Main Source: Counter Trade, some guidance for exporters (Project and Export Policy Division. Department of Trade and Industry, London, UK. May 1987). Reproduced by permission of Her Majesty's Stationery Office.

recourse to a monetary transaction. That is to say, the good old-fashioned 'exchange of perceived values'. It is easy to see how such contracts may be complicated by, say, time, when already manufactured goods may have to await harvest time before the exchange commodity is available, or when more goods or parties to the contract are incorporated. The magic words that appear in most texts on the subject refer to the 'double coincidence of wants'. The likelihood of such a coincidence is comparatively rare and so simple barter deals are few and far between, and recourse is usually made to other methods.

Counterpurchase
Under such arrangements a seller is given a wider range of options whereby an order is made conditional upon an undertaking to buy goods to a specific value of the main contract from a specific list of products. Clearly, the wider the list of products and the greater the opportunity to negotiate lower percentage values of the main contract the more attractive the proposition becomes.

Switch Trading and Swap Deals
The build-up of uncleared credit surpluses from bilateral trade arrangements between countries can sometimes be used to lubricate deals between other countries. The redistribution and redocumentation of goods required by such arrangements (i.e. switching) often relies on a series of back-to-back arrangements and currency deals and is therefore rarely an area where the novice can afford to be involved.

Buy-Back, Evidence Accounts, and Offsets
As deals assume greater value or complexity, the involvement of foreign investment countertrade arrangements become a little more subtle. Buy-back requirements are most likely to affect capital equipment suppliers who will be asked to accept payment for their plant through the supply of goods produced by that plant. The proposal can be intensified so that equipment, or a loan to buy it, is fully repaid by the offtake of product. Such arrangements are sometimes referred to as compensation trading. The Russians tend to favour the former arrangement and the Chinese the latter, and in both cases it is not only the economics that appeal—doctrinal thoughts also play a role.

Evidence Accounts

The principle behind such arrangements is usually that a local operation of an overseas company pays its way by showing evidence in its accounts that sufficient foreign currency has been earned to pay for either the import of raw materials and components or the externalization of funds.

Offsets

The simplest proposition is that an exporter incorporates in his products an agreed level of raw materials or components produced by the importing country. Wider meanings may arise in Government to Government contracts, for example, where purchases are conditional upon the sponsorship of other requirements such as the setting up of related or high technology joint ventures.

It will be seen from the above résumé that countertrade is a tool of considerable flexibility and potential. It can be a sharp tool in the hands of a third world adviser to benefit financial, doctrinal, or development needs (infrastructure or skills). Equally, such arrangements may be an instant response in time of need for those whose economies crack or become war torn. In general, however, the major incidence of countertrade activity has been with the Eastern bloc and with developing countries.

It is as well to remember that there is hardly a text on countertrade that does not warn that activities such as buy-back and switching require specialist advisers, where no fully trained in-house team exists. Barter, offset, and evidence accounts often have to be handled on a company-to-company basis. Specialist services are not in short supply, with banks, consultants, and brokers providing staff knowledgeable in the area. The discount (sometimes known as disagio) required for reselling countertrade goods can be considerable, particularly when the quality is unknown or suspect. Figures of up to 30 per cent are not unusual, making it imperative that information on the rate likely to be charged is obtained before a deal is contemplated. Clearly, the risks can be high and it is useful to guard against them by understanding the nature of the proposed deal, beyond reasonable doubt, namely:

(a) The exact nature and specification of the goods involved.
(b) How and where the goods will be supplied and any limitations on transport.
(c) How and where the goods may be disposed of with as few limitations as possible.
(d) The exact linkage between the main contract and the countertrade deal, obligations and penalties.
(e) How enforcement of the other parties' obligations may be ensured.

In concentrating on the wider international issues involved it is important not to overlook the importance of countertrade to trade with political groupings such as the Eastern bloc. On an interregional basis such activity strengthens economic ties and interdependency and self-sufficiency. In the future other trading groups may well come to hold the same views as planners in Eastern Europe. The main advantages sought elsewhere appear to concentrate on saving currency outflows and using up excess plant capacity, with ancillary implications for employment. The main deficit is the way countertrade blunts a nation's view of the markets that it may want to serve and denies it the knowledge of the distribution channels and competitive product benefits.

The arguments against countertrade and the emotion and frustrations that build up in companies that simply want to trade is easy enough to understand. There are, however, alternative views of merit which can be tabled. For example, Rolf Mirus and Bernard Yeung have tried to state an alternative view by arguing that countertrade is a valid business tool for dealing with market imperfections. In this way it can be suggested that participants are in fact taking decisions to forgo other market alternatives, and that in those markets where investment is either unwise or impossible countertrade offers a viable alternative. In a buy-back situation, for example, there can be a 'coincidence of needs' in say, raw materials. The 'seller' may require a long-term off-take of product and technical development, while the 'buyer' may require to protect his supply but not feel that he wants, or be allowed, to invest. In such circumstances both parties benefit from countertrade. The idea can then be extended to incorporate buyers of technology who find it difficult to assess the quality of the know-how they are being offered. Through a counterpurchase arrangement some assurance would arise with regard to the marketability of the final product. The final 'twist' of the argument concerns the pressure that countertrade could exert on the selling price of technology by ensuring that the seller reveals his hand through the negotiation of value of the goods purchased after the application of know-how.

It can also be useful to review countertrade as an attractive proposition in bringing forward a sale that might otherwise be put at risk by the entry of new competition before a currency allocation comes forward. The advantage of using home plant capacity now that may not be available later can also be a valid consideration.

From the above appraisal two important considerations arise:

1. It is worth keeping an open mind about countertrade and if its merits are greater than its complications then its introduction as a marketing tool when others run from it would be an advantage.
2. Countertrade may have a greater value than short-circuiting currency problems and pampering to doctrinal differences, if it is specifically adapted so as to secure quality and negotiating benefits in any deal.

If the advantages begin to look attractive in any review of overall strategy it will become necessary to carry out a full investigation into the impact of such activity throughout the company. Such a review would incorporate current purchasing relationships, production planning, cost allocation, stock financing, and labour relations as a minimum. It is apparent that international divisions should not be allowed to act unilaterally in this matter and that there must be total co-ordination throughout the organization. From a structure point of view some may wish to see countertrade as part of a scheme of events within international physical distribution; there are many similarities in moving goods both inwards and outwards.

It is hoped that this appraisal of countertrade makes a useful contribution by showing that the subject is not of immediate necessity a 'black and unnecessary art', but rather an interesting business tool that is worthy of deeper thought. Nowhere has it been suggested that such activity is easy nor in general a remit for amateurs. The view that countertrade should be seen as a possible part of the strategic process, both within its own right as a business tool and because it is more likely to be used in the future than discarded, has, I hope, here been canvassed. The outline is also useful in forming a link with the following Chapter on know-how and technology transfer which, although a much freer subject-area, raises questions of valuation for which it may now be considered that countertrade has a novel answer.

References

1 K. R. Cho, 'Using Countertrade as a Competitive Management Tool', *MIR* 27 (1987).
2 Christopher M. Korth, 'Barter: An Old Practice Yields New Profits', *Business* (Sept./Oct. 1981).
3 'Barter Trade', *Economist*, Feb. 1982.
4 Rolf Mirus and Bernard Yeung, 'Economic Incentives for Countertrade', *Journal of International Business Studies*, 17/3 (1986).
5 'Countertrade', Project and Export Policy Division Department of Trade and Industry (1984. United Kingdom).
6 Stephen Markscheid, 'Compensation Trade: The China Perspective', *China Business Review* (Jan./Feb. 1982).

7

Technology Transfer

From the earlier Chapters it will have been appreciated that the exchange of technology is often not just the simple application of another international business tool. Between North and South it is often an emotional issue when technology is judged as the cornerstone of industrial and commercial maturity, considered over-protected, and out of reach. Equally, elsewhere strong feelings can be generated concerning the 'throwing away of birthrights and potential' or the implied 'failure' of being taught by another business. Such considerations have a conditioning affect on the people involved which tends to make the practical aspects of technology transfer difficult to handle.

Within the spectrum of traditional international activity technology transfer marks the divide between straightforward exporting and a variety of closer business collaborations. It is to be hoped, however, that a more succinct and professional approach to agency arrangements, with a more careful participation in selected territories will, as already suggested, lead to a smoother transition between all forms of international activity. In this way more meaning would certainly be given to the generally accepted view that their should be a continuous strategic link from successful trading through to direct investment in proven markets.

The transfer of technology can take place in a variety of forms, the simplest of which is giving permission (a licence) to another to do something that they would, or could, otherwise be prevented from doing because of existing rights such as patents or trademarks. The more complicated methods are embodied in wider arrangements where not only knowledge is transferred but also an amalgamation of support activity within the broad scope of what most people understand as the 'know-how show-how' range of agreements. Such activity may be through wider licences with additional service agreements (sometimes generically called 'industrial development agreements') or embodied as supplementary agreements themselves within, say, a Joint Venture agreement where the granting of the licence is probably a secondary consideration.

In this Chapter and the following Chapter on management contracts the emphasis will be placed on the simpler forms of technology transfer where knowledge is passed to another organization for use by itself, or to be managed on its behalf. The idea that is common to both situations is the finite duration of the relationship and the absence of any long-term co-operation or profit responsibilities.

The range of methods for transferring technology needs to be understood at the outset since once a business takes the decision to transfer knowledge it has to reconcile itself to either straightforward transfer and loss of control or controlled transfer and an increase in risk through added profit responsibility.

For completeness, a third alternative can be noted whereby a level of continuity might be achieved through the exchange of complementary technology between two companies to optimize their R & D resources.

Important considerations flow from the basic understanding of the composition of technological knowledge. Dunning's version serves well: 'the body of knowledge that is applicable to the production of goods and the creation of new goods, and the way in which resources are converted into commodities'. (Based on F. R. Root, 'The Role of International Business in the Diffusion of Technological Innovation', *Economics and Business Bulletin* (1968) and R. Jones, 'The Role of Technology in the Theory of International Trade', NBER (New York, 1970).) Clearly, there are many ways of 'skinning the cat' but the definition serves to place an emphasis on the practical ways of producing products for markets. The question is therefore not simply one of 'how'?, but equally of 'how effective'?, and 'how beneficial'? in cost and market terms. The simplest of examples serves to make the point and to explain the differences. A company can be licensed to draw metal through a die, and, so that the elements of a technological transfer are thought to exist, let it be agreed 'special metal', 'special die'. A substantial improvement in benefit might, however, take place for the licensee if the know-how of rolling to within the minus tolerance is also taught, as it does not take many tonnes of throughput to bring cost benefits. Further, if the licensee is shown how to market a particular indentation on the drawn metal so that his customers are sold on the idea of new benefits (say, better grip and therefore shorter length for the same application and, as a result, higher prices or volumes are obtained) then the value of the basic knowledge has increased further.

The importance of the argument lies in highlighting from the start that there is often technology for sale in companies which might consider themselves to be low technology based or intellectually modest. The value of the argument can be particularly pronounced when applied to North/South technology transfer since the chemical formula without the 'stick and the bucket' and an element of temperature and effluent control is probably not very useful.

Therefore, it would be wise for a business in pursuing its international strategy to value its activities more carefully and to draw up a knowledge inventory of what it might have for sale, like the following:

- Kit (capital equipment);
- Know-how (functional skills);
- Knowledge (what people know).

Looking at the three 'K's will often yield good results and Millman's quotation has a ring of truth about it: 'Know-how is a sleeping asset—it lies hidden in people's heads, their desk-drawers and filing cabinets—a potential source of income waiting to be packaged.' It is therefore clear that useful skills in international technology transfer are not necessarily going to be the prerogative of the large company, albeit that they are off to a good start with patent departments and the like, as many smaller companies will find that they too have considerable assets, particularly in the 'know-how show-how' area.

Further, any mature company looking at its manufacturing side will probably find that its capital equipment is not unique but is supplied by others who are more than prepared to sell such equipment elsewhere with knowledge on how to install and use it packaged in as a 'loss leader' to gain competitive edge. A mature firm, however, that lives cheek by jowl with strong competition is likely to be strongly honed in competitive skills. Skills in marketing are to be expected, but skills in cost control and maintaining the financial benchmarks for running the business might be just as valuable. Easy-to-understand examples often occur in service industries where, for example, route density and route planning are of paramount importance: learning the skills the hard way often requires shareholders with very deep pockets.

Particularly with reference to the North/South transfer of technology, but by no means exclusively so, the passing of information is meaningless unless there is the capacity to absorb it. This is not to suggest that there is an intellectual league table of brain power, which would be a difficult concept to establish when there are people with Ph.D.s driving buses in Calcutta, but rather it is to draw attention to the fact that in the industrialized world career growth has usually incorporated a large measure of business experience that is not necessarily paralleled elsewhere. Countries new to the industrializing process often have experience gaps particularly at middle management level. Therefore one is again prompted to widen the scope of knowledge transfer in order to improve the capacity to absorb: naturally there must also be greater financial rewards for the wider product offer.

The capacity to absorb should be of concern to both parties and should take precedence over just 'getting one's hands on the information'. Some argue that it was European receptivity that was in reality the driving-force behind the industrial revolution. To quote A. R. Hall: 'Europe would yield nothing of the eminence of its religion and but little of its philosophy, but in the processes of manufacture and in natural science it readily adopted whatever seemed useful and expedient'. The basic idea seems sound since by now most are aware that the Chinese invented virtually everything! A modern equivalent may well turn out to be the Middle East OPEC countries where only history will be able to tell if the wide strategic thinking of some Arab businessman, who installed large plants in the Gulf, affected the course of world industry.

It is therefore not surprising to discover that the world's governments have also taken a keen interest in the terms of technology transfer and sometimes strongly influence what may be given (with regard to, say, military goods) and what might be taken by, for example, preventing unhelpful economic clauses such as those concerning export/territorial limitations and 'tie-backs'. The discussion on countertrade also demonstrated that ideas such as buy-backs can be government sponsored and can act as a safety check on the quality of goods produced from the technology given.

As an introductory summary one might conclude that technology transfer is keenly sought both in its own right and for national, social, and economic reasons. The process need not be as intellectual as it at first sounds: it is open to all who can correctly value and package their skills. The methods of transfer are very wide but can be broadly categorized as 'one shot' or 'participative'. Overall, the capacity to absorb is as important as the capacity to give.

Although at first sight the approach appears scientific McDonald and Leahey have put together a very practical list of 'pros and cons' for the inward and outward licensing of technology. This is reprinted as Appendix I at the end of this chapter. Both attitudes are incorporated as it is always important to understand both the 'sale' and 'purchase' positions.

The current cost of R & D comes through strongly thereby raising the general question as to whether or not a company considers technology sales as part of its international strategy from the outset. It may be necessary to 'bend the knee' to shareholders who feel that a quicker return is required on research expenditure which is often a high risk/high value cost centre. The extension of the value of current technology by putting it to use elsewhere massaging other companies' product life-cycles is also important.

The 'give and take' arguments can be set out schematically for ease of reference and to allow a better focus on the calculation of value of the 'finite' or 'participative routes' Figure 7.1 shows the overall assessment of costs and values between licensing and investment routes. Essentially, the equation turns on licence or investment revenue, both less technology transfer costs and opportunity costs of the chosen strategy.

Two important ideas emerge as one builds up towards the technology sale:

1. Technology transfer costs are never free, and experience indicates that intangible costs can be much higher than anticipated particularly when the capacity to absorb is weak.
2. Whichever strategy is chosen there are risk elements to consider. Revenues depend upon the unhindered remittance of funds by both the customers and governments concerned. Return predictions can be no better than market forecasts.

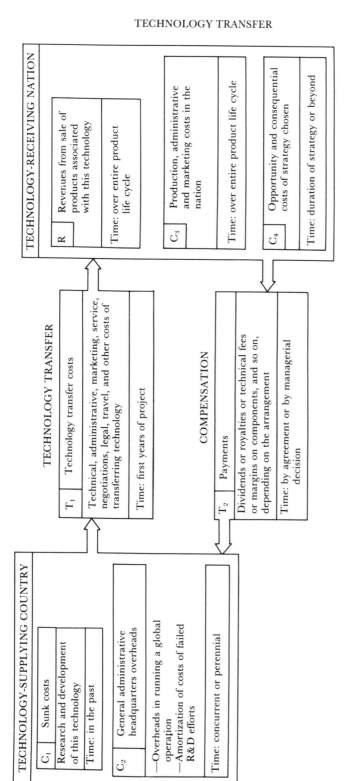

Figure 7.1. Schematic of International Technology Transfer Costs and Compensation in either Licensing or Direct Investment

Source: F. J. Contractor, 'Choosing between Direct Investment and Licensing', *Journal of International Business Studies* (Winter 1984), 169.

It would therefore appear that there is a remarkable similarity between the requirements for the preparation of a technology sale and for the use of agents in exporting. This is so in practical terms because no estimate can be made of the transfer costs of technology unless the nature of the recipient is researched and the ability to absorb technology assessed, or in other words: what level of support cost will be required to keep royalty payments flowing? Moreover, the returns from technology transfer are suspect unless the value of the market is known together with the financial and legal characteristics of the licensee's territory which will control the value and quality of fund remittance and perhaps the content of the agreement. In these terms the general principles of sound market research and partner selection apply as well as the security of joint activity, albeit with different emphasis.

With regard to the selection process there are key considerations apart from those discussed elsewhere and which require more emphasis:

Company structure
(a) Shareholders and their activities and what other interests might they have in the licensed information?
(b) Overseas connections, where else might the technology or the products flow?

Production facilities
(a) What are the provisions for quality control if we are going to be associated with the end-product?
(b) What are the customer service criteria?
(c) What are the career records and backgrounds of key technical staff; what also is the length of service and loyalty?
(d) Past experience in absorbing new know-how and current workload in absorbing new processes, etc.
(e) Relationships between R & D and production functions.

Relationships
(a) Who will we work with day to day?
(b) Who controls the day-to-day staff and what is management's motivation?
(c) Why was the decision taken to purchase technology?
(d) Who has been responsible for absorbing technology in the past, where are they now, and what was the track record.

Financial
(a) If the deal is successful could the company expand further?
(b) Records of overseas payments and a clean record with the local authorities.
(c) Who advises on legal actions, what is the style, and what is the record.

Market

(a) Are the sales personnel adequate to the task and adaptable.

(b) Is there confidence below sales-leadership level that the volumes are there?

(c) Is there any evidence of formal market planning for new product introductions?

(d) Nature and accuracy of sales budgeting and forecasting.

(e) What will the addition of technology transfer costs do to the product price and its relationship to competitors' prices?

Overall

(a) If we link up with this company what conclusions will our customers and our competitors draw.

(b) If this deal goes through will we have a good case history which will make it easier to sell technology elsewhere?

Later discussion can cover the nature of negotiation and the style of the agreement and its clauses but before that stage is reached the licenser needs to have a firm view as to how much he wants to charge for all or a combination of the following:

(a) Down payment for an agreed first disclosure of technology information.

(b) Interim payments for further stages of disclosure.

(c) Minimum royalty (Fall back position if nothing happens in the market place).

(d) Ongoing royalty rate (usually a percentage of the selling price or an agreed value per unit).

(e) The value of any special provisions such as buy backs tie-ins purchase of raw materials or components) or future options of say either more technology or equity participation.

In the overall terms the answer to all of these expectations lies in the assessment of:

licence revenue less technology transfer costs less production and sales costs.

The estimated answer shows what is available to be shared between the participants. The alternative basis is to 'set the clock' by the supposed industry norm and follow the simple mathematics of 2 per cent being less than 3 per cent and 4 per cent being a happy event!

The preferred suggestion that participants should work together to determine the assumption on market size will therefore come as no surprise. It certainly fulfils the main requirements for both parties in determining what quality of working relationship can be anticipated. There are also negotiating benefits: if the licensee says the market is weak then the licensor is drawn into horse trading front-end benefits to get the licence off the ground. If the market is said to be substantial he is tempted towards the 'jam tomorrow' by the running royalty. Both stances have obvious traps, but both can be negated, with a sound view of market potential.

Products can be sold by samples and brochures but technology should not. The value of technology should be shown through obvious skills in passing knowledge on and through interest and understanding of its use in the market-place. A wise purchaser will want to know as much about the donor as the donor wishes to know about him, and for this reason the wise seller will set his stall out not only in his briefcase but also in his own factory and offices.

Transfer costs, industry norms, and the length of time that patents have to run are all important, but like every other commercial deal the main consideration is what the market will bear. Therefore market size, profit generation, and who else is trying to sell are more important considerations. It is worth noting that from a negotiating standpoint a combination package of 'intellectual property and know-how' is likely to offer higher perceived values, be more competitive, and is less open to straightforward cost comparisons.

The scope of a 'combination package' can be considerable:

(a) Intellectual property (Patents, Trademarks, Copyright etc.)
(b) Product processes
        procedures;
        layouts;
        training and training aids;
        quality control;
        worker compensation packages.
(c) Commissioning procedures
        testing performance (speed, quality, wastage);
        sampling;
        safety tests;
        environmental tests.
(d) Sales
        training and training aids;
        joint publicity;
        PR packages;
        marketing plans;
        product launch plans;
        literature, etc. (blanks without words if language intrudes).
(e) Finance
        accounting procedures;
        stock control.
(f) Trouble-shooting
        crisis package;
        holiday cover for key staff;
        regular management 'surgeries'.

All of the above, plus many other ideas, need expression in some quantifiable form such as man-hours, or the number of visits, if technology transfer costs are to be controlled. The use of the wider combination offer might also allow the splitting of intellectual property into smaller tranches sensibly traded off by improving the licensee's ability to absorb. This may lead to a longer relationship through the 'drip feed' of technology which would allow for a longer royalty revenue life. Such sales are easier when based on a successful and vibrant working relationship.

The overall negotiation requires careful planning by the licensor and the basis of his case will rarely be scientific; almost invariably his presentation will revolve around the demonstration of benefits. There is much discussion amongst marketeers concerning benefits and it is sometimes easier to take the simplest route; challenge a benefit with the question 'so what?'. If a valid answer is available the benefit exists, if this is not the case move on quickly!

In many ways technology transfer is about taking short cuts so 'negative benefits' should not be overlooked. Saving time by avoiding the selection of the incorrect methodology, or by having widely dispersed information presented 'on a plate' are all quicker routes to profit. Reducing risks and avoiding the risks of market-testing faulty choices are obvious tangible benefits. 'Saving face' with owners or shareholders can be another advantage.

The way to start building value is through confidentiality. It is the seller's responsibility to create value—everyone else is working in the opposite direction. Clearly the starting-point is to ensure that patent protection exists or that at least copyright is established. All documents will be marked 'confidential' and, most important of all, the route for disclosure will be meticulously mapped out and managed *throughout* the donor organization. The phrases that stick in the mind, and possibly in the gullet too, are: 'I thought it would be helpful', and 'I didn't realize'. Negotiation teams are like army platoons—they should do what the lieutenant tells them if they wish to achieve objectives; if there is nothing to do they should fall out and go to sleep!

Once sufficient information has been passed to the potential licensee to confirm credibility and interest, a confidentiality agreement should be signed. Such an agreement should be tightly drawn and in sensitive areas the schedule of information to be passed will be extended to incorporate the minutes of meetings or the file notes of telephone conversations if necessary. In this way what has been passed on is on record and the value which the seller attaches to his knowledge is kept to the fore.

Again, the imposition of discipline, possibly to an extent which is neither normal or generally sought after in today's organizations, is emphasized. The seller's ability to cover the ground with decent speed and to act confidently adds value; delays can cause suspicion, apprehension, and weaken values. It follows, therefore, that at the start of the negotiation the seller should have established three important criteria:

1. That the seller's negotiating team have a remit and the authority to conclude a deal.

2. That the recipient's negotiator has similar authority.

3. That there is an agreement on how and where the legal negotiations will

be pursued and that the legal representatives have a common brief on the scope of the commercial arrangements. This can be done either through a Heads of Agreement document (less formal) or a more formal Options Agreement.

It is most unlikely that this point will have been reached without the joint agreement on:

1. Whether the agreement is exclusive (which means what it says), or 'sole' (which will allow the seller some continuing rights).
2. The territory in which the grant can be used.
3. The effect of local legislation on the proposed terms.

Additionally, the seller will need to have established his negotiating stance which as a result of his researches will, one hopes, fall within the aspirations of the purchaser.

It has been implied throughout that the negotiation is a stepping-stone for the pedestrian or a springboard for the enthusiastic and poses the question of how to ensure the continuity and durability of the arrangement. The style of the negotiating team is therefore a matter of some importance in securing a smooth transition from discussion to action. This is best achieved if both sides get up from the table feeling that they have a fair deal, sensibly negotiated, and with no 'scores' to settle at the first opportunity. The negotiator's password is empathy. The word has occurred previously in this book and the concept is important for crossing cultural frontiers. On this occasion we shall eschew the dictionary and seek clarity through pictures rather than words.

There is a Japanese woodcut in the Victoria and Albert Museum in London called 'The Great Wave' executed by Katsushika Hokusai (Plate 1). Herbert Read in *The Meaning of Art* suggests we have the choice of feeling concerned about the safety of the men in the boat, which would be 'sympathy', or of projecting ourselves into the scene and of feeling *with* the men the danger of the wave about to engulf them, which would be 'empathy'. In negotiations, if one can feel the tensions and understand and respond to them then international strategies will be that much easier to achieve. Feeling 'with' produces results in a relationship which will be fundamental to long-term profits.

THE LICENSING AGREEMENT

A typical licensing agreement is set out in skeletal form below.

Broad outline concerning whom the agreement is between, where they carry on their business, and what they have to give one another, followed by the euphoric WHEREAS:

Article: To defining the terms used in the agreement to make it self-contained.

Licenser's Obligations

Empathy: "feeling with" – People the 5th P. (See preface)
Source: Hokusai, *The Great Wave*, reproduced by courtesy of the Board of Trustees of the Victoria and Albert Museum.

Article: Scope of the licence and, most importantly, whether it is exclusive or sole, and making the licence subject to following articles.
Article: Governing law and language.
Article: Duration of the agreement and when it is to start.
Article: Permissions with regard to trade names, etc.
Article: The exact nature of what the licenser agrees to do.
Article: Provision for what happens if he improves the technology.
Article: Provision for what happens if licensee improves technology.
Article: Limitations of licenser's risks and obligations.
Article: Rights to cancel and reasons for so doing.

Licensee's Obligations

Article: When the use of the technology will commence.
Article: Restrictions on the use of information.
Article: Initial payments and for what.
Article: Royalties (minimum and running), how paid, how recorded, and how audited.
Article: Responsibilities for tax.
Article: Limitations on exploitation, e.g. exports.
Article: Use of trademark, patent, etc. assignments.
Article: Permission for inspection, marking of products, warranties etc.
Article: Local registration.

Joint Activity

Article: Arbitration.
Article: Ending agreement (determination).
Article: Addresses for communication.

Signatures.

Schedules and any secondary agreements referred to in the main articles.

In the above outline, as in lawyers' agreements, 'the singular means the plural' if you want it to, and some sections may expand into many articles with subclauses if the grant is a complex one. Equally, some advisers like to change the order. While the agreement may seem a little arid and the language old-fashioned, the main contribution that it makes is to determine beyond reasonable doubt what has been agreed. If it all gets a little long and perhaps even tiresome, it is the negotiator's task to maintain interest and to ensure momentum. The attitudes of legal advisers can have a considerable conditioning effect but in the end their task is to express the commercial view as best they can. They should certainly not be left alone to knock it out on a 'three of sand and one of cement' basis!

Will it all have been worth it? If the detailed preparatory work has been done and the motivations understood, then there is an above-average chance of a positive answer. Business, however, does not stand still, neither does technology, and it is important that the negotiators meet regularly not only to review progress (that is fundamental) but also to confirm that their original information and assumptions are still valid. It would be wise to check (discretely) if the licensee is getting value for money, because if he is not then the seeds of discontent may start to germinate. It is also important to assess whether or not changes in legislation might affect any arrangement.

Technology transfer can be a powerful business tool but it is clearly not easy to handle and not risk-free; careful consideration is required before making a commitment and considerable effort necessary to get the full rewards. The fact that the content can, and perhaps should, be wide opens up opportunities for many companies if they value their stock of knowledge correctly. Technology transfer not only give momentum to individual companies but it also plays an important strategic role in bridging the North/South gap. The capacity to give, however, is limited by the capacity to absorb. The main dangers in the technique is the loss of a very substantial measure of control by the donor and a very real difficulty in assessing the value of what is being offered by the recipient. One of the important differences from an organizational point of view is the necessity to involve more members of the team than is generally necessary for straightforward exporting. More revenue may be squeezed from the technique by the skills associated with management contracts and the provision of skilled management labour, and this will be looked at in the next Chapter. Overall, it is clear that in the spectrum of international strategies, knowledge is the bridge between selling to and working with.

References

1 D. W. McDonald and H. S. Leahey, 'Licensing Has a Role in Technology Strategic Planning', *Research Management* (Jan./Feb. 1985).
2 J. D. Major, 'Some Practical Intellectual Property Aspects of Technology Transfer', *International Journal of Technology Management*, 3 (1986).
3 A. F. Millman, 'Licensing Technology', *MD* 21/3 (1983).
   A. R. Hall, 'Epilogue: the Rise of the West', in Charles Singer *et al.*, *A History of Technology* (O.U.P., Vol. 3, 1957), pp. 716–17.
4 F. R. Root and F. J. Contractor, 'Negotiating Compensation in International Licensing Agreements', *Sloan Management Review* (Winter 1981), 23–31.
5 F. J. Contractor, 'Choosing between Direct Investment and Licensing', *Journal of International Business Studies* (Winter 1984).
6 K. Mason, *Standard Clauses in a Licensing Agreement* (Kenneth Mason Publications: London, 1970).
7 D. E. Brazell, *Licensing Check-Lists* (Kenneth Mason Publications: London, 1974).
8 W. A. P. Manser and S. Webley, 'Technology Transfer to Developing Countries', Royal Institute of International Affairs, Chatham House Paper No. 3.
9 J. H. Dunning, 'Towards a Taxonomy of Technology Transfer and Possible Impacts on OECD Countries', OECD Analytical Studies (Paris 1982).
10 'The International Transfer of Industrial Technology Past and Present', OECD Analytical Studies (Paris 1982).
11 E. M. Graham, 'The Terms of Transfer of Technology to the Developing Nations', OECD Analytical Studies (Paris 1982).
12 J. Delorme, 'The Changing legal Framework for Technology Transfer'.
13 H. Read, *The Meaning of Art* (Pelican Books: Harmondsworth, 1954).
14 P. Lasserre, 'Selecting A Foreign Partner for Technology Transfer', *Long Range Planning*, 17/6 (1984).

APPENDIX I[a]

Pros and Cons for the Inward and Outward Licensing of Technology

Advantages of Licensing-out

1. Allows full exploitation of technology while it is still viable and increases the return on technology investments.
2. Helps to justify R & D expenses. May also result in additional R & D being done by the licensee(s), particularly when the licensee has resources and know-how not held by the licenser.
3. Improves value of patent position by adding know-how sales and technical assistance to the package.
4. Helps to avoid litigation and reduces the incentive of others to develop ways to circumvent the patents.
5. Upgrades the knowledge and performance of the technical staff involved because of their external contacts and the need to stay informed about competitive developments which may affect the firm's licensing position. This is supported by an Industrial Research Institute survey that indicated that licensing of patents resulted in increased innovation.
6. May enhance the growth of the industry and make the technology more valuable.
7. Can help to sell products, equipment, and/or services. Licensing may also help unrelated companies get to know each other, possibly resulting in other mutually profitable relationships.
8. Frequently allows for grant-back of improvements made by licensees. In addition, having

Disadvantages of licensing-out

1. May dilute the firm's technical developments to sustain the effort required to sell the licensing package and, if successful, to provide the necessary support for it.
2. Could be very expensive. Securing and maintaining worldwide patent protection can be costly (and may also dilute the R & D effort). Likewise, foreign trade and tax laws can be complex and require continuing attention by in-house staff and/or consultants.
3. May cause unwanted legal entanglements. In non-exclusive agreements, the licenser generally bears the cost of policing to assure non-infringement. Also, the licensee may subsequently contest the validity of the patents.
4. May result in competition from licensees who have certain advantages such as lower labour or raw material costs.
5. Can be risky, due to lack of control over licensee's manufacturing and marketing practices with resultant product liability risk.
6. Might result in unlicensed technology and future potential developments either being given away or obtained by licensees at a very low cost.
7. May lose opportunity for expanding participation in the market beyond the original licence terms.

[a] Taken from D. W. McDonald and H. S. Leahey, 'Licensing Has a Role in Technology Strategic Planning', *Research Management* (Jan./Feb. 1985).

Advantages of Licensing-out

several producers manufacture under a licence can establish industry standards for products and processes that may result in competitive advantages.

9. Permits participation in certain international markets where direct investment would either be prohibited or unattractive. May also result in access to low-cost and/or raw materials.

10. Allows a firm to test market a product indirectly through a foreign licensee.

11. Provides an opportunity to profit from technology that the firm does not intend to exploit, such as developments that do not currently fit into the business strategy, or those that fit markets that are too small to be of interest.

12. Can help sell a subsidiary company.

13. May help to avoid antitrust actions or trade regulations.

Advantages of Licensing-in

1. Is an approach for buying time; it can result in faster commercial production and market entry, or assist in gaining market share and/ or improving profitability if the licensee is already a participant in the industry.

2. Can be significantly less expensive than internal development and can eliminate or reduce the firm's commitment in staff and costly facilities.

3. Can have much less risk than internal development.

4. Can provide specialized knowledge and skills that are beyond the capability of the licensee to develop in a reasonable time and enable the technology function to focus on projects where it has the greatest competence and highest odds of success.

5. Can generally provide for

Disadvantages of licensing-out

Disadvantages of Licensing-in

1. Is an investment in the current state-of-the-art technology of the licenser at best, rather than in technology which will be superior to all others.

2. May create substantial problems in translating the technology to the licensee's operations, particularly if the licenser is located in a foreign country with language and cultural differences.

3. May require significant scale-up, resulting in additional costs and delays in commercialization.

4. Does not necessarily result in the in-depth technical knowledge and training of personnel gained from internal development.

5. May require grant-back of improvements made by the licensee. These improvements may flow from the licenser to other licensees who are competitors of the

Advantages of Licensing-in

continuing technical assistance from the licensee through the licence agreement and may result in access to new development from the licenser and, in some instances, from its other licensees through technological 'pool' arrangements.

6. May avoid a patent or trade secret
- dispute or a costly effort to circumvent existing patents.

7. May permit use of a trademark or result in immediate market recognition based on the good reputation of the licenser.

8. May stimulate the licensee's technological development and help overcome a 'not invented here' attitude. Relying solely on internally developed technology is introspective and can be costly. A sophisticated licensing staff can also act as technological 'gatekeepers' by monitoring outside developments.

9. Is sometimes easier to 'sell' management on investing in proven technology from outside than in an internally developed technology.

Disadvantages of Licensing-in

firm making the improvements.

6. Can have adverse effect on morale of the R & D staff, who may interpret licensing-in of technology as a vote of no-confidence.

7. May require the licensee under exclusive licences to bear the cost of policing the market for infringement and of subsequent litigation if required to resolve a dispute.

8. Last but not least, could be so expensive that the cost of the licence is a significant drain on the business.

8

Management Contracts

Management contracts may be considered the ultimate technique in transferring knowledge in so far as they combine the movement of information with the people to show how to apply that information, but without the responsibility of ownership. Such contracts share with other technology–transfer techniques the key characteristic of a planned finite life.

As is so often the case in international business the historical background is long yet simple. Since the earliest days of industry people have seen techniques elsewhere which they believe would be of benefit to them and have invited skilled practitioners to come and set up a similar operation for them. It has always been acknowledged that in the process local people will learn the skills and benefit from the new ideas and the new ways of doing things.

Herbert Minton's appointment in 1848 of Leon Arnoux, the celebrated French potter, in order to bring the colours and designs of Sevres to Stoke-on-Trent is a good example. An even earlier instance would be Henry VIII's use of Pietro Torrigiano to bring the style of the Renaissance to the English church and the albeit forced use of French and Flemish carpenters and joiners can be seen as a part of the same process.

There is, however, comparatively little written about management contracts. The subject was raised in a meaningful way in 1967 when Peter Gabriel published his analysis of four case histories. There was a surge of activity around a somewhat arid report in 1983 but thereafter it was left substantially to Michael Brooke who in 1987 in a major analysis, supported by the Leverhulm Trust, brought some life into the subject that business had already begun to appreciate could add value to technology transfer. The later work, commenced in 1974, was able to draw on over forty substantial case histories and much greater business awareness.

Governments have long used the technique in key areas such as mining and public services (e.g. railways and electricity). Management contracts are also well known to the hotel industry but the general idea of using the management contract as either a defensive tool to retain a presence in a territory, or as an offensive device to generate more revenue from territories where investment is not contemplated, or where the finalization of a consultancy or turnkey project would have led to a cessation of activity, is a relatively new approach.

The essence of a management contract is relatively easy to define: one party provides the capital and retains beneficial ownership, and the other provides the management for a fee and has obligations to the owners. Within the overall concept it is important to understand that managers' negotiating strengths and power is greatest at the outset of a project, but as skills and information is supplied the manager's influence weakens and the owner's real power strengthens. Therefore, however tough and clever the clauses are in the agreement between the two parties reality will condition application and the balance of power will change to the extent that the manager's ability to negotiate an extension of the arrangement will be considered suspect from the outset. This is an important aspect of the understanding of management contracts since it will have a conditioning affect on relationships as the contract matures, and should be taken into account when considering strategic options.

When management contracts are dressed up in their added value roles by becoming an adjunct to a know-how contract or a turnkey or consultancy arrangement there is a temptation to blur images, but it has to be remembered that despite the substantial advance in relationship, there is no participation, and in consequence none of the rights of ownership. Quite simply, it is as well to remember that managers can always be sacked. In a competitive world it is not beyond the bounds of possibility that another organization is trying to engineer that sacking! Nevertheless, the management can be a powerful cementing agent and a sound platform from which to play for the continuation of commercial arrangements, but the inherent weakness remains that a company's market presence can be curtailed fairly smartly.

Overall, however, it is difficult not to share in the new enthusiasm for the concept which certainly fulfils the local business and national requirements in many parts of the world of getting 'hands-on' experience in the use of new technology and a soundly based organization. Equally, for the managing contractor the technique can provide a very valuable training ground for an international management cadre at someone else's expense. If as a result of the contact further opportunities arise to transfer further technology, or the confidence arises to transfer the activity into a joint venture to harness the full potential of the project then the full value of the technique as a planned and practical selling tool will have been harnessed. If the catalytic effect can be used to generate further profitable opportunities the subsequent negotiations may not be subject to the same competitive pressures that might otherwise have applied.

As management contracts are less well known than other international business techniques it is perhaps useful to look at an outline contact at an early stage and to draw inferences from the content requirements.

The main considerations that form the body of the agreement are:

1. Scope: The main concerns are regarding the overall parameters of the arrangement and the extent of the manager's control. The spectrum of choice is not unlike the exclusive and sole arrangements that applied to agency agreements. From the manager's standpoint probably anything short of absolute control on a day-to-day basis is going to threaten the achievement of essential results, possibly linked to the payment of fees. In a practical sense one of the most important value judgements is the extent to which the manager is in a unique position in terms of skills and knowledge, which will enable him to retain a large measure of control until the operation is handed over. If this is not the case it may be in the manager's interest to limit the scope and to ensure that areas in which the owner wants to make some input are clearly his responsibility. It is an important feature of shared operations that there is clarity of control—without it staff left with the day-to-day duties flounder.

Generally the manager contractor is going to have to satisfy himself that he can offer control, services, and advice in the following areas:

- Planning.
- Organization.
- Day-to-Day operation (production, sales and marketing, purchasing, financial control, personnel and training).
- Further Development and sometimes the mobilization of capital.
- Performance against any other appended agreements.

It therefore becomes clear from the outset once again that the scope of the contract, if it is not to be a function of the imagination, had better be based on market research and a knowledge of the owners and their business record. Equally, unless expenses and a flat fee have been negotiated, performance against a wide scope of activity requires a firm knowledge of the market requirement. For example, the performance of a pressing plant is substantially different if the average piece weight is 5 kgs against the manager's 10 kg in the home plant and run volumes average 5,000 units as against the normal 25,000 units.

2. Pre-Contract Activities: It is not unusual for managers to be given the task of 'setting up' or plant construction. The combination makes very good sense to the owners as it packages the activity and combines the responsibility. Such a combination may, however, be outside the general scope of the manager's normal activity. Ideally, therefore, this activity should be the subject of a separate contract (albeit cross-referenced) where the specific issues, responsibilities, and payments are negotiated against defined arrangements of a specific activity like, say, bringing a plant on stream with agreed criteria within a specified time limit. It is wise to see that the cost and penalties of one activity do not affect the potential revenue stream of other agreements. Equally important is to understand where the authorities for procurement are going to fall and to ensure that expediting and commissioning are seen 'in the round'.

3. Owner's Control: The difficulties for the owners are readily apparent since the information on which they are going to rely to exercise their own rights and obligations is going to be controlled by the managers. It follows that the owners have to decide on levels of 'interference' and restriction. There is a tendency for many managing contractors to favour wide-ranging clauses which allow for wider interpretation, and from a general negotiating standpoint including its possible shortcuts, this is clearly attractive. From the day-to-day operational point of view, however, such clauses can lead to untold difficulties. It is suggested that it would be mutually beneficial if both owner and manager (not his representative on the ground) have a clear understanding of the areas of control and the limits of authority. Without this neither side will be able to approach day-to-day management with any degree of certainty. Similarly, day-to-day management will, without clear rules, spend more time negotiating than trying to achieve objectives.

The key clause is: 'The manager shall not do any of the following unless specifically authorized by the board of directors of the owner'. Negotiate it, then let the buck rest!

It has already been mentioned that one should be wary of the adage about never looking at the agreement once it has been signed. Here is one instance where the sentiment may be perfectly acceptable, providing that the negotiators have agreed with one another who does what. It is certainly true that once all is clear the agreement is only of consequence to those who have weak memories.

Usually in this section another subclause will reside stating exactly what information the manager will provide to the owner and the timings of the submissions. As the object of the exercise is either profit or for a services and utilities cost-effective operation, it is also important to agree at an early stage which accounting conventions and methods are to be used. The area is of sufficient importance to see the detail of the accounting procedures and key conventions agreed in a separate schedule. If the management fee is to be related to profit in any way it makes good sense to understand the basis of the calculation, and to 'freeze' the rules before agreeing to the formula.

4. Owner's Obligations: The requirement for clarity is again obvious, and should directly relate to the manager's view as to what he needs if he is to succeed in achieving his agreed objectives. The well-meaning clause is no friend. Best endeavours to assist in any local matter are a long way from appointing a full-time liaison officer who will accompany the general manager to all meetings with local authorities, including police, customs, hospitals, and so on. One approach is more likely to get the goods out of the docks, or a staff member released from a delicate situation, than the other.

Overall, the manager will be looking for logical contributions that ensure that the day-to-day management can operate effectively (regarding matters such as power, visas, licences, etc.) and to relieve the day-to-day management of activities in which they are relatively inexperienced in the territory and where the owners have superior knowledge (in such things as credit ratings, government regulations, renting accommodation, etc.).

5. *Human Resources*: Appointments, payment, treatment, training, and career progression are key areas and full of sensitivity since it is the people who do the selling and manufacturing that determine the future success of the operation, and in the vast majority of cases the owner will have set his heart on having his own team at some stage in the future. The interrelationships with people building up to an eventual handover will be critical, and the speed and the manner in which this is done needs to be controlled. The finding, acceptance, and training of local employees needs to be tied into job descriptions, manpower specifications, training programmes, and task qualification, assessment, and termination rules.

It is not unusual for there to be conflict between the manager's requirements for his staff and the owner's requirements to see some form of equality for local employees. Overseas packages and local packages rarely align and the agreement of broad terms for different grades of employees is best spelt out before they are employed. 'House', 'car', 'school', and 'annual leave' are of course all too vague and failing to qualify them numerically in the overall negotiation can be a costly omission in terms of employee relations. Overall, neither the manager nor the owners should have to act as a 'court of appeal' in these areas; the ground rules should all be set before the operation begins.

6. *Business Objectives*: It is a wise precaution to have these fully set out and to ensure that the manager fully understands the owner's requirements. It all sounds so obvious, but it must never be assumed that the owner wants a repeat performance of what goes on in the manager's home country. There will be other pressures arising perhaps from his view of his own economy, the local, competitive situation, and the financial pressures in other parts of his operation. In combination these and other considerations may well generate a set of requirements that the manager has to be fully conversant with, not only to run the business overall but equally to take into account when making all the secondary decisions. For example, staff selection cannot be attempted without consideration of the main skills needed to meet the objectives.

While it may appear to be the owner's responsibility to set out his requirements , in practice it is up to the manager to assure himself that he fully understands what the key tasks are.

7. *Special Project Provisions*: Here one would expect to see a tabulation reflecting the owner's way of carrying out business in his area as well as any special arrangements between the parties concerning raw materials, spare parts, special purchasing arrangements, etc.

Thereafter the contract will be following well-trodden ground with clauses on:

- Expenses and fees (formulas, indexation, allowances, etc.).
- Liabilities and termination.

- Duration and extension.
- Resolution of disputes.

Michael Brooke's check-list for the evaluation of management contracts is reprinted as Appendix I at the end of this chapter and serves well to highlight many of the points of concern which should receive attention at the outset. It is equally important to re-examine each item in this or any other check-list to ascertain if today's view would change if the balance of power between the parties were different. For example, if a clause concerning staffing confers equal rights to select, but with the owner's approval being final, it may not matter overmuch when the project can only be started with employees trained by the manager. Later on, however, there may be real concern about achieving objectives unless the manager has final control over staff in key areas, such as quality control.

In this sense there is a similarity between management and joint venture contracts; once international activity moves towards combined working arrangements both the management and the relationships between the parties have to be controlled to limit conflicts of interest. As will be seen in the following Chapter the joint venture starts with a considerable advantage because it is founded on common interests and objectives mutually agreed. Correctly constructed the blending of relationships can develop the joint venture into a powerful entity in its own right; in a management agreement, however, the changing balance of power and the certainty of termination can exercise considerable strains on relationships and weaken day-to-day management motivation.

One issue that arises in the use of management contracts is the need to have staff working overseas and assigned to another organization. It has already been mentioned that management contracts can be of use in providing an excellent training-ground for an international management cadre but this is an overall 'cream-on-the-cake' argument. The heart of the matter is to find staff capable of performing overseas and to ensure that they receive a suitable package of terms and conditions that ensures that they spend the maximum amount of effort running the business and not running the children to school! At this stage it is important to accept that certain personal characteristics are required for people taking overseas postings and self-discipline, self-sufficiency, and empathy will feature strongly. Further, there will be technical requirements which may not arise in larger organizations in the manager's country, such as running 'live bank accounts' and controlling cash flow day-by-day. Diplomacy will also be required as the political issues are for real and distant from the fourth-form horse-play that resides in clever in-house memorandums, fence-sitting, and personality-baiting that can be tolerated in well-established organizations.

Given that suitable people can be found, not only do they have to perform but they have also at some stage to be fitted back into the donor organization as a persuasive force to advocate that others take the same route, without the fear that 'out of sight is out of mind' and therefore a weak career option. Clearly, when considering management contracts a host of fundamental organization and structure problems are raised. With such a background in mind it will come as no surprise to find that the manager's requirements are often in conflict with those of the owner, who simply wants the best person at the lowest price for three years, and, if he approves, a 'twin' to replace him or her. A wise practitioner in this area will give considerable thought to staffing at the outset and fold into the negotiation the careful selling of his candidates using their availability and willingness to add value to his proposition.

CONCLUSION

For the supplier of technology management contracts are sound but complicated formulas for adding value to know-how transfer. Offensively they provide a good opportunity for short-term market entrenchment without the risks, obligations, and capital commitments of ownership. Defensively such contracts provide the opportunity to retain an integrated position in weakening markets where for example, the retention of ownership is under threat.

For the purchaser of management skills the opportunity is there to obtain technology as well as the organization and trained staff to put it to best use with the minimum of experimentation. The considerable advantage is the retention of absolute ownership and control as well as the preservation of the 'purity' of national business in those areas where such considerations matter. The element of 'gamble' is in the ability to withstand the withdrawal of practised management and in the skill of sustaining development of the technology, if appropriate, with further help.

For both partners serious issues arise in the control of relationships and the integration of staffs from different cultural backgrounds. In these areas there are similarities with joint ventures, which is dealt with in the next Chapter, but the major difference is that in a joint venture the opportunity is there for continued market development by mutual consent whereas in the management contract the arrangements are generally short-term and finite and the balance of power changes substantially between the parties during the life of the contract.

References

1 Michael Z. Brooke, *Selling Management Service Contracts in International Business* (Holt, Rinehart, and Winston: London, 1987).
2 Peter P. Gabriel, *The International Transfer of Corporate Skills* (Havard University, Division of Research: Boston, 1967).
3 United Nations, *Management Contracts in Developing Countries: An Analysis of their Substantive Provisions* (New York, 1983).
4 Paul Atterbury, *English Pottery and Porcelain* (Universe Books: New York, 1978).
5 Ralf Fastnedge, *English Furniture Styles, 1500–1830* (Penguin Books: Harmondsworth, 1964).

APPENDIX I[a]

Check-List for Evaluating Contract Terms

| | Check for priority to | | | | | |
	(1) Client	(2) Contractor	(3) Whether monitoring required	(4) Whether to be included in legal document	(5) Role of contractor (advisory or executive)	(6) Comments
1. THE BOARD						
1.1. Composition						
1.2. Rights of veto or limitations of power						
1.3. Frequency of meetings						
1.4. Reserved decisions						
2. APPOINTMENTS AND PERSONNEL						
2.1. Right to appoint senior staff						
2.2. Overseeing of staff changes						
2.3. Recruitment						
2.4. Personnel policies						
2.5. Management training						
2.6. Other staff training						
2.7. Stock options						
3. PLANNING						
3.1. Long-range planning						
3.2. Policies that will continue after expiry of contract						
4. FINANCE						
4.1. Borrowing						
4.2. Budgets						
4.3. Expenditure						
4.4. Dividends						
4.5. Fees						
4.6. Credit						

[a] Taken from Michael Z. Brooke, *Selling Management Service Contracts in International Business* (Holt, Rinehart, and Winston: London, 1987).

9

Joint Ventures

Joint ventures are words that have been on many lips and even the most casual reader of daily papers and business and management journals will be aware of the intensity of activity on a world-wide basis. In the North much of this activity has been centred on restructuring and realignments in industry, although by no means exclusively so. The Middle East and, to a lesser extent, perhaps South America, based their developments in the late seventies and early eighties on joint venture operations. What was newsworthy then has become more commonplace now and major comment, rather than recording, nowadays tends to be reserved for the more difficult areas of operation such as Russia and China, respectively perhaps, the ultimate expression of perestroika and the breakthrough into inscrutable insularity. In neither area is the idea startlingly new. China's joint venture law was first promulgated on the 8 July 1979, and if one accepts Émile Benoit's definition that recognizes that it is not ownership but the right to share management and benefits that characterizes joint ventures then Russia and the Eastern satellites have practised this form of business activity for some time both at home and, when times have been more politically favourable, overseas.

In the *Handbook of International Joint Ventures*, for example, a global view of activity has been set out and there is no need to reiterate such detail since evidence abounds that the process marches on. Reference to Figures 2.1 and 2.4 are useful reminders of how the governments of the world have set their rules to cover joint ventures and, by definition, when total ownership is restricted, acquisition. It will suffice for current purposes to bring the matter up to date by borrowing the words of John Lloyd from *Financial Times* as he assessed the strains and opportunities of the Russian market:

> Co-operation between foreign and Soviet enterprises is of a piece with much else in the economic reform movement at present going on in the Soviet Union—as with, for instance, co-operatives, self-financing by enterprises, and leasing of land and equipment.

It is the subject of a huge piece of legislation, is being boosted by senior figures and the media—but as yet has produced very little. Like perestroika itself, of which it is a part, it remains very largely potential. Potential there is, though: the Government has earmarked 320 ventures for development over the next seven years, including 69 in agriculture, 60 in chemicals, 50 in the 'social sphere', 48 in machine building, and 33 in construction.

Of the total, some 140 are expected to use advanced technologies—perhaps, for the Soviet Union, the most important single element.

But that growth will only come—as Soviet planners recognize—from foreign partners seeing that profits can be made and that their assets are secure, a belief which will take time to spread.

For the moment, the base is small: some 70 joint ventures, of which all but 11 are between Soviet and capitalist partners.

A lengthy analysis of this new sector by Dr I. Ivanov, deputy chairman of the Foreign Economic Commission of the Council of Ministers, in the current issue of Kommunist, underscores its fragile nature.

Of the total, 48 have a capitalisation of less than Roubles 5m, with only 10 over Roubles 10m. Total investment to July was Roubles 530m, of which more than one third is foreign.

West Germany is easily the most important partner, with 13 joint ventures so far; Finland, the traditional western conduit, has nine, Italy eight, the US seven, Austria six, France four, Switzerland and Japan three. Australia, Britain, Canada, Ireland, Spain, Sweden and Syria all have one or two at the most.

An earlier study by Ernst and Whinney, the British business services group which has secured the contract to audit the books of most of the joint ventures in association with the Soviet office of Inaudit, shows that workforces are often in no more than double figures—though a refrigerator company founded by Sovital Prodmash and the Italian company Fata employs 2,500 and a Soviet–Swiss construction enterprise has 460 workers.

The limiting factors are taxes, quality of local components and service, the repatriation of profits, and access to the domestic market.

At present, the Western partner can only repatriate that share of the profit earned in hard currency, and hard currency must also pay for all machinery and supplies not sourced in the Soviet Union, and the salaries of non-Soviet staff.

Further, an effective tax rate of 44 per cent was, under the terms of the original decree of joint ventures of January 13 1987, paid on all repatriated profits: that figure has been lowered, and is anyway subject to negotiation.

In addition, the quality of local products of all kinds is said to be variable. One or two of the more recent US joint ventures have attempted to overcome this and other problems by establishing a series of joint companies which can both supply each other and co-operate on profit repatriation.

The original design of the Soviet authorities was to insulate the joint ventures from the domestic market, allowing them to trade only through trade associations. That had the advantage of guaranteeing a stable level of profits, though under pressure the enterprises are now being allowed direct access to the domestic market.

Even when gained, however, access to the market is only the beginning of the matter: for many enterprises, especially those in technically advanced sectors, the larger problems are trained staff, a sales infrastructure and a market ready to buy their goods.

Take the case of the computer company Interquadro, one of the handful of joint venture companies now beyond the documentation stage. It is a joint French–Italian–Soviet venture, to market personal computers and software.

Easy enough, in a vast, relatively well-educated market which has an estimated 1,000 personal computers in all? No—because there is not the training, nor the infrastructure, nor yet any more than a tiny computer culture, on which to float.

Interquadro has its own client training programme, and is looking for big orders from the agriculture ministry (which owns 35 per cent of it) and from Moscow diamond and watch factories. But Mr Alexandre Kaplan, the French deputy general manager (the 'chief' must always be a Soviet citizen), knows he is in for the long haul.

The reservations are not all on the western side: in Dr Ivanov's Kommunist article, he relates fears generally felt that the foreign partners will 'exploit' Soviet workers and consumers: and that if Soviet companies establish production facilities abroad, they will themselves become exploiters.

Dr Ivanov dismisses these fears: Soviet law can take care of its workers, and Soviet companies abroad would export not imperialism (as some Western companies, he says, do through investment) but technology and a socialist example.

Dr Ivanov is concerned to persuade his readership—the Party élite—that the Soviet Union has no choice but to insert itself gently into the 'international division of labour' and that this cannot be done any longer simply through distant trade relations.

In Soviet discussion of the issue, it seems apparent that the authorities are moving towards a position where the rules governing such ventures are flexible, geared to attracting and keeping doubtful foreign partners.

Dr Ivanov, for example, suggests that they could be relieved from many of the labour laws (there is a similar debate going on about co-operatives) so long as they agreed to undertake collective bargaining with the unions.

New partners including corporations like McDonalds' fast food chain, are now coming forward. But no one expects anything big for a while.

While accepting the wide application of joint ventures it is perhaps useful to examine the definition, antecedence, and the theoretical rationale which makes joint ventures such a promising business proposition, not only in terms of the company's external development, but also in terms of the changes which are taking place in the world's industrial and economic climate. Finally it would remiss at this stage not to acknowledge that many joint ventures fail; we should try to understand why.

DEFINITION AND ANTECEDENCE

Lee Adler, writing in the *Harvard Business Review* in 1966 took an early view on the practice of joint ventures and showed a mature appreciation which has stood the test of time well. Akin to many of those who have since followed him, Adler started by searching, in the first instance, for a working definition. He eventually adopted the term 'symbiotic marketing'. Though he may be faulted for using a somewhat clumsy combination of words, the definition does succeed in uniting two very important ideas: namely, the harmonious living together of dissimilar organisms and the marketing concept. Moreover, the notion conveys an analysis of business activity that goes deeper than mere trade relationships, since it concentrates on the deliberate alliance of resources between two independent organizations in order mutually to improve their market growth potential. This strategy of developing market penetration jointly leads to the existence of a third entity which then generates its own force and momentum. Looked at in this perspective, it is easy enough to go along with Adler's enthusiasm for 'symbiotic marketing' which, he claims, puts 'the multiplier into individual companies'.

In some ways it could be argued that the business world, however much it may have compensated for the failing in the last few years, has been slow to take up such a basic theory which had in fact been identified and put into practice as early as the end of the Middle Ages. Although long ago merchants saw the clear advantages that could accrue to them from overseas trade, they took a very pragmatic view both of the risks involved and of the long time span that needed to be endured (with all its adverse cash flow connotations) before they could get an adequate return on the initial investment. To offset this, they combined their resources to exploit the opportunities and share the risks. The thought-process of the merchant adventurers of yesteryear is thus remarkably similar to that of the joint venture operators of today, who not only see the rich prizes available in expanding technology and in assisting the Less Developed Countries (LDCs), but also perceive the inherent wisdom of combining resources to achieve a common purpose. Likewise, the lessons of failure were also there to be learnt in the olden days. There were those tragic occasions when ships did not leave the harbour, or when they were sunk—just as today a factory might remain a mere plan on paper, or an industrial plant become an economic white elephant. Even worse was (and is) the continuing possibility of watching a lame venture becalmed on an unresearched market.

Moreover, if somewhat wayward thoughts are allowed to intrude, it may be observed that in spite of all the technical and other improvements that have taken place over subsequent years the evidence to hand suggests that it still takes as long in the twentieth century to achieve success in a joint venture as it did in the Middle Ages—two to three years remains par for the course. Further, perhaps the joint venture general management fraternity would add a comment on the luck or otherwise of their ancient mariner counterparts who were out of touch with senior management for months on end!

RATIONALE THAT MAKES A JOINT VENTURE A PROMISING BUSINESS OPPORTUNITY

Having sketched a background to the subject, it is important to look in a little more detail at some of the main reasons why companies may wish to consider joint venture opportunities.

1. One of the prime attractions of the joint venture as a business tool is the clarity of purpose that arises as a precondition to its existence. For, whereas an industrial company may have lost a sense of direction (and a practical examination of any set of business plans will demonstrate how easily chief executives and their staff can lapse into the role of maintaining and defending long-standing company traditions, practices, and structures), participation in a joint venture, ensures renewed and strengthened business purpose. Indeed, without a clearly spelt out objective no viable platform exists for the two (or more) companies to negotiate upon. Given that this determination of common purpose is present, the joint venture will almost certainly start off as a superior enterprise, and with the judicious application of research stands more than a reasonable chance of being a continuous profit earner.

2. Another important factor is that a joint venture often possesses a number of comparative strengths over other possible routes to the various business improvements that are desired. Assuming it has already been decided that the organization's strategic interests lie outside a purely internal readjustment, there are a number of theoretically 'co-operative' options available. These include joint venture, merger, or acquisition. There is an important distinction to be made here that is not just a matter of semantics. The word 'co-operative' has been deliberately emphasized because two businesses co-operating through a third entity become a joint venture, whereas one incorporating another into itself is a merger or an acquisition. In the latter cases control is substituted for co-operation, and one management subjected to another.

The initial confusion that often arises here is based on the fact that typical lists of reasons for justifying mergers and acquisitions would also justify participation in a joint venture. The following list, drawn together by Paul Van der Stricht and quoted by Adler in his *Harvard Business Review* article, makes this point well:

   a. To acquire a means of distribution.
   b. To penetrate a specific geographic market.
   c. To acquire skilled marketing executives.
   d. To enter a new business field.
   e. To achieve vertical integration of existing products.
   f. To acquire a manufacturing base or raw material source.
   g. To expand existing product lines.
   h. To learn newly developing market needs.
   i. To buy time.
   j. To improve the effectiveness of existing marketing efforts.
   k. To avoid cyclical or seasonal instability.
   l. To acquire consumer franchises.

Therefore, embarking upon a joint venture operation might be seen as a deliberate decision to achieve new business strengths (such as those outlined above) without the use of a merger or acquisition strategy, based on the clear advantages of such a decision in terms of risk reduction. As always, a price has to be paid for reducing the risk: in the case of joint ventures the profits are shared with chosen partners.

Thus:

(a) The joint venture affords the maximum opportunity to control and develop a structure which is consistent with a clearly stated purpose. It can adopt its own style, has no need to assimilate inherited business strategies, and has no resistance to overcome within its own infrastructure. By comparison, a merger or acquisition is largely an 'all or nothing' technique inviting a large number of possible frictions. If, as generally happens, all the business is effectively transferred from one company framework to another, this can cause an immense diversion of management time and effort, personal problems for the staff involved and the inevitable emergence of functional duplications which have to be smoothed out. The interaction of these elements can have further damaging ramifications. However professionally the operation is handled, and however friendly the business atmosphere, there is bound to be a general upset in the companies concerned, and some confusion for customers.

(b) A joint venture need contain no 'winners' or 'losers'. Instead it can and should harmonize the varying skills that the partners are able to contribute in the interests of the joint business mission. By contrast, a takeover strategy usually results (albeit inadvertently) in the subordination of certain qualitative issues—such as skill utilization—to the overriding question of restructuring, new control systems, and operating guidelines.

(c) In terms of business development, the joint venture operation is so clearly isolated from the existing structures of the participants that both sides can measure the activity generated and react in a way that is often not possible in the context of a merger or an acquisition.

(d) Within the framework of a joint venture it is possible to concentrate management thinking purely on the growth of the new business in its selected market-place.

3. Another important attraction of joint ventures is that they possess an inherent flexibility. They can be moulded and shaped in a wide variety of different ways to suit the specific needs of the partners and of the market. A valid testament to the many forms in which joint ventures can be set up is the lucid set of fifty-four case studies (spread over Latin America, Asia, and Europe) which was published by *Business International/Management Monographs* in 1972 under the umbrella title 'Recent Experience in Establishing Joint Ventures'. These texts adequately cover a number of possible arrangements, including the following variations:

(a) Joint ventures started 'from scratch' with another company, where neither side holds shares in the other, with equity variations from 10 per cent to 90 per cent for either participating company.

(*b*) Ventures where an overseas organization improves a local company which retains its own indigenous management and identity.
(*c*) Ventures where local ownership is widely distributed and has little direct say in the management process.

The variable ingredient in all these is the percentage of equity held by the partners, with all that this entails. In this context it is worth mentioning two additional forms of venture which are still relatively infrequently used but have a considerable future potential.

(*d*) Decreasing equity joint ventures—these could give an opportunity to prospective technical partners who might have reservations about the long-term viability of the market place, or whose corporate strategies could not allow for finance or management skills to be stretched too far and too wide for too long. They could also provide an opportunity to compete for business in an area where it is necessary to generate local confidence by taking some equity in the early stages, and then to execute a planned withdrawal. For local partners, decreasing equity joint ventures can satisfy the requirement for actively increasing the level of control as their experience and expertise develop.
(*e*) Increasing equity joint ventures—these give the opportunity for partners to improve their share of the business when they have gained a deeper knowledge of the market place. This form can be used by any partner, to secure a higher level of continuing interest on what can amount to 'payments by results': in some cases additional equity rights are granted specifically as a performance bonus.

For both increasing and decreasing equity ventures either side may build into the agreement positive facilities for transferring equity at set times and prices to an agreed valuation formula or to adopt looser option criteria.

DIVESTMENT

Lastly, and thinking particularly of Western Europe, it should be mentioned that joint venture formation can also be used in a rationalization/divestment role. For example, a British-based international engineering group recently joined up with the nationalized steel industry in Britain to form Allied Steel and Wire Ltd.—a 50/50 joint venture for a range of basic steel products. The implications were that the private sector industry wished to reduce its dependence on a product range which was failing to meet its strategic needs, and the nationalized industry (under a right-wing administration) was searching for a practical vehicle for partial denationalization and ways and means to incorporate impetus from private enterprise in a politically acceptable form. Both sides could also secure the benefits of rationalized production resources in very depressed markets. Therefore the joint venture solution provides an adaptable tool for both sides in the context of a defensive strategy. The joint venture worked out very satisfactorily for all parties and Allied Steel and Wire is now an independent company, quoted on the London Stock Exchange and with a good rating at that! There is a growing awareness of the potential for joint ventures used in this way. Numerous instances in the automotive, electronic, and communications sectors, where alignments have been engineered to counter aggressive markets, come to mind.

Mention should be made, however, that in the developed world antitrust legislation and EEC Law 83, for example, act against the pooling of resources and therefore, on occasion, mitigate against joint venture arrangements. The overall matrix of opportunity is obvious enough, vertical for growth, for pioneering, and for the organization of capacity and parts supplies and horizontal to curtail capacity, to restructure, or partially divest.

RELATIONSHIP TO THE SHRINKING WORLD AND WIDER MARKETS

The advantages of the joint venture outlined so far tend to be related to companies and their strategies. It has been shown, however, in terms of the North/South argument that it is going to be difficult not to bend the knee to indigenization and national requirements. Equally it would be difficult to defend today's exports and licences without a deeper commitment to chosen market places, and perhaps impossible to generate international economic growth without releasing the potential of today's less developed markets. As such joint ventures appear more and more as the key to participating in tomorrow's markets.

One can see the cycle of events clearly in the Far East, where Japan, the success story of fast industrialization, is now having to face up to the costs and implications of it's own progress. It has become necessary to move some of its manufacturing base into other Asian countries to take advantage of cheaper raw material and labour. Further, it has to be reiterated that the freedom with which loans have been granted and the upsurge of wealth that followed 'oil shock' have enabled substantial infrastructures and basic industries to be set up and there is no valid reason to suppose that all that activity will be allowed to go to waste.

Within the more developed countries associations have developed, such as the European Economic Community. Its wheels might grind somewhat slowly but the incorporation of countries remains an ongoing process, and even the Eastern Bloc now recognizes the Community. The planned reduction of barriers in 1992 will lead to many threats and opportunities, but language and culture will still take their toll and many will need the power of combined resources through the medium of a joint venture to garner the benefits profitably.

History may of course find the growth of steel mills and fertilizer plants and the reduction of a few tariff barriers of only moderate significance if the billions of pounds invested in the development of new medicines, crops, fertilizers, and pesticides through the biotechnology route pay off and get the approval of legislators and environmentalist lobbies. What transformation could a pest-resistant crop make to one of today's weather-peened economies?

It takes a certain strength of blinkered conviction not to sense that economic evolution is as pervasive in crumbling the hegemony of today's economic order as the oceans are in their erosion of the shores.

SUCCESS AND FAILURE

As a generality, in the previous Chapters the considerable advantages that accrue, and the improvement of performance that is derived, from effective working relationships has been distilled out. These benefits occur just as much in what might be considered the 'lower forms' of international activity as in the more complicated relationships. The effectiveness of working relationships is something that can be planned for and it stems from considerations of policy and structure. This is easily enough verified by reference to any organization that refuses to grasp the nettle by amending its structure; staff are unclear of their responsibilities and objectives and live on the 'high' of fourth-form politics. The results are obvious and the people problems often tragic; further comment for those with business experience is unnecessary. The concentration of people towards common objectives clearly remains the goal and to achieve this in a joint venture is not easy. To see why not it is necessary to understand three main issues which constitute the essential paradox of this form of business.

1. Joint ventures are neither self-supporting nor self-sufficient yet they need to be self-determining in their objectives.
2. Whatever the equity percentage no partner can be constantly overruled otherwise co-operation ceases.
3. In real joint ventures no partner sleeps.

In a successful joint venture there is constant professional attention from partners who co-operate towards stated goals that arise from the self-determining nature of the enterprise as it responds to its chosen market place. It is as simple as that!

JOINT VENTURE FAILURE

Though any list of companies involved in joint ventures would certainly put the *Book of Genesis* with its extensive genealogy into the shade, it is none the less necessary to consider that for such a popular business solution the road is still littered with failures. The failures do not stem the tide, but they provide an essential lesson for prospective participants in demonstrating that the joint venture option is not necessarily a short cut to quick profits, that it needs careful consideration and planning, and that it will not succeed without a willingness to develop co-operation and understanding. All this particularly applies to overseas ventures where the frequently irresistible urge to achieve quick-fire solutions does not leave the necessary time for seeing to all the attendant cultural and business implications.

The extent of the failure-rate can be gauged from a recent survey by Jayanta Sakar which indicates, for example, that 40 per cent of Indian overseas joint ventures were considered failures, and, in Saudi Arabia, 70 per cent of potential ventures fell foul of problems in the very early stages prior to formation. The reasons for such unfortunate occurrences are of course as many and varied as the participants involved, but in essence may be reduced to three major areas:

(a) Lack of adequate pre-planning—the breadth and depth of the planning that is necessary to provide any joint venture with a reasonable chance of success is bound to be great in a complex industrialized setting. It has to incorporate not only the practical functioning of the operation, but also the whole gambit of skill application and business appreciation. Gone are the days when merchant ships returned home, the goods were divided, and the crews simply returned to their next task. For, today there are legal agreements, local trading rules, tariffs, technology exchange rules, labour laws, social legislation, tax and profit repatriation aspects, and other considerations to contend with. These are vital areas of understanding for determining a successful venture. Failure to grasp that joint ventures are complex tools which need to be honed on the whetstones of business understanding, rather than used as blunt axes to 'chop out' a bit of market, causes many difficulties.

(b) Lack of attention and flexibility—there are all kinds of reasons why the parties to what is essentially a co-operation agreement may fall out, disagree, or diverge on policy. The important thing is to realize the very real possibility of this happening within the joint venture framework, and to be prepared to invest time to understand, to adjust, and then to negotiate as the situation demands. Unilateral decisions, even if impeccable in management judgement, are seldom successful in joint ventures.

(c) Lack of policy agreement—the general experience is that joint venture partners have most trouble over dividend policies, capital increases, investment plans, and transfer prices if materials or parts are supplied by one side. Equally, any move by a participant to threaten the venture's self-determination—for example, by flexing its activities to align with a supporting company's global production or marketing strategy—is bound to generate difficulty. Moreover, as the *Business International* text already referred to makes abundantly clear, even simple differences in business practice can provide their own headaches.

Broadly speaking, experience suggests that one businessman will remain suspicious of another until the necessary degree of trust and confidence has had time to establish itself in the relationship. Even when the venture has been going for some time, this spirit of understanding can be frittered away by just one simple, thoughtless action. Whatever the technical ramifications of the arrangement, human relationships will always be central to its success.

As and when difficulties occur they will have to be handled with consummate care, because the essence of the joint venture is the continuing motivation of all sides to operate in the creation of a long-term business entity with a permanent and viable role in the market place. This is why all concerned will want to establish their rights and viewpoints within a more permanent framework than is necessary when merely doing a business deal, shaking hands, and moving on to the next scenario.

It is clear overall, therefore, that joint venture failure and 'people' failure, particularly when they fail to reconcile to the inherent paradox of the method, are closely aligned. Natural management style, currently seen as drive, guts, and entrepreneurial flair with business mission oozing from every pore, is not a natural sharing mode. This is well summed up (and, in the context, a justified outburst) by the CEO of Grand Metropolitan who, when introduced to the board of a newly acquired company as 'the shareholder's representative', reportedly commented: 'Hell no, I run the bloody thing!'

THE BASIC STEPS INVOLVED IN SETTING UP A JOINT VENTURE

For those people who are generally conversant with and practised in commercial development work joint ventures will hold no surprises. They will have already suffered the frustrations and the 'no-progress time-lags' that are inherent in creating change and in doing new things. Business developers will know that, despite verbal and written protestations to the contrary, harnessing people power, particularly if the people report elsewhere, and keeping projects within even broad guidelines, requires diplomatic skills, strength of purpose, patience, and above all else a carefully thought-out plan. The overall plan for a typical joint venture can be encapsulated in the following nine basic steps:

1. Internal policy decisions.
2. Market research.
3. Partner selection.
4. Support team and staff.
5. Feasibility plan; derived action plans.
6. Negotiation.
7. Starting the business.
8. Running the business.
9. Developing the business.

The basic criteria which govern policy, research, and partner selection are already common ground as these aspects have been discussed in previous Chapters. It therefore suffices here to reiterate the key principles and to examine the scope that is required to ensure quality and professionalism in a joint venture.

The basic policy decision needs to be clear and authentic to the point where a written brief emerges that can be linked to a board minute—always a wise precaution when subsequent equity discussion is involved. Overall, this gives strength, purpose, and conviction to those involved in the proposed joint venture, and although formal negotiation appears well down the scheme of events, in practical terms it has to be acknowledged that the first meeting with a prospective partner is, in fact, the first step in the negotiation process.

In the bluntest of terms a close interrelationship has been drawn between partner selection and research. Initially, partner identification is itself a research process and preferred to casual and secondhand contact. Thereafter, the involvement of partners in research, the sharing of assumptions, and the joint involvement in the feasibility study and its financial predictions are imperative. In this way secondary motives are discerned and isolated, the viability of what partners can contribute more readily assessed, and project aims confirmed. When all parties can see what the others can contribute and have confidence in the profit projections then formal negotiation is worth while.

The quality of this joint research and appraisal can be very sharply focused through setting out a critical path for the venture and assessing how the product or service is going to be 'translated' into the market-place. Figures 9.1 and 9.2 show the complexity for a typical venture which could be much improved if initials and completion dates are allocated to individuals on both sides. There is a considerable tactical advantage to be gained though quantifying contributions to the venture in real terms rather than promises. If progress can be made thus far then it can be claimed that partners have their feet on the first rung of the ladder.

Viewed from the standpoint of high-quality information and a worthwhile feasibility study, and with a good knowledge of a partner's attributes and contributions as set out in Table 9.1, stronger views can be taken with regard to support staff requirements and legal requirements.

To discuss these issues in greater detail it is necessary to examine the company's attitude towards the venture and ensure that a clear approach is promulgated. There are two basic alternative policy approaches; at the one extreme the policy will reflect that the venture must stand on its own two feet and will not require any other support apart from that specifically agreed under the joint venture agreement. At the other extreme the policy recognizes that while the venture is not wholly owned, it will as far as possible be treated as part of the technical partner's own company. There are naturally many policies in between the extremes.

The point at issue is not so much the policy in itself but clearly to set out for all concerned in the support company, right down the line, how relationships are to be conditioned. Without guidance, a situation can be

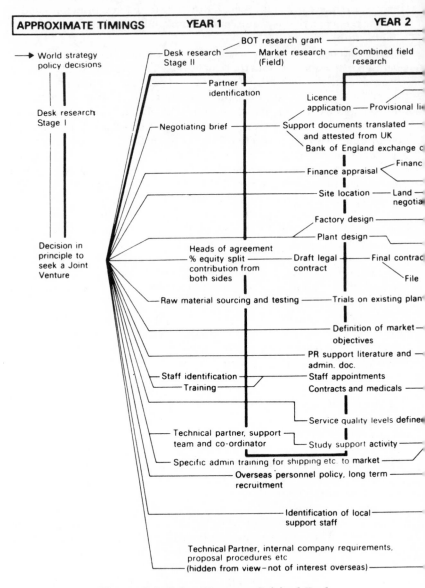

Figure 9.1. Joint Venture Critical Path

The thick line shows the suggested critical path for initiating a joint venture and bringing the project to full production in a developing country.

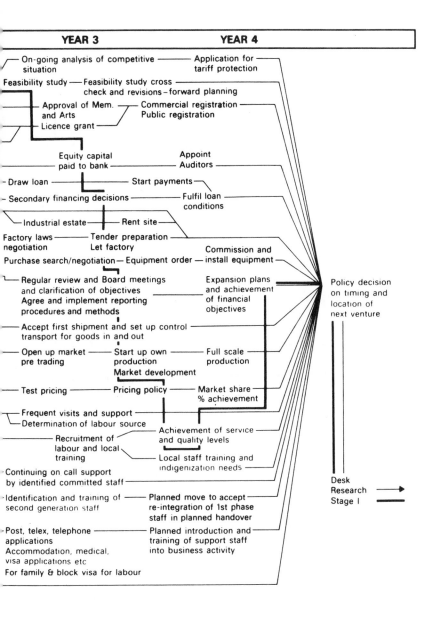

YEAR 3   YEAR 4

On-going analysis of competitive — Application for
situation   tariff protection

Feasibility study — Feasibility study cross
check and revisions – forward planning

Approval of Mem. — Commercial registration
and Arts   Public registration
Licence grant

Equity capital   Appoint
paid to bank   Auditors

Draw loan   Start payments

Secondary financing decisions   Fulfil loan
conditions

Industrial estate   Rent site

Factory laws — Tender preparation
negotiation   Let factory
Purchase search/negotiation — Equipment order — Commission and
install equipment

Regular review and Board meetings   Expansion plans
and clarification of objectives   and achievement
Agree and implement reporting   of financial
procedures and methods   objectives

Accept first shipment and set up control
transport for goods in and out

Open up market — Start up own — Full scale
pre trading   production   production
Market development

Test pricing — Pricing policy — Market share
% achievement

Frequent visits and support
Determination of labour source
Achievement of service
Recruitment of   and quality levels
labour and local
training   Local staff training and
indigenization needs

Continuing on call support
by identified committed staff

Identification and training of — Planned move to accept
second generation staff   re-integration of 1st phase
staff in planned handover

Post, telex, telephone — Planned introduction and
applications   training of support staff
Accommodation, medical,   into business activity
visa applications etc
For family & block visa for labour

Policy decision
on timing and
location of
next venture

Desk
Research
Stage I

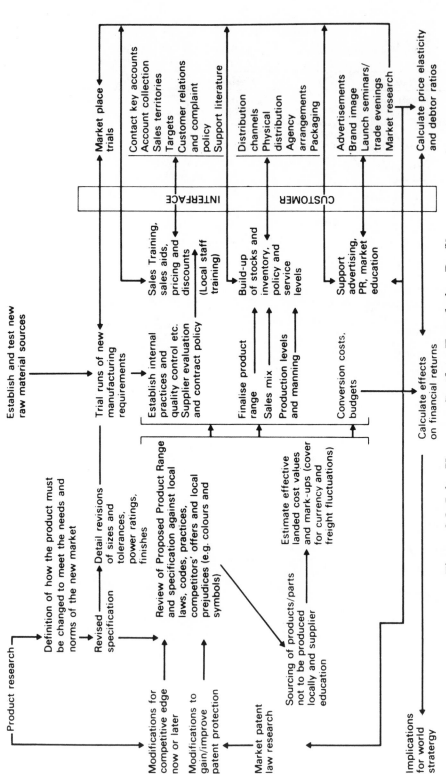

Figure 9.2. Joint Venturers Product Translation Profile

Table 9.1. Possible Allocation of Duties Between Partners

Duties	Partner(s)	
	Technical	*Local-Commercial*
Joint sponsored market research	•	•
Feasability study	•	•
Appointment of key staff	•	•
Factory design/plant layout	•	
Purchasing recommendation of machinery and materials	•	
Check testing of material and product quality	•	
Commissioning, spares list, annual plant inspections	•	
Operational cost control, installation of financial systems	•	
Continuing technical know-how	•	
Strategic planning and development	•	
Nominating board members (and their availability) experienced in the business	•	
Training of key staff	•	
Dealing with all matters relating to the registration of the company and its continuing conformity with local law		•
Negotiation of local financing arrangements, land, planning permission, etc.		•
Advising upon, translation, and submission of local documentation		•
Ongoing advice and assistance to ensure the venture's continuing conformity with local laws (e.g. labour law, social security, etc.)		•
Providing all necessary work visas, permits, etc., for personnel and representing personnel in the event of local legal proceedings against them		•
Ensuring the supply of all local services		•
Provision of local accommodation, temporary offices, and communication services		•
Assisting in local import and export procedures		•
Negotiating and securing the cost effective supply of local products and services		•
Ensuring the local availability of competent staff to assist the venture at all times (including public holidays, etc.)		•
Specific market-place tasks		•
Formal appraisal of economy on a regular basis (say twice yearly)		•

postulated where, for example, spare parts will only be supplied with difficulty and perhaps on letter of credit terms; the sales department will surreptitiously continue to export into the area while the technical department will flood the venture with new know-how irrespective of the cost, and the personnel department will excel itself looking after children on half-term holiday.

The free division of the company's attitude between 'they are part of us therefore we do not have to try so hard' and 'they need to succeed so we will do everything we can to help them' and possibly 'what they are doing is so much more interesting than what I am meant to be doing that I would prefer to help them' creates havoc at both ends. A clear definition of attitude is integral with the considerations discussed above concerning the calculation of the values of participation.

The decision as to which is the correct policy to lay down is dependent upon the appreciation of several important factors:

- Prevailing financial conditions in the support company.
- Whether the venture is one-off, one of many, or the first so far.
- The value of the total deal to the support company.
- The type of relationship existing with the joint venture partner.
- The quality of support staff.
- A frank assessment of interdepartmental cohesion and communication in the support company.

Whatever the policy, it goes without saying that it has to be effectively and consistently marketed to the joint venture staff. It may be that on balance a strong supportive policy will yield the best long-term results, providing clear rules for the payment of services are understood and accepted. This reasoning depends upon the assumption that people are the 'unknown factor' and that the success or otherwise of people's contributions finally makes or breaks the venture. Therefore, total commitment to help those people ensures that the correct quality personnel go and stay there and, equally important, that there are others who want to follow them. There are usually problems in finding key staff who will be successful overseas and, if the choice is between a known employee or an 'unknown' chosen after two or three interviews, it is clear that the safest policy is to send people who know the support company, its methods of working and its products. This situation is often more readily achieved under a supportive policy than under other policies.

In practical terms it should be remembered that the joint venture partner is in a strong position, not only because he probably has the majority holding but also because he is always available. Without wishing to seem to advocate politics with senior staff, the key question might be seen as determining how, from a distance and in a minority holding position, the support company can ensure that adequate involvement is possible for them to the extent that is necessary to protect the investment and the well-being of the business. Optimum relationships with staff are of crucial importance, particularly as joint venture partners are (or should be) active working colleagues and the whole team needs to pull together.

Sometimes one feels that borderline deals, where the technical partner only achieves his minimum requirements, work against maximum contributions. Some ventures would be more successful if the commercial partner, having negotiated a strong position, was prepared to negotiate away some of his rights in the interest of getting stronger and more detailed commitments from the technical partner.

The creation of a good-quality home support team is an important prerequisite for effectively marketing whatever policy is adopted towards the venture. However that policy may have been construed there are obligations to be fulfilled and, when the venture starts operations, the technical partner's head is once again on the block to see if his actions are as good as his words. In the first stages of the venture, action is best seen in terms of continuing negotiation and continued selling. The surest way to draw the maximum help and co-operation from the joint venture partner is to try to set the pace. It should be remembered that the local partner is often part of a business community that has to go back to the same sources for licences and investment funds time and time again; success or failure will be reflected in his own standing with his peers and national institutions. The start-up situation is one where, with correct handling, two and two can equal five.

It is possible that, in the build-up of the feasibility study, staff will already have identified themselves as logical support team members although, unless there are many active ventures in a company, the support work may not have to be full-time.

The original negotiator does not have to head the support team and, indeed, because of the amount of time that he is likely to spend in the field, it may be that he should not fulfil that role. The negotiator does, however, need to have conferred on him formally by his own organization the full control and right of decision, without question, on any policy matters that may have to be considered. In the first instance the joint venture partner needs to see that the negotiator is still committed to the success of the venture and, second, if any suggestion appears that there is an alternative decision-maker, it is tantamount to inviting the reopening of negotiations, which is tactically unsound.

On the assumption that the negotiator is not leading the support team, a co-ordinator is needed who is generally available, who can appreciate the main venture concepts and policies, and who has the time to find out and to absorb a reasonable level of background knowledge about the venture territory. A technically biased co-ordinator is often useful in overseeing all practical aspects of getting into production and will frequently complement the skills of a more commercially orientated negotiator. The co-ordinator needs to be at a level in the organization where he can discuss on equal terms the allocation of work priorities, and he should be capable, by persuasion, perseverance, and reputation, of getting things done on time by drawing the best out of any key people nominated to assist in other functions.

The skill in choosing the support team is in getting together people who are practical problem-solvers; in a stereotyped organization, where to quote the cliché 'experience equates to the same thing done time and time again over twenty years', such people are not easy to come by. Setting up joint ventures is not necessarily a science but perhaps more the art of doing the practical effectively and quickly. To see this in context, one can think of a technical question posed by telex on a Thursday morning and answered on a Monday afternoon which, at first sight, might appear reasonable. In certain areas of the world, however, such as the Middle East, this results in the loss of three working days due to differing weekends. The support team's simple expedient of asking for a telephone discussion or sending an unclear or political reply will go down like lead within the venture for it will commit some key person to an unreasonable amount of time in trying to make contact to right the situation.

In summary, people in the team should be responsive and interested, technically competent, and practical problem-solvers who get things done. Ideal candidates are those who, perhaps at some later stage, will themselves take up overseas appointments.

The local partner's support team is of equal consequence. For discussion purposes, it can be accepted that in a sophisticated environment the local partner can exercise similar decisions to the technical partner and teams can be equally matched. This is not the situation in developing countries. It is probable that there will not be the wealth of support talent to draw upon, not because developing countries contain an unfair share of inadequate people but rather because there is not the depth of detailed working experience available. So often the business society will have developed out of people who have been subject to a sudden burst of education and have then moved directly into areas where they are most concerned with wider business issues. Therefore, their curricula vitae do not contain, like those of their counterparts in the West, detailed specialist application in their formative years.

The technical partner should therefore not be looking so much for business competence as adaptability and a twenty-four-hours-a-day and 365-days-a-year presence. In other words, an 'on-tap' local adviser (with a substitute for holidays) who will *live with and learn about* the venture and its needs. The main advantages of such a person are often initially in time saving; as an adviser on local practices, as a translator, as an adviser on credit risk, as an assistant in debt collecting and an administrator in the visa and local documentation area. In other words, the local support acts as a heat-shield to allow technical and commercial venture staff to concentrate on the business rather than its local administration.

In those areas where there is a requirement for training and development of local staff, it is usually better to opt for planned integration through the medium of this type of support role rather than to accept a sudden implant who does not have any knowledge of the business.

This discussion on support teams finds its place in the early scheme of events because adequate people are hard to find, and they need to be identified early on so that they can have some commitment to the development of the project. Certainly either partner who can bring his support team to life during the negotiations can give confidence that there is real activity and skill and determination on his side to back the venture.

THE FEASIBILITY STUDY

The study can, of course, be considered as a paper exercise to achieve the limited objective of getting a loan or a licence but to treat it in this limited way is to lose a major opportunity. The feasibility study should effectively act as a bridge between the theoretical side of the venture and the actual operation.

The key questions that should be asked of any study are:

1. Is it directly relevant to the market and, throughout, does the logic follow from what has been learned about the market-place?
2. Is the study a blueprint for the first five years of activity and will it still form a sensible basis for discussion over time?
3. Is the study professional, will it stand comparison with other studies on an international basis?

These questions probably appear simple and even a shade naive but, to anyone who has been able to check-read some feasibility studies, they will make abundant good sense. The traps which business people seem to fall into are as fundamental as the questions.

There are studies based on similar ventures elsewhere or study packages conceived in the technical partner's home country. Throughout such studies, one is constantly aware of the abstract nature of the presentation.

The second key question concerns the longevity of the document. In practice, the technical partner is not going to be able to make an input to the development of the business from miles away by telex, telephone, or memorandums; therefore the important consideration is that the general manager has a relevant and well-thought-out course of action which he can adopt in the knowledge that the whole board knows the priorities and can support him in pursuing them. In this way, the fear of two partners advocating different business paths or objectives can be eliminated in advance. Financial projections will follow from the plan and not vice versa, thus at one and the same time the study has also in effect set up a numerate control and review system.

Lack of professionalism in the study can stem from the failure to appreciate that the study is the first, albeit marginal, effective move within the relationship from the theoretical to the practical. A local partner may not have been in a position to judge technical partners' professional competence through lack of detailed information: the presentation of the feasibility study, however, allows just such a judgement to be made. A shrewd partner will have no difficulty in getting a specialist second opinion and, in many developing countries where loans or licences are required, the formal submission of the study to authorities will immediately put it in comparison with other studies of a similar nature from many parts of the world. This ability to cross-check also raises the question of integrity: in a venture where the equity holding is set and the value of any other management agreements accepted, it is wise to consider the package as the total negotiated payment for participation. To attempt to go on from there and start making 'a turn' on the equipment, for example, may well end up as a bad error of judgement: at worst it will be seen as cheating; at best the technical partner's inability to shop around wisely to obtain competitive prices will have been exposed. This is much too early a stage in a working relationship to run the risk of causing real damage through mistrust.

There is frequently a supplementary problem arising for technical partners at this stage which needs consideration. If the feeling is beginning to develop that honesty has perhaps become one-sided, the provision of the full feasibility study may be seen as the final straw in so far as it releases too much sensitive information which reduces negotiating strength and which is simply not commercially prudent. This need not be the case if sensitive information is put into supplementary documents which may be viewed but not left to become the property of the company until negotiations are finalized.

The definition of sensitive information depends upon the nature of the business as well as upon the personalities of the main characters in the technical partner's organization. Some will want formally presented flow-charts and machine operation instructions, etc., protected; to others, training manuals and accounting procedures may well be considered as valuable know-how. There is a common tendency for technical partners to place more value on such information than local partners but, nevertheless, it remains a wise provision to view the know-how content of the study judiciously.

In fact, in joint ventures the question of suspicion, particularly in the early stages, arises time and time again and the best working rule is to accept that it cannot be eradicated. It is better not to complain about suspicion but to determine how to live with it. Men of the world, with integrity, might even come to accept that there is an element of reflection in the distrust that is so readily perceived. Distrust and suspicion, sometimes more readily disguised as 'politics' and 'hard negotiation', are rather like ivy on a tree where it is only when growth gets out of hand that suffocation occurs.

So much for the pitfalls, but what about the study documents themselves?

A study might well contain the following elements:

- The overall feasibility study.
- Supporting market survey.
- Financial considerations.
- Accepted quotations for plant and equipment.
- Rejected quotations for plant and equipment.
- Applications and attestations.
- Confidential supplementary and sensitive documents including factory specification and proposed tender documents.

A more detailed look at the suggested documents is required; the object of the exercise is not to set out a rigid set of rules or to seek claim to a magic and unchangeable formula but rather to describe the situation on a case-study basis and to leave any intending partner to amend and improve, to show the full extent of his own offer and professionalism.

The content of the overall feasibility study should start with a concise summary mentioning the economic viability of the business, the estimated market, and the proposed strategy for developing that market. The nature of the plant, its location, site services, manning, raw materials, and so on should all be summarized to give a practical view of the operation. The timing of strategic stages of development and proposed management structure should be dealt with briefly; it is also wise to highlight any crucial assumptions that have been made for it is better that these are plain and clear for all to see, rather than that they be hidden as afterthoughts in footnotes. It is useful in international competition clearly to state in the early stages the important efficiencies so that, when comparisons are made with other similar operations (which may be based on the impractical 100% efficiency level), due allowance can be made. In all, this concise summary probably will not cover more than two or three pages.

The main body of the report should then deal with the estimated market size, total and regional growth predictions, structure of the market, structure of the industry, assessed attitudes towards the product, and existing industry competition. Prices should be dealt with and there should be incorporated a full discussion of a logically determined strategy for obtaining and retaining a certain market share.

In a good study the realism will shine through and the charge of over-optimism (so often relevant) will have been avoided. The second section of the study should deal with plant and processes in all aspects including manning, labour, welfare, raw materials, and, most important of all, the relationship of the product range/production mix to the market-place and the development and extension of the range to predicted changes in the market. (Clearly the use of diagrams and pictures helps to lighten the load on the reader, but such considerations are negated if the visuals are not specific to the market or not of good pictorial quality.)

The criteria for plant selection together with salient details concerning factory structure and layout need to be readily understandable and clearly demonstrate that modifications have been made to meet the requirements of local conditions. This practical section can end with the summary of fixed assets, their costs and the contingency assumptions made on price movements which it has been considered wise to provide.

The final section will be a financial summary but set in the context of the logic of the market assessment and reflecting the key aspects of financial understanding that largely determine the viability of the business. To this end, the section should incorporate some form of sensitivity analysis, for it is wrong to suggest, or let others suppose, that the business is other than dynamic and that assessments are other than *reasonably* correct. Most businesses, as mentioned earlier, have three or four key sensitivity factors which control their financial viability and these can be tabled to show the sensitivity of financial performance to change. Clearly this work can be

Table 9.2. Sensitivity Analysis

Conv. cost (per x units)	Output m	Unit selling price					
		Surplus $000	% ROA	Surplus $000	% ROA	Surplus	
	1.5	6000	30	6250	31	6500	
5000	1.75	7500	35	7750	37	8000	
	2.00	8250	39	8500	42	8750	
	1.5	5500	28	5750	24	6000	
5500	1.75	7000	33	6250	31	7500	
	2.00	7750	37	7000	33	8250	

done by computer but very often a simple tabulation such as that given in Table 9.2 suffices, other key factors can be displayed in a similar way.

The first supplementary document suggested was the market research study. This document should deal exclusively with the findings of desk and field research and set out the questionnaires and research methods used; the sample of people selected as respondents, research resources, and documents should also be clearly evidenced.

The second supporting document is a financial one which should give a much greater depth to the financial case; it will provide detailed analysis of cost build-up, estimated operating statements, and DCF (discounted cash flow) calculations. It should also contain the accounting procedures and control documents that it is intended to install in the venture.

Supporting documents concerning the accepted and rejected quotations for plant and equipment need to be shown and there must be evidence beyond reasonable doubt that the selection has been fair and in the interest of the joint venture business. It is therefore wise to set out the quotation requests and any terms and conditions that may have been specified. In the acceptance file, a list of all manufacturers approached and the major sources not approached (together with reasons for not doing so) should be given. It helps to indicate in separate tabulated form the countries in which manufacturers have been approached for major items in order that the search for quality, service, and price can be seen to have been completed on an international and not a parochial basis.

The 'rejected' file will clearly and justly show the detail of manufacturers' offers that have been rejected. Comparative summaries of offers are difficult and time-consuming; the most useful short cut derives from the original clarity with which offers were sought. The determination of currency, FOB, C&F, and CIF prices on identical terms, length of the offer, the method of determining commissioning charges and credit arrangements are all examples and considerations which need to be clearly specified if the comparison of offers is to be simplified.

The next study document considered should be that of 'applications and attestations'. The purpose of the document is to achieve both confidence and speed. This is done by filling in, in detail, any forms and submissions that may be required by local authorities and utilities.

Finally, the additional supporting documents are derived from the technical partner's own requirements for security and commercial safety, or perhaps even his own negotiating style. It would not be unusual for a detailed site plan together with tender documents and specifications for the factory building to be evidenced in this way.

The outline of the feasibility study given above will be adequate for most purposes, but it still remains essentially a two-dimensional document. If it is to form the effective bridge that was mentioned earlier between the theoretical and practical stages of the venture, it will need to become three-dimensional. This may be achieved simply by answering many of the 'how' questions.

Once signed, the joint venture document requires the partners to put their hands in their pockets and probably put themselves at risk by guaranteeing some loans and overdrafts. This is the moment of truth. How quickly the venture can develop its own funds and begin to pay its way and reduce the exposure to risk will suddenly become a prime consideration. Therefore, attention will have to be given to the detail of who will run various aspects of the venture during site development, machine commissioning, and the opening up of commercial activities. There are all of the site problems to be solved; the co-ordination of services that will not only be needed when production commences but will also be required in order to enable the factory to be built. A good feasibility study will incorporate a bar chart of practical relevance which will take into account local shortages and working conditions.

Naturally all of these considerations tend to make the feasibility study a weighty document, but there is a strong case for arguing that once submitted it should never be necessary to expand the study; the main value of the document should be in its relevance to developing the business so as to service the funds that are invested in it; it may also be used for authorities and banks.

In summary, the case has been made that the overall task of setting up a joint venture is wide-ranging and complex; it therefore needs careful planning from beginning to end if people are going to be kept on course.

For discussion purposes it has been found possible to analyse joint venture activity by reference to nine action areas. The first five such areas, comprising internal policy decisions, market research, partner selection, support teams, and staff, have been examined together with the feasibility study which forms a bridge to the areas of practical application. These need to be held in abeyance, however, while the legal documentation is dealt with before the project can be brought actively to life.

FORMALIZING THE AGREEMENT

Discussion of the legal agreement has deliberately been left to this later stage, not only so that it can take its rightful place in the nine-step pattern but also to reflect the personal prejudice of briefing lawyers early, giving them time to be well-versed in the laws of the land in question, conversant with the totality of the scheme, and then used as allies, at the right time, to achieve a document which is a means to an end rather than an end in itself. After all, what is required is a document which reflects the working agreements and understandings already reached.

Shining through the text, whatever the language and legal wording, should be the business intent clearly showing what needs to be done by the participants before the business starts, how the business will then be organized, run, and monitored, the nature of continuing support, and the provision for sharing both the profits and the losses.

The overall scope of legal agreements has already been outlined above when reducing and increasing equity ventures were mentioned: the number of participants is a variable, as well as the partnership percentages. Further, it is going to be necessary to superimpose factors which adjust the value to any participants over and above that which the mathematical ownership percentage requires. Finally, it will be necessary to reflect local legal requirements.

As has been mentioned so many times previously, the venture is a very flexible tool: the legal document can give formal expression to that flexibility yet nevertheless the clauses and the words are rather like reinforcing steel and cement combining together to give a structural form to the venture and then holding it together under a variety of stresses.

A viable relationship clearly does not exist if the partners only deal with one another through the terminology of fine print. However, a sound document allows for good understanding and once it has been drawn up and has made a firm impression on the partners, then, perhaps, it can be filed and forgotten.

It is important to remember for the set-piece 'signing ceremony' that all the documents should come forward for signature at the same time as a reflection of the fact that a complete agreement has been reached; that is to say that the memorandum and articles of association should be locked into the joint venture agreement and any management, technical, or royalty agreements. There is a clear risk from a technical standpoint in not signing all the documents at the same time. More importantly, if all documents cannot be agreed, it indicates a breakdown of understanding between partners as to the benefits that they will allow one to the other.

The outline of the typical clauses can be structured in the following way:

Memorandum and Articles of Association
    Statement of participants in which the participants' nationalities and often passport numbers for easy identification are quoted. Partner's

nominees should be stated as having been appointed in accordance with the regulations of their own boards.

Section I: Main Objectives, Duration and Head Office of Company
Article confirming company name.
Article stating the company's objective which will need to be in accordance with any industrial licence both in terms of product and capacity.
Article on the duration of the company. This is open to negotiation but anything less than ten years may be limiting to the overall thinking.
Article confirming the location of the head office.

Section II: Capital and Shares
Article stating the total share capital, the value of each share, and the respective contribution of individual shareholders in value and percentage terms.
Article stating the nature of the shares. It is important that equal rights and indivisibility are made clear. It is also useful to provide that any joint shareholders should nominate one person only to negotiate on their behalf.
Article providing for increases and decreases in shareholding being done in such a way as to give first preference to existing shareholders but not altering the ratios between shareholders without agreement.
Article stating share transfer rules. Care is required here to ensure that the original partners stay together and, within the inheritance laws and the acquisition activity of developed countries, that the original shareholding team does not develop into a fractured committee.
Article confirming the setting up and the maintenance of a register of shares.

Section III: Management of the Company
Article giving the composition of the board and their voting rights.
Article stating the powers of the board. Although generally this article is widely construed, it is worth spelling out the relationship and delegating those powers that are necessary for specific people to effectively run the company.
Article appointing a chairman.
Article appointing a managing director.
Article providing for stand-in and alternative directors.
Article giving rules for calling board meetings and determining the number of meetings per year.
Article defining any agreement where a simple majority of the board shall not be acceptable. This article is worthy of considerable thought and negotiation.

Section IV: Auditors
Article making the appointment of auditors and their payment necessary. The need for providing information and co-operation with auditors can be spelt out.

Section V: General Meetings
Article giving rules for calling general meetings, including provision for recording of non-majority views.

Section VI: Company Fiscal Year and Budget and Annual Accounts
Article determining the fiscal year and due date for accounts.

Article dealing with the treatment of profits, including provision of statutory reserves and any board remuneration.

Section VII: Dissolution and Winding Up
Article of the reasons for winding up and the powers of the board and shareholders *vis-à-vis* the liquidator.

Section VIII: Arbitration
Article providing for the appointment of an arbitrator, where he works, and what laws he may apply.

Section IX: Miscellaneous
This miscellaneous section is traditionally used by the lawyers to tidy up loose ends and to pat themselves on the back for managing to keep the document in accordance with the laws of the country and the like.

Apart from giving his legal colleague a clear original briefing, the lay businessman often has a continuing advisory role to fulfil. For example, provisions for the calling of meetings by mail, with the proof of posting being the main criterion, are often not practical. It is more practical to have rules compelling the use of telex. A good lawyer working with a thoughtful businessman will blow the dust off some of the more time-honoured clauses.

THE JOINT VENTURE AGREEMENT

The opening preamble of the joint venture agreement would give the date and the participating parties. Set out under the euphoric WHEREAS is a statement of what is going on and the state of the relative authorities giving permission for the venture. The first article will define general business intentions further and, importantly, will lock the agreement into the memorandum and articles of association in completed and signed form. The memorandum will be incorporated as a schedule to the joint venture agreement.

The articles of the joint venture agreement essentially determine what has been agreed between the participating shareholders. Typically:

Article: Secondary Agreements
Note should be made of any other arrangements such as management, royalty, licensing and any documents covering these should be attached in schedule form.

Article: Management of the Business
Clauses are needed to determine clearly how the day-to-day business is to

be organized and how the major appointments are made. Any special provisions for auditors (e.g. by nationality or experience) should be included here.

Article: Operation of the Company

Here it is clearly set out what each side will provide to the joint venture and how partners agree to receive or waive payment for such services is also stated. It is normal for the technical partner to be reimbursed for the direct costs involved in providing the services.

Article: Dividend Allocation

Prior discussion to achieve understanding is a prerequisite before an attempt is made to write this clause. It is wise to appreciate that in the examination of the value of the agreement to both sides the value can vary over time. That is to say that a tax-free holiday can yield a surplus for division which is almost certainly fair, but when tax is applied at a later stage the take-home values to the shareholders often move adversely against an overseas technical partner.

Article: Non-Disclosure, Secrecy, and Confidentiality

The intent is clear enough but, whatever the legal text, the value of the clause in practice must be considered to be suspect. Even so, it is worth securing approval that the survival of such interests lasts for a considerable time after any break-up takes place.

Miscellaneous Clauses

Normal practice is to include a series of clauses governing the duration of the agreement, support, breach, applicable law, arbitration, general rules of the agreements, rights, waiver, modifications, the effects of headings, and the meaning of the entire agreement and other decisions that are the legal man's own domain.

The language of the document and how it is arrived at is also a matter worthy of some thought. Assuming that it has been agreed that a dual text will be provided but conceded that a local language will take precedence in the case of a dispute (not an unusual combination), translation then becomes important. The only safe procedure is to provide for an independent translation of the foreign language as a cross-check. Such procedures are time-consuming but frequently turn out to be worth while.

The actual signing can, naturally, be a heady moment as the tension eases with the flourishing of pens. The signing needs, however, to be matched with fast action to provide the funds for setting up the business—a matter in which delays, however justifiable, tend to cause a disporportionate amount of bad faith at the very outset. Otherwise, given that practical matters for setting the business in motion have been attended to and provision has been made for running the business, the legal document should be what we intended it to be: a means to an end, a way of getting into business.

As a practicality, it would indeed be strange if there were no clauses precedent at this stage which did not attract the attention; such clauses need to be clearly allocated for action to the partners and their resolution subject to a clearly defined timetable. Delegation to an incoming general manager should not be tolerated.

It is important to examine broadly what happens at the first shareholders' meeting and to give some thought to other areas which will enable the business to start off both quickly and effectively.

The main set piece event is the initial shareholders' meeting which gets the company under way. No matter how well the main personalities may think that they know and understand one another, there is a considerable risk involved in sitting around the table and extemporizing on a free-ranging agenda.

There is merit in drafting the minutes prior to the meeting in as many working sessions as it takes and confining the meeting itself to an hour's formality. This formula can serve both sides well for the whole range of general and board meetings. Meetings are usually infrequent and their form is too rigid to ensure that full exchanges take place. Additionally, attitudes struck during a hasty appraisal may be difficult to move away from without loss of face, and considerable damage can be done. An appropriate amount of argument and counter-argument before home board meetings to iron out major problems and viewpoints is fairly normal. In a joint venture, this evolution of thinking often has to be synthesized and prior drafting of minutes in dual text is a useful formula to achieve this.

There is much to commend allowing sufficient time to get up to date with venture activity before attending any substantial partner meetings, formal or otherwise. Impressive travel schedules and the trappings of the business jet-set are poor fare as a substitute for examining some of the details of the business, and listening to the staff. A lot can happen in three months, and the chances are the local partner knows more about the business than a visiting director.

A typical first meeting will include most of the following together with any other salient issues of principles that have been agreed:

First Shareholders' Meeting Held on . . . at . . .

Agenda
  1. Incorporation of the Company.
  2. Appointment of Directors.
  3. Appointment of Chairman.
  4. (i) Appointment of Managing Director.
      (ii) Powers and Authority of Managing Director.
  5. Special Agreement.
  6. Bank Account, Bank Overdraft, and Form of Guarantee.
  7. Fund Loans and Necessary Guarantees.
  8. Rental/Purchase of Land.
  9. Appointment of Contractors to Build Factory.
 10. Capital Expenditure:
      (i) Building—Signature of Contract.

(ii) Plant and Machinery—Signature of Orders.

(iii) Rules for Further Capital Expenditure.

11. Contracts of Employment.

12. Appointment of Auditors.

13. Tabulation of Major Business Items that Require Board Approval, e.g. sales contracts in excess of value x; raw material purchases in excess of value y.

The key areas in the whole agenda are the managing director's power and authority and the determination as to how the company is going to be run. The normal policy formulation processes will not apply, nor are the 'staff tugs' going to be around that normally 'nudge the boat into harbour'. The managing director either directly or through a general manager is going to control events through his interpretation of what is required. Effectively to limit his operating freedom may appear down-grading or commercially unwise but on the other hand, here is a business set up and planned to achieve certain financial objectives and it was on this basis that money was invested. Further, the terms of the licence and the bank or government loan are specific and any flights of entrepreneurial fancy outside the planned operation may generate problems with the authorities. Harassed civil service administrators may be one thing today but quite another when they have spare time on their hands.

Into the managing director's brief should go clearly stated broad business objectives and detailed reporting procedures that will be installed and maintained, as well as any other reports that will be submitted regularly; there will also be the more traditional limits of authority.

So it is that with a signed agreement and money in the bank, the joint venture partner and the technical partner can begin in earnest to do what they really wanted to do in the first instance—get on with the business.

RUNNING A JOINT VENTURE

The planning is over, the legal aspects settled, the intial shareholders' meeting has taken place, and the venture moves to the practical stage.

The appointment of key staff is a matter of considerable importance and the UK *Personnel Management* journal was, for example, intent on keeping the matter in the public eye with its headline 'The Cost of Picking the Wrong Expatriate is Terrifyingly High—the failure is more often due to an inability to adapt to cultural change than to lack of skills'.

To put the matter in perspective, Holmes and Piker of ORC New York and the UK, respectively, argue that assessing potential candidates for adaptability to cultural change can reduce expatriate failure rates from 45 per cent to 25 per cent. It is argued that people responsible for expatriate selection should have a clear understanding of the attitudes, values, feelings, and beliefs which affect social adjustment and thereby contribute crucially to a candidate's adaptability. The argument continues that evidence of mental flexibility, communication skills, previous cross-cultural exposure, breadth of experience, positive attitudes towards change, social adaptability, tolerance for frustration, physical and mental stamina, and resilience indicate a strong likelihood of cultural adaptability. Assessments of potential candidates and their spouses should be made, with these matters being considered of equal importance to technical skills.

This somewhat lengthy and perhaps even awesome appraisal is further broken down into more readily assimilated factors which are perhaps more meaningful for a layman having to handle such a selection.

Adaptable people are more likely to exhibit the following tendencies:

- Empathy;
- Self-awareness;
- Role differentiation and reversal;
- Absence of dogmatism;
- Tolerance of ambiguity;
- Respect for equality;
- Non-verbal communication skills;
- Self-esteem.

The *unadaptable* are likely to exhibit:

- Escapist tendencies;
- A desire for change for change's sake;
- A desire for change for financial reward alone.

These broad hints give adequate food for thought and individuals will clearly determine the validity of establishing a process to establish adaptability, or of using the background thinking on a more subjective and personal basis.

In the more traditional approach to staff selection, the armed forces—although often criticized for lack of refinement in personnel skills—may well have the simplest and most appropriate answer for handling a new market attack: 'send the best man'.

Deciding what 'best' means may be problematical. The best often has a simple way of confirming himself or herself by saying 'Yes' quickly to a genuine opportunity when it has been offered. With apologies to the man-management scientists who may find such a simple appraisal a trifle naive, the alternative of negotiating a person into serving overseas once he has said 'No' has proved to many to be a disastrous mistake. If people are being nominated by departmental heads, look at the motivation. If there is any suggestion that this person can easily be spared, think long and hard about the appointment. If the proposed candidate weakens the home organization when appointed and someone shouts loudly that he is irreplaceable, or that he is the top person in the sales team, or that he has the lowest man/unit volume ratio in the production team, then you are probably on the right track.

To decide between the good and the not-so-good, the following non-exclusive list of tell-tale signs sometimes helps to identify the weaker candidates:

1. Being the subject of carefully worded assessments.
2. Unusual job titles.
3. A lot of time spent on courses.
4. Trail of superfluous memorandums or minutes.
5. Excessive social style of doing business.
6. Political protégé.

Some of the above may be considered blatantly unfair, but the end justifies the means and, if the message has got across that people failure is high and that the price to be paid in joint venture partner confidence and venture progress for inadequate selection is unacceptable, then the provocation is worth while.

For well-motivated, confident, and competent people who are likely to be successful, the most difficult stumbling-block that the support company probably faces is to answer honestly the question concerning what happens at the end of a successfully completed contract.

Key joint venture appointments are very often not as well understood as home appointments because of the newness and uncertainty that surrounds the position. It is therefore very useful to help to determine the acceptability of the candidate by setting out a simple job description. A well-written job description can be more helpful than a man specification for it will generate a business reaction which is assessable.

What the job specification should do beyond reasonable doubt is to highlight to the candidate that he is isolated and without cover; it is his task to achieve a set of numerically expressed objectives. A good candidate will grow towards rather than shrink from the task. All key personnel will share responsibilities as individuals for creating and running a business, not as departmental or works staff within a company where they are propped up by staff specialists and an existing regime of action. Good candidates will translate numerical objectives into key questions about business prospects and the commercial environment.

Within the general job description layout, the following is an example of the style suitable for a general manager appointment:

Responsible to: Board of Directors.

Immediate subordinates: Sales Manager (expatriate); Works Manager (expatriate); Accountant (national); Local Adviser (national).

Responsible for:
  (a) Ensuring the continuance of a balanced and good working relationship between the joint venture partner and technical partner.
  (b) Bringing the plant into successful operation by [date] and achieving single shift production by [date].
  (c) Achieving sales values and volumes in the pre-operation year, and increased values in subsequent years.
  (d) Achieving production volumes in given time units.
  (e) Achieving the following financial objectives:
      (i) x per cent return on assets;

    (ii) capital expenditure within the budget of x value;

    (iii) conversion cost of value x per unit;

    (iv) trading results substantially in line with financial appendix attached;

    (v) keeping cash flow within stated guidelines as appendix attached.

(f) Making effective use of all resources and ensuring the long-term success and competitiveness of the venture specifically by:

    (i) market development;

    (ii) quality control (factually expressed);

    (iii) service levels (factually expressed).

The emphasis is balanced to ensure that joint venture relationships based on known project objectives are maintained. The exact *work* content is spelt out beyond doubt. Although the manager's contract is often for a relatively short period of time (say three years), the judgement of success also rests on providing for the *future development* and well-being of the business.

At the selection stage the far-sighted technical partner will also give thought to the replacement of key staff, particularly if the policy is to supply from within. To many this will appear an unnecessary refinement because few Western businesses can afford to carry surplus staff in today's conditions. On the other hand, hard-pressed senior management is often dismayed to find out how short a three-year contract really is!

The final selection process has to be carried out by face-to-face interview with the joint venture partner and a measure of acceptability gained no matter how reluctant the joint venture partner may be to give this: full acceptance is unlikely to be forthcoming in a two- or three-hour discussion. The investment of having new staff in the territory for a week or so during interviews is small beer compared with what is at stake.

Key staff working for a separate entity need a contract of employment and this should be agreed well in advance with the joint venture partner. The contract should carry major shareholders' signatures and have full board approval as there must be unequivocal acceptance not only of the money but also of the full terms.

Contract acceptance is frequently difficult to achieve with the local partner. This stems partly from a natural desire to see performance and day-to-day work attitudes before giving too much away. There is often genuine concern at the high overall costs of expatriate packages, which frequently lie between £50,000 and £100,000 ($90,000 and $180,000) and moral indecision as to whether it is in fact correct to invest that amount of money in non-national staff.

Prior internal determination of contract policy is essential before discussions with any potential candidate or local partner takes place. The extremes of option are wide; either high salary and limited commitment to ancillary parts of 'the package' or low salary and total commitment to providing trouble-free living conditions. Considerations for deciding the most appropriate course of action are varied and both schools of thought have merit.

Undoubtedly high salaries attract into the selection process a good calibre of candidate and readily show the importance that is attached to the job.

Lower salaries, whilst not having this attraction, do have the advantage of making reabsorption technically easier and cause less abraison throughout the home organization. However unwarranted, stay-at-home employees often show an undue interest in the overseas remuneration situation.

The crucial factor, however, is the philosophy behind the low salary package. In essence, it can be so designed as to ensure that staff have no worries about their personal well-being and survival in an alien environment. The time taken in third world countries to get the wherewithal to secure acceptable living conditions is considerably more than in Western countries. Finally, any aspect of local need that has to be negotiated by an outsider can dig a deeper hole in the pocket than if the task is undertaken by local people on the company's behalf. This is particularly true of accommodation, for example.

Reverting to the basic view that creating a business is difficult and that there are particular problems in doing this overseas, there is a strong case to be made for having key staff concentrating on the job and ensuring when they move away from it that there are reasonable conditions in which to relax and have their families around them.

The cost implications of a full package become clear from the sample contract suggested later in this Chapter. Such contracts might discriminate against older candidates with large families, but this limitation may not be too onerous since the consensus of opinion is that pioneer business and expatriate life in the industrial field is best suited to the younger man. The success and vigour of a younger man holding a position that he would not get in a developed country, supported by an agile-minded wife, making full use of the overseas adventure, and with youngsters in the background acclimatizing faster than either husband or wife, is borne out in practice—the failure rate on contracts is demonstrably less within the younger age groups.

Genuine 'bachelor packages' need adjusting to allow more time for home leave but thought should be given to the amount of total absence and the need for cover that occurs if too many bachelors are employed in key positions. With family appointments it is better if the husband arrives in advance and finds his way around and acclimatizes, so that he can help the family to cope on their arrival. This is better than having everybody floundering together and possibly commiserating with one another. While long flights are not necessarily the trial mothers believe they will be, coping with the luggage, kids, the handbag fumble for tickets and passports as well as staid airport officialdom causes strain: companies that do not see expatriate families 'in' and 'out' are missing a trick.

The outline of a typical contract based on 'low salary' and 'high package' is set out below:

1. Contract heading and definitions.
2. Engagement: position, title, and duration.
3. Remuneration:
    (*a*) Salary.
    (*b*) Expenses.
    (*c*) Salary reviews.
    (*d*) Assessment schemes.
    (*e*) Entry fees to local clubs.
    (*f*) Home entertaining allowances.
4. Duties:
    (*a*) Job and appendix job description.
    (*b*) Confidentiality.
    (*c*) Medical rules and examinations.
5. Family: agreement that spouse and children live in the territory.
6. Kit allowance for clothes, etc., prior to departure.
7. Leave:
    (*a*) Paid month at home.
    (*b*) Paid 14 days locally.
    (*c*) Extra payment for leave not taken.
8. Fares: for all home to territory expenses at commencement of contract, and of contract, and on home leaves.
9. Personal baggage payments to take a certain level of personal effects to and from the territory.
10. Living accommodation: fully furnished/air conditioned/centrally heated; electricity, light, water bills to be paid by the company.
11. School: full cost of local school or schooling in a preferred third country. Fares for children to visit the territory on holiday.
12. Car: type of car, full maintenance, and change every 100,000 km, company driver.
13. Health:
    (*a*) Full salary during illness/injury.
    (*b*) Full cost of medical treatment for himself and his family with a nominated doctor and private medical centre.
14. Pensions: preservtion of all rights, inflation-proofed during contract.
15. Miscellaneous: termination rules and clear statements as to who pays what in a broken contract.

Whatever the salary, it is a wise provision to express it in local currency terms only, unless senior management has a particular penchant for exchange rate discussion.

Getting senior expatriate staff effectively installed is also worthy of more detailed planning. Whilst a general manager, for example, may be known to the joint venture partner, it is unlikely that a strong working relationship exists. This often has to be created by ensuring that there are programmed and predetermined times for meetings and discussions. (It may be that in developing countries the local equivalent of 'British Raj' is a 'local partner elusiveness'.) The point that is being worked towards is that it is equally important for the technical partner to lock into the venture a positive measure of the local partner's time and interest.

If the joint venture partner has nominated a local adviser to become an employee of the company (and this has a lot to recommend it), it is wrong to assume that a good working relationship will spring up automatically with expatriate employees. There are many natural problems arising from upbringing and approach which will mitigate against this and the gradual development and working together of a multinational team may well rely upon the careful work of a relative outsider. Not least of the problems may be in coaching local people to accept the time disciplines of industrial employment, and to accept the obligations of team membership rather than being a 'partner's stooge'.

The installation of the general manager may also require a practical approach. However well-travelled and mature he may be, it is unlikely that he will emerge unscathed in his first encounter with everyday local life in a new territory. In the early days, when he is feeling his way towards a working relationship with a joint venture partner, it is not wise to leave him struggling to perform with the business and groping with day-to-day living difficulties.

To deal with the problem effectively means ensuring that the general manager is out of his hotel and living in his accommodation, has his driving licence, his car, and begins to cope with normal life in the shortest possible time. A hard philosophy, perhaps, but certainly a very therapeutic one.

To make a start on the job he needs his temporary office, office equipment, and ready access to (preferably sole use of) telephone and telex facilities. Once there is a semblance of normal life and a working base, a lot of time can be saved if he is physically shown how to reach main customers and important work contacts. Getting around and finding offices and outside locations is difficult: the more extensive the help that can be given, the shorter the time to the first order and the more adept the general manager will be in playing the significant leadership role in settling down other people.

If it can be arranged for two expatriates on temporary bachelor status to work together in the first stage of the venture, it is preferable, as the work situation can become very intense: a shared burden can help the settling-down process.

To determine when it is safe to back off, there are four checks:

1. Assuming trading before operations commence, when the first delivery has been made and when the money is in the bank.
2. Assuming family postings, when facilities permit the arrival of the first family.
3. When the contractor has started on site.
4. When the general manager has ready access to funds and methods of making financial settlements.

Pausing for a moment to think of the implications behind each requirement will highlight how this stage of the venture can easily be the busiest
time in anyone's working year. Speed is a function of preparation and
preplanning. The normal time taken to install the general manager will
often be in excess of three to four working weeks.

The long-term integration of senior local staff is also a matter of
considerable importance. Whilst the local advisory role may be time-
absorbing and interesting in the early stages of the venture, there comes a
time, and there is indeed a need, when local staff should contribute
positively to the business. To do this effectively requires an understanding
of what the business is about; the time taken in training both on the spot and
possibly in the technical partner's factories, for example, can yield rich
rewards.

HANDLING INEVITABLE CONFLICTS AND KEEPING ON LINE

When structure and strategy were reviewed in Chapter 3 a generous insight
into the sights that exist between 'headquarters' and overseas operations
was outlined (see Table 3.3). It is most unusual if no relationship problems
arise; often they are spontaneous and can be rationalized, or they can be
planned for by either side to find out where the 'brink' really is. It is
.herefore wise to have a plan for handling conflict when the different
business cultures appear to clash. One way of achieving this is based on the
assumption that some form of misunderstanding has occurred. When the
real cause for conflict is not clear, and it is evident that more words and
telexes than normal are being used, it is worth while to get everyone around
a table on which there is only one piece of paper. The paper will be headed
'Frame of reference' and will list in columns areas of friction. The rules of
the game are that all have to agree that the frame is complete and that there
are no other issues to be tabled. Step two is to grade the columns in
importance and, finally, step three is to discuss each area in turn taking the
least important items first. As agreements on the action required to put the
situation right are reached and actions allocated, they are entered in the
appropriate column at the bottom of the frame.

A frequent presence is important in ensuring that misunderstandings do
not increase and become flashpoints. Again the point has to be emphasized
that expatriate contracts pass quickly, that there are staff failures, and at
any point the original negotiator has to be available, and still be acceptable
as a man with the good of the business writ plainly on his heart, to step in
and give confidence and continuity.

As discussed when dealing with the first shareholders' meeting, it is
usually a wise provision to have full discussion on the agenda and contents
of board meetings prior to the meeting, leaving time for the alignment of
views and to eliminate the risk of a positive stand being taken at a meeting
where resolution will require loss of face by one side or the other.

It is equally important for both partners to appreciate that any general manager or managing director who is put in the unenviable position of deciding a particular issue by voting with one partner or another may be subjected to an unrealistic strain. It is better for partners to accept advice from a senior person on the basis of what he believes to be the best course of action for the venture and then to resolve the matter exclusively between themselves. To deny any chief executive or general manager voting rights at board meetings is sound policy and not an act of degradation.

It is important that the staff responsible for running the venture should have a crystal-clear brief: to achieve this, it is necessary to start at the top and to ensure that local partners in an executive or even in a non-executive role agree on broad priorities. It is an unfortunate fact of life that senior people often like to participate in the venture from time to time without giving detailed thought as to the validity of their actions. It is disappointing to see how often good intentions are at variance with strategic design; therefore consideration could be given to attaching to the managing director's brief, for example, an appendix of broad priorities which can serve him, and incidentally the rest of the board and management team.

The objective is not to set down a rigid policy document for all time but to state what needs to be done first. When it is necessary to change direction, then there is a platform for discussion and major shifts of policy can be readily substituted. A simple policy sheet is shown in Table 9.3. To use a cliché, 'it is only the goals that count, kicking the ball is not good enough'; the Table shows in which direction the goals are.

Whether the managing director and general manager are one and the same person or not is immaterial, in so far as the day-to-day management needs must be clearly understood. It is better to spell out the needs rather than let people try to swim with copies of the feasilibty study under one arm and the articles of association and the joint venture agreement under the other.

In an ideal situation, the general manager will have had an extensive programme of orientation, training, and familiarization with the negotiator and the co-ordinator of the home support team prior to departure. The general manager will also have been the prime architect for a forward business diary.

An example of the type of entry that may appear in a forward business diary is given below:

March 198—
1. Quarterly report.
2. Building steel erected—stage payment value x.
3. Site services, electricity, and water to be available.
4. Raw material order 1,000 units delivered works price x maximum.
5. Orders on hand———average value per unit———.
6. Plant and machinery to be shipped.
7. Works manager due to arrive.
8. Overall finance estimates: (i) Equity loan.

Table 9.3. Priorities for Opening Up a Market for Building Greeches

Customer priorities	Geographic priorities	Production priorities
1. x major companies which have an association with project through shareholders	1. Contracts within 100 km of plant location	1. Maximum production runs for products a, d and f to xyz national standard
2. All European contractors	Concurrently government consultant	2. Maximum production runs for products a, d, and f to abc national standard
2. Contracts in x geographical area		
3. All pre-cast industry	3. Contracts in y geographical area	3. Major customers with annual offtake in excess of 97 units
4. Local and Asian contractors	Private local consultants	4. Production of b, c and e products
4. Exports		
5. All other contractors	Overseas consultants	5. Development products

The main purpose is to compare business opportunities on a simple 'who, what, where' basis to ensure best decisions and effort to support profitability predictions. The chart also acts as a guideline for the required relationship between production and sales. It also gets 'lay' shareholders looking in the right direction and acts as a 'hedge' against getting the business bogged down with interesting but unprofitable orders.

(ii) Estimated outgoing.

(iii) Bank balance.

9. Pre-occupational trading account estimate.

The opportunity which the forward business planning diary provides is that it allows for rapid identification of things that are not happening on time; resources can then be focused and action taken to secure short-term tangible objectives.

It should also be borne in mind that pacing of work is of prime importance; if time is short, it is wise to concentrate on tight schedules early on, rather than allow problems to accumulate. In this way there is sufficient clarity about objectives for internal management to:

1. Build and run a successful, free-standing, autonomous enterprise.
2. Relate that enterprise operationally in a predetermined way to the international organization of one or more of the partners.
3. Work on an agreed basis to achieve the agreed objectives of the partners.

The preceding paragraphs give a tight construction to the management of day-to-day issues and imply that there is a constant and valid understanding between partners. The delegation of partner negotiations is not a viable proposition because it mixes two fundamentally different processes: that of harnessing resources and co-ordinating aims and that of driving the business forward. In a joint venture the first is the continuation of a long-term negotiation and the second a service to all of the partners.

THE OPERATIONAL SIDE AND 'THE MEN'

Building the factory and commissioning the equipment are two operations which will demonstrate beyond reasonable doubt whether adequate attention to detail has taken place. Overall, these are specialist areas combining skill and experience. A common danger is for non-practical people to underestimate the requirements: looking for a 25 mm rebar in sand or mud makes an impression never equalled by the 'make believe'!

The development of the site and the construction of the factory are almost by definition some of the most well-charted areas of the venture. Keeping to the time schedule and the specification may be the sole function of the contractors on paper, but for day-to-day working purposes, achievement can depend upon how flexible and adept the client is in adjusting to problems as they arise.

A similar philosophy will almost certainly have to be applied to commissioning. Frequently insufficient attention is given to pre-planning and, although it may seem an expensive extra, it is worth while for all the parties to be involved in pre-meetings that define beyond reasonable doubt how the dovetailing of specialist operations will take place. If there is any shortage of facts, or weaknesses in local knowledge, ways and means have to be found of getting the answer fast and prior to departure (no matter who holds the nominal responsibility for getting the information). A favourable settlement on a claim or a commercial 'sweetener' is often chicken-feed compared with the loss of profit that arises from late start-up.

The schedule of spares to be held in the venture is one of the most important single judgements made on the operational side. Whilst a sensible approach can be made by the support team, the final determination should be by the works manager when he has done his own local research to ascertain what he can buy, what he can make, and what he can have made. So often the shortage of parts which will stop a machine in Europe for ten minutes can put a plant out of action for days in a developing country. Even air-freighted parts get lost, get held up by customs, or become broken in transit. The definition of spare parts often leaves a lot to be desired, particularly in complex situations where a large number of equipment manufacturers are involved. There is no certainty of understanding until both support team and venture have parts classified and numbered in identical manuals.

Finally, whatever the pressures, the nationalities, working staff deserve and will respond to honest man management and training. The works manager may need to have patience and moral fibre as well as all the other skills to create a workforce of high standard and morale. Again it is an area that costs money, again it is an area where both partners should take an interest, again it is not easy. One may like to raise the question as to whether this is 'preaching?' It is not: workmen who sign for second contracts in hard business terms are very valuable commodities.

THE SALES SIDE

Market information and intelligence are often more readily available in Western press articles and documentation than in overseas territories. In support companies, someone should hold the responsibility for sifting out such information and forwarding it to the venture on a regular basis. Within the venture, the setting up of records is a laborious but essential task that has to be started on the first day. Customers, their background, contact telephone numbers, addresses, directions, together with alternative contacts in their organizations and trading records with the venture need to be meticulously kept. The increased profitability that comes from adjusting terms according to payment records and being in a position to send people quickly and directly to factories, sites, and offices repays generously the cost of keeping the records.

Often the post is not a safe way of dealing with orders, invoices, or money payments and receipts. If the sales force is going both to sell and to act as postmen, then prime selling time is going to diminish. The general manager needs to look at total staff deployment to ensure that the attack is kept up on the main priorities, particularly in large territories.

There are frequently fewer opportunities for press advertising and public relations work, and trade journals often originate out of the country. The promotional mix, therefore, will often have to ensure high impact and recall from sales presentation. Emphasis will need to be given to multiple customer presentations in segmented territories such as trade evenings and seminars. Working factories are news; local manufacture and local availability is news. The use of the factory and its stocks and the delivery and use of products by others on their premises all make centrepieces for business meetings and discussions. Action orientated presentations can overcome language barriers and get practical people understanding one another with a minimum of words.

If it is difficult to contact customers, then it is equally difficult for buyers to find the venture. The liberal use of signs with clear telephone numbers is one of the strongest sales aids in developing countries.

There is a tendency, perhaps, to take short-cuts when the venture's products are in short supply, but quality and service are keys to a safer future market and the standards have to be set early on if a reputation is to be built that will defeat the competition in the longer term.

Often price differences are likely to appear to favour imported products. Where high volume orders can be negotiated in weak world markets, advantageous prices can be obtained: the sales team has to be well-versed and convincing in the arguments for local purchase. The main elements of these arguments are that local purchase:

- reduces financing costs and eliminates letter of credit charges;
- is negotiated at an exact price—many customers do not know how much they really pay and the full cost of getting goods from ship to works;
- reduces delay and the cost of stock held;
- allows a longer time before final product specification is necessary and purchase modifications are easier;
- allows reductions of contingency purchases to cover scrap and damage;
- is cost effective for ordering, servicing, complaints, and payments;
- allows continuous long-term alignment to purchaser's quality needs whereas frequent changes of suppliers in the world market might cause quality problems.

Such arguments are not natural conversations for salesmen schooled in domestic industrialized markets.

Preparing the market may not be possible for all ventures but, in many instances, a pre-occupational trading exercise can be set up using imported products. If this can be done in a profitable way, then it is advantageous in generating cash to offset the constant outgoings before the operation starts. It is, however, likely that the combination of price, low volume, and debtors may make an overall profit difficult to achieve. Early trading does, however, confer other benefits that may well be worth paying for.

Pre-operational trading should be considered because:

- if it takes a year to build a factory and commission plant, this dead-time can be used to open up the market and to get ahead of or turn away competition;
- it forces the team's attention on to the main task, which is not building the factory but building sales for production to cut into;

- it enables the team to be sent out early and become acclimatized to the business;
- it begins to prove what is practical, and weaknesses in marketing theory can be adjusted at an early stage;
- as a practical participant in the market-place, the venture can have some influence in discussions on local standards, etc.;
- it may engender some exports that the support company would not have achieved;
- it enables any errors of judgement in personnel selection to be sorted out early. (The effect of such problems should not be underestimated in terms of the joint venture partner's confidence. In some cases, it will also enable families to get over their first home leave successfully—one of the key signs of stability.)

Overall there is a very strong case for pre-operational trading. A host of minor points also emerge that may well seem insignificant from a distance but are important on the ground; for example, the staff will find their way around, particularly amongst customers, so that at the stage when production requires sales, attempts are not being made to decide why the call rate is so low.

RUNNING THE BUSINESS AND FUTURE DEVELOPMENTS

It defeats the purpose to have a special set of rules for running overseas business when the total objective must be to run the venture as nearly as possible to the same high professional standards one would want to see at home. Support visits are, therefore, not just exercises in personal relationships but also provide the basis for a sensible and planned maintenance of business standards. While most people would agree that insisting on sand being kept out of the compound, in a Middle East venture, for example, is nonsense; the overall tidiness and good order of the factory is a non-negotiable requirement.

The most significant difference expatriate managers are likely to find results from their lack of experience in dealing with cash flow and real bank accounts. Many will find themselves dealing for the first time with having to organize the business on a day-to-day basis so that the flow of funds into the bank account is adequate to meet the outgoings and to build a reserve from which dividends can be paid. Money management and developing the ability to see day-to-day actions as cause and effect mechanisms on the bank balance can usually be readily assimilated, but prior training often offers rich rewards.

Joint management meetings with all the top team present, as well as major shareholders, if at all possible, are invaluable if the strength of both sides is going to be kept working for the venture. Quick routes to changes of purchasing policy in customers' joint ventures, for example, obviously lie through discussions between major non-Western shareholders. Also, one of the swiftest ways of establishing credit ratings and getting debtors back in order can be to use local influence. The regular management meeting is a neat and tidy way of leaving the business open to examination and determining who can best do what. The value in keeping the joint venture partner interested and involved in the venture, no matter how many other irons he may have in the fire, is crucial. The main way to keep the interest is through the value content of the venture, that is to say the money in the bank and the dividend payment.

THE FUTURE

Most people appreciate that businesses are dynamic and come to some arrangement that matches the only certain knowledge that exists about the future: that tomorrow will be different from today. Frequently, however, in sluggish world markets, with weak economies and high taxes, the response to change has become muted; it is often the case in developing countries that survival depends upon development and diversification. In a success-ful long-term venture, technical and commercial support has to match this need; this brings the whole wheel full-circle since it requires a match in attitude of mind between the partners. The fundamental research that was so essential to the original venture has to become the corner-stone again— first for the evaluation of the correctness of the original research, and then, by refining the methods, for appraisal and the knowledge to allow the identification of the next profitable growth opportunity. As in any business, the way to protect the future is to assess the present and plan for change. In planning for change in developing markets it is necessary to plan for growth, recognizing that growth depends upon the maintenance of customers, plant, people, and technology that gives product advantages. However busy the people are, however distant the venture may be, however varied the business background of the partners, it is likely that setting aside time for forward planning will turn out to be the only sensible way of pulling knowledge out from the venture and determining the most appropriate way to keep abreast of the market.

Technical partners frequently tend to assume that a market in a developing country will follow the product evolution pattern in terms of sophistication and time that occurred in the originating company. Sometimes this is the case, but in many instances the process is subject to considerable contraction in time, and the unwary are caught out by their own preconceptions.

CONCLUSION

This Chapter covers very briefly some of the practicalities of running a joint venture in its first and subsequent years. Nothing substantially new is being proposed but, rather, confirmation of the need to adhere to simple business effort and principles. The quest was to avoid failure and to show the joint venture as a successful business proposition. It is true that in many parts of the world there are additional risks, but seeing and setting a course for rapid pay-back is often a fair compensation; by and large, judging risk and matching activity to it is the skill that the businessman should pride himself upon. As a way of doing this, the problem that the joint venture poses is to find ways and means of sharing management with people who have different ways of doing things, in the knowledge that one cannot have a continuing partner relationship where one of the partners is regularly overruled. There, then, is the rub; one negotiates to get value for contribution and reflect it in equity percentages but, on a day-to-day basis, the business has to be run as a co-operative. An important skill in avoiding joint venture failure is to use methods and practices and set standards that acknowledge this paradoxical state of affairs.

References

1 K. R. Harrigan, 'Joint Ventures and Competitive Strategy', *Strategic Management Journal*, 9 (1988).
2 R. P. Nielsen, 'Cooperative Strategy in Marketing', *Business Horizons* (July/Aug. 1987).
3 D. Morris and M. Hergest, 'Trends in International Collaborative Agreements', *Columbia Journal of World Business* (Summer 1987).
4 P. Lorange and G. J. B. Prabst, 'Joint Ventures as Self-Organizing Systems', *Columbia Journal of World Business* (Summer 1987).
5 B. Gomes Casseres, 'Joint Venture Instability: Is it a Problem?' *Columbia Journal of World Business* (Summer 1987).
6 M. A. Lyles, 'Common Mistakes in Joint Ventures by Experienced Firms', *Columbia Journal of World Business* (Summer 1987).
7 P. W. Beamish, 'The Characteristics of Joint Ventures in Developed and Developing Countries', *Columbia Journal of World Business* (Fall 1985).
8 *Joint Ventures in Eastern Europe*, Praeger Special Studies (New York).
9 Philip Hill, 'The Long Arm of the Comecon Multies', *Vision* (Feb. 1977).
10 Emile Benoit, *The Joint Venture Route to East-West Transactions*, American Management Association Monograph No. 119 (New York, 1968).
11 James M. Barkas and James L. Gale, 'Joint Venture Strategies—Yugoslavia: A Case Study', *Columbia Journal of World Business* (Spring 1981); *Business Eastern Europe*, 28 June 1980.
12 Jayaza Sarkar, 'New Dimension for India', *Far Eastern Economic Review*, 30 May 1980.
13 Zillay Zaidi, 'Success of Indian Ventures Abroad', *Insight*, 25 Aug. 1980.
14 Herbert Glazer, 'Capital Liberalization' in R. J. Ballon (ed.), *Joint Ventures and Japan* (Sophia Univ., Tokyo in conj. with Charles E. Tuttle: Vermont).
15 Kenneth Gooding, 'An Increase in Joint Ventures', *Financial Times*, Commercial Vehicles Survey, 24 Sept. 1979.
16 Pierre Beauregard, 'Oracle Feature', *Car*, July 1979.
17 'Euro-Trucks: Sisters Under the Skin, *Economist*, 27 Oct. 1979.

18 William Holmes and Fred Piker, 'Expatriate Failure: Prevention Rather than Cure', *Personnel Management* (Dec. 1980).
19 Ulrich E. Wiechmann and Lewis G. Pringle, 'Problems that Plague Multinational Marketers', *Harvard Business Review* (July/Aug. 1979).
20 Lee Adler, 'Symbiotic Marketing', *Harvard Business Review* (Nov./Dec. 1966).
21 *Recent Experience in Establishing Joint Ventures*, Management Monographs, No. 54 (Business International: New York, 1972).
22 James D. Hlavacek, Brian H. Dovey, and John Biondo, 'Tie Small Business Technology to Marketing Power', *Harvard Business Review* (Jan./Feb. 1977).
23 Lee Adler and James D. Hlavacek, *Joint Ventures for Product Innovation* (Amacom: New York).
24 Peter Drucker, *Management Tasks, Responsibilities and Practices* (Harper and Row: New York, 1974).

10

Money Matters and Conclusion

It is probably one of the supreme ironies of international activity that for all that can and needs to be done in the growth and development of the economy there is no real shortage of money. In the broadest of terms, earlier on note was taken of the near indiscriminate and almost ovine rush to lend. More specifically, one only has to read the updates on the management buy-out scene, in the USA and the UK to understand that there is too much money chasing too few projects. A few years ago it was a privilege to be allowed to put one's house on the line and borrow to buy a company out. Today the venture capitalists complain about overcompetition and ratcheting—the incentive by which managements (to the financiers' detriment) get an increasing share of the equity if they are successful. 'Flood of Finance' and 'Pressure of Finance' shout the headlines; perhaps the opportunity to put power into international diversification projects is being overlooked.

Taking a step backwards it is easy enough to understand the problem; the optimization of capital investment is the highest return with the minimum of risk. The ultimate expressions of such criteria are of course hard to find and a judgement has to be made on the likelihood of better-than-average performance for agreed levels of risk. This perception can only be achieved sensibly if the financier gets closer to the business entrepreneur to understand the true nature of the international opportunity of wider markets in the shrinking world. If there is a gap between supernational, national private money and the international opportunity it is necessary to understand why this may be so. It is important to acknowledge that financial institutions overall have a long history of supporting both exports and overseas' long- and short-term projects. Today there is ample evidence that such institutions are becoming more ingenious than ever before in an effort to become more involved. The impediment is that their products are complicated ones and do not readily translate into field sales tools. Compare the situation, for example, with home consumer markets where the finance package is a leading edge in securing the sale.

In international work the financial dialogue is often confined to the company's finance arm and the financier; the finance department is not usually blessed with risk-taking qualities and its relationship with sales is often restrictive, through credit control, or near-panic-driven through asking for help in collecting cheques. It can be very cosy to blame the accountants again and beat them with their own 'stick-in-the-mud' stick but generous criticism is also due to the marketing fraternity who fail in the internal sell by neither realizing or demonstrating that international finance can be a powerful tool. The Treasurer spelt out the problem in a succinct and meaningful way:

> For many years the Treasurer's main contribution has been in developing the skills and techniques required for successful cash and currency management and funding in times of high volatility in the financial markets. A detailed series of case studies and interviews of UK exporters that we have recently completed indicates that . . . at times Sales Directors have seen major opportunities for profitable exports being lost because the finance package was not competitive. If these sales opportunities are to be exploited we believe new financial techniques must be introduced and awareness within the company of their profit potential increased. This challenge must be picked up by the Treasurer just as much as the marketing team. Based upon our recent experience with companies in this area of trade finance we outline below how a company should proceed in overcoming the high risks associated with the challenge and reap the substantial rewards.

> It is commonly accepted among Treasurers that there is a growing emphasis upon the provision of credit in export markets. . . . But it is also a result of the general shift in power that many feel has taken place in UK exporting sectors away from the supplier to the buyer. This demand for credit coinciding with the international debt crisis and increased volatility on world financial markets has combined to significantly increase the sovereign, commercial and exchange risks facing the exporter who offers delayed payment. The Treasurer is often caught between his natural caution in the face of this situation and pressure from his Managing Director and colleagues in line management for increased export turnover. . . .

> The problem is acute and is not going to disappear. We have explored with a number of UK Treasurers the ways in which answers can be found and it is clear that they do not lie in reliance upon the use of traditional export finance methods. . . . Advance payment or confirmed letters of credit meet with increasingly stiff customer resistance or the frequent unwillingness of banks to increase their exposure to difficult countries. . . . This is resulting in the exclusion of any marketing effort to some countries where for example we found margins of up to 80% could be earned. Furthermore many Treasurers saw no means of obtaining sufficient credit to allow their company to take full advantage of the continuing trend of faster growth in world trade levels.

> From our work in this area we have found that significant impact on turnover and profitability can be achieved by exploiting the available opportunities. But to do so requires companies to take at least three essential steps:

> —the first is a thorough understanding of the expanding range of new and revised financing techniques available to exporters. Their characteristics can be summarised in [the following] Table:

Financial Product	Characteristics
A Forfait	Non-recourse discounting of trade bills guaranteed by a bank in the buyers country
Non-Recourse	Finance provided through a Confirming House with or without insurance cover for 100% of the export value.
Countertrade	Covers a variety of possible forms of trading through barter, partial payment or other arrangements.
Leasing	Used particularly for fixed capital goods where finance to match the economic life of the goods is needed
'Credit Mixte'	Taking advantage of the aid funds available internationally to offer softer credit terms
Private Insurance	This can be on a whole turnover basis or used selectively to fill gaps not covered by ECGD
Risk Switching	The transfer of risk from the country concerned to the buyer of its exports in a more stable country
International Factoring	Purchase by a factoring company of foreign receivables with or without recourse

Virtually all the major UK and foreign banks in London have the capability to offer these services though we have seen that the standard of service varies considerably.

—the second step involves internal adaptation in order to enable the company to make the products available. This, in our view, poses the major constraint. A key requirement is for close co-operation between the Treasury and Marketing Departments. Only in this way can an optimum plan be developed that takes into account both the benefits of improved credit control in the form of reduced bad debts and also the costs of such control which show up in lost sales and inventory financing charges. We have found few companies that could really assess the true costs and benefits of a change in export credit policy.

—Finally the third step concerns bank relationships. In our view it is essential to treat trade finance relationships in a very different way from general banking relationships. The later can be handled by generalist account officers involve pricing through trade-offs between deals and over time; and are often judged by the Treasurer on the basis of the overall price paid for the bank's services, the quality of the account officer and other banking staff and the banks long term commitment to supporting the company. Trade finance relationships however can only be handled effectively by specialists—and we have seen that finding these exports who work behind the account officer can be a real problem for a company. Pricing is wholly dependent upon the economics of the particular deal since there are no rules of thumb for assessing difficult trade transactions. Their cost and benefit have to be worked out individually. Finally, the key criteria for judging the relationship should be its impact on export turnover and profitability. The bank and the company have to adopt a somewhat more flexible and entrepreneurial outlook in trade finance—and work to find solutions that achieved these criteria. . . . This culture shows some of the differences that should exist between the two types of relationship and recognition of this should lead to better management of the relationship. The goal must surely be to end the selling of standard products by the banks but instead develop a 'demand-driven' relationship that delivers solutions to particular export finance problems. This special type of relationship would soon bring to an end the succession of callers from banks asking 'what can we do for you?' and then only delivering on the deals that fit into the standard product line in low risk countries.

In summary, we believe that there are major hidden opportunities in the area of trade finance. Furthermore the present world economic situation is making this an increasingly important function within the company. In order to overcome the difficulties of providing export finance and to exploit the opportunities that are available in this field the Treasurer must increasingly be prepared to:

—understand the complicated new or revised financial products that exist;
—develop his company's understanding of the economics of export transactions;
—establish a specialised form of banking relationships

But most important he has to ensure that there is very close cooperation at all stages with his Marketing Department and that he becomes very closely involved in the direct marketing effort of the company's products overseas.

Source: G. Fletcher, D. Paige, D. Bond, 'The Treasurer's Role in Exploiting Hidden Opportunities', *The Treasurer*, March (1984).

A schedule of the application of financial instruments for all markets is out of the scope of this book and the pace of change, particularly in risk assessment, would make the summary a transitory one at best. The article in the *Treasurer* does, however, propose a course of action that is worth while. The discussion underwrites the need for ensuring in organizational terms that the financial arm should come into the company structure, and do much more than simply adding up the score to one side of it.

For many financial decisions there is a safety-net against the risks through the medium of insurance. ECGD (UK), COFACE (France), MITI import/export Division (Japan), SACE (Italy), HERMES (Germany), and the EXIM bank in the USA are all examples of government-based operations giving insurance for international trade and projects. Such organizations have varying reputations for supporting or countries moving into higher-risk categories. Most developed countries also have a well-defined private insurance sector to draw on. At the end of the line, when the debt repayment looks long at the best and unlikely in the foreseeable future at worst, some financial institutions have yet another new idea–debt equity conversion. In this way the existing debt is exchanged for equity participation. Perhaps this form of self-enforced international participation is not a natural long-term occupation for bankers but yet another new opportunity exists for companies to absorb the equity and to bring their own and possibly more practical skills to bear.

On a day-to-day basis there clearly needs to be a good relationship between finance and the achievement of international strategies. There are, however, many occasions when one is left in doubt as to whether either side draws the best out of the other thereby letting many opportunities go begging. It is wise to keep in mind that international credit arrangements can be a highly competitive business and it is important to be able to understand the strengths that any competitor may have in this area. For example, the Netherlands, amongst others, recognized this point officially with their Matching Fund whereby they would subsidize interest rates for overseas credits if competition from a subsidized foreign offer was proven. The ultimate free-for-all that might be envisaged in this area is curbed from time to time by twenty or so of the most involved countries agreeing through a consensus pact to align rates. As always with so much at stake, loans in the pipeline, and others with years to run the 'bite' of implementation, is often not as bad as the 'bark' of the press release.

Another area requiring careful attention is that of tax treaties. Such treaties can have a significant effect on any two companies of different nationality examining the same opportunity. Particular attention needs to be given to the existence or pending negotiation of double taxation treaties and the movement of tax rates that make ingress into dividend and royalty payments. The Table between pages 214 and 215 gives an overview of the international tax situation.

CONCLUSION

The most formidable of the world's institutions that concern themselves with the operation of international capital flows are the World Bank and its affiliate the International Finance Corporation (IFC), and the internationally subscribed International Monetary Fund (IMF). There is an important set of regional second-division players in the OPEC orbit, for example, which are worthy of both research and consultation depending upon the part of the world in which a company has a special interest. All of the world institutions produce excellent reports and the World Development Report, published by the World Bank, in particular, focuses on the contribution that international capital makes to economic development. The annual report (some 250 pages, generally) seeks to trace the financial links between the policies of developed and developing countries and the various mechanisms for transferring capital. As a deliberate short cut, the contents page to a World Development Bank. Report is included as Appendix II at the end of this chapter in order that anyone who is not familiar with range of analysis may readily see what is available and in broad outline the mental process of the analysis. This Appendix should marry up well with Appendix I at the end of chapter 4 as it is research oriented towards the country and its economic environment; the earlier Appendix concerns research within the country to see what opportunities exists for a particular product or service. All of the evidence points towards there being enough funds and an adequate financial infrastructure.

That business is not fully aware of the facilities that are available is a black mark to the would-be international operator: if, however, it is more a case of not understanding how the various financial instruments work then that clearly is the fault of the people who sell them. If neither side gets the best out of the other then that is a pity because it does not have to be the case.

Treaties and pacts with:

Treaties and pacts by:	Austria	Belgium	Denmark	Finland	France	West Germany	Greece	Ireland	Italy	Luxembourg	Netherlands	Norway	Portugal	Spain	Sweden	Switzerland	Turkey	UK	Canada	USA	USSR and Eastern Bloc	Argentina	Brazil	Bolivia	Chile	Colombia	Ecuador	Mexico	Peru	Uruguay	Venezuela	India	Pakistan	Sri Lanka	Honk Kong	Indonesia	Japan†	South Korea	Malaysia	Philippines	Singapore	Taiwan	Thailand	Australia	New Zealand	Iran	Iraq	Israel	Saudi Arabia	Egypt	Ghana	Nigeria	Kenya	Zaire	Zambia	Zimbabwe	South Africa	Sudan
Austria	—	15/10	10/10	10/10	15/10	25/0	●/0	10/10	25/10	5/10	10/10	15/10	15/5	10/5	10/10	5/5	20/10	10/10	15/10	5/0	●	15/15	15/10	—	—	—	—	—	—	—	—	0/0	10/20	—	—	—	10/10	—	●	15/6	—	—	—	—	—	—	—	20/10	—	10/0	—	—	—	—	—	—	—	—
Belgium	15/10	—	15/0	15/0	10/0	15/0	15/5	15/0	15/0	15/0	5/0	15/0	15/5	15/5	15/0	10/0	Ø	15/0	15/10	15/0	●	Ø	15/15	—	—	—	—	—	—	—	—	●	Ø	—	—	15/10	15/10	15/15	15/10	15/25	15/0	—	15/15	15/10	15/10	—	—	●	—	—	—	—	—	—	—	—	—	—
Denmark	10/10	15/0	—	5/10	0/10	10/—	—	0/—	15/0	Ø	0/●	5/—	0/10	10/6	5/—	0/0	—	5/—	5/●	5/0	●	—	●	—	—	—	—	—	—	—	—	●	●	—	—	—	10/—	●	●	●	●	—	●	Ø	Ø	—	—	●	—	—	●	Ø	●	—	●	—	—	—
Finland	10/0	15/5	15/0	5/0	0/0	15/5	13/10	●	15/5	15/5	●	15/0	15/10	15/5	15/0	10/0	Ø	5/0	15/15	15/0	●	Ø	25/15	—	—	—	—	—	—	—	—	25/30	—	15/10	—	—	15/10	15/10	15/5	25/25	15/10	—	25/15	15/10	15/10	—	—	15/10	—	10/25	—	Ø	—	—	15/15	—	—	—
France	15/0	10/0	0/0	0/0	—	0/0	●	10/0	15/0	15/10	15/0	15/0	15/5	10/6	15/0	15/5	—	15/0	15/10	5/5	●	Ø	15/15	—	—	—	—	—	—	—	—	●	●	—	—	Ø	15/10	Ø	●	Ø	●	—	●	●	15/10	●	—	●	—	—	—	—	—	—	—	—	—	—
West Germany	●/0	15/10	●	●	●	—	●	●	●	●	●	●	Ø	●	15/—	●	Ø	●	●	●	●	15/—	●	—	—	—	—	—	●	—	—	●	●	—	—	Ø	●	●	●	Ø	●	—	●	●	Ø	20/10	—	●	—	●	—	Ø	●	—	●	—	●	—
Greece	●/10	25/5	—	0/10	●/5	25/0	—	—	25/0	—	35/5	Ø	—	Ø	●/5	35/5	—	0/0	—	●	—	—	—	—	—	—	—	—	—	—	—	●	—	—	—	Ø	—	—	—	—	—	—	—	—	—	20/10	—	—	—	—	—	—	—	—	—	—	—	—
Ireland	10/10	15/0	●	●	●	●	—	—	●	●	●	●	—	●	●	●	—	●	●	●	—	—	—	—	—	—	—	—	—	—	—	—	●	—	—	—	—	—	—	—	—	—	—	—	—	—	—	—	—	—	—	—	—	—	—	—	—	—
Italy	15/10	15/5	15/5	10/5	15/0	0/0	25/0	15/0	—	15/10	●/0	30/0	15/12	15/14	10/5	15/5	—	5/0	15/10	5/10	●	15/10	15/15	—	—	—	—	—	—	—	—	—	●	—	—	Ø	15/0	—	●	Ø	Ø	—	●	—	●	—	—	25/0	—	30/0	—	—	—	—	●	—	—	—
Luxembourg	5/0	10/0	5/0	5/5	5/0	10/5	—	5/0	15/10	—	2.5/0	5/0	—	—	5/0	—	—	5/5	—	5/0	—	Ø	15/10	—	—	—	—	—	—	—	—	0/21	—	—	—	—	10/10	10/10	10/15	—	10/5	—	15/15	15/10	15/10	—	—	25/0	—	0/15	—	—	15/15	—	—	—	—	—
Netherlands	15/20	15/20	15/20	15/20	15/20	15/20	15/20	15/20	15/10	15/20	—	15/20	Ø	15/20	15/20	15/20	Ø	15/—	15/20	15/—	●	Ø	—	—	—	—	—	—	—	—	—	Ø	20/20	—	—	15/20	15/20	15/20	—	Ø	15/20	Ø	15/20	15/20	15/20	—	—	15/20	—	—	—	—	—	—	15/20	—	15/20	—
Norway	15/0	15/0	15/0	10/10	15/0	0/0	—	0/0	●	●	0/0	—	10/0	10/0	15/0	5/0	—/13	10/0	15/0	10/0	●/Ø	—	●	—	—	—	—	—	—	—	—	●	—	—	—	—	●	Ø	●	Ø	●	Ø	●	—	—	—	—	●	—	●	—	Ø	●	—	●	—	—	—
Portugal	12/10	12/5	10/10	10/6	12/5	12/10	12/—	12—	12/12	12/—	12/—	10/10	—	10/5	Ø	10/5	12/—	10/5	Ø	12/—	Ø	—	12/10	—	—	—	—	—	—	—	—	—	—	—	—	—	Ø	—	—	—	—	—	—	—	—	—	—	—	—	—	—	—	—	—	—	—	●	—
Spain	10/5	15/5	10/6	10/0	10/5	10/5	—	—	15/4	5/10	5/6	10/5	10/5	—	10/10	10/5	—	10/10	15/10	—	●	Ø	15/10	—	—	—	—	—	—	—	—	—	—	—	—	—	10/10	—	—	—	—	—	—	—	—	—	—	—	—	—	—	—	—	—	—	—	—	—
Sweden	10/10	15/10	15/10	5/0	10/0	15/0	0/5	0/0	15/5	15/0	15/0	15/0	Ø	15/0	—	5/0	15/—	5/0	15/0	15/0	●	●	—	—	—	—	—	—	●	—	—	●	15/0	5/0	—	—	15/0	15/0	0/0	20/0	15/0	—	20/0	15/10	15/0	—	—	15/0	—	0/0	—	Ø	25/0	—	15/0	—	●	—
Switzerland	5/0	10/0	0/0	5/0	5/0	15/0	5/0	10/0	15/0	—	0/0	5/0	10/0	10/0	5/0	—	Ø	5/0	15/0	5/0	●	Ø	—	—	—	—	—	—	—	—	—	Ø	15/0	10/0	—	●	10/0	10/0	5/0	Ø	10/0	—	Ø	15/0	15/0	—	—	—	—	5/0	—	—	Ø	—	—	—	7·5/0	—
Turkey	0/—	●	—	Ø	●	●	—	—	Ø	—	●	—/13	—	—	●	—	—	●	—	Ø	—	—	—	—	—	—	—	—	—	—	—	—	—	—	—	—	Ø	—	—	—	●	—	—	—	—	—	—	—	—	—	—	—	—	—	—	—	—	—
UK	●	●	●	●	—	●	●	●	●	●	●	●	●	●	—	●	—	—	●	●	—	—	—	—	—	—	—	—	—	—	—	●	—	—	—	●	●	●	—	Ø	●	—	Ø	●	15/—	—	—	●	—	Ø	—	●	●	—	—	—	●	—
Canada	—	15/10	●	●	●	●	—	●	Ø	—	●	●	Ø	Ø	●	●	—	●	—	●/10	Ø	Ø	—	—	—	—	—	—	—	—	—	●	●	—	—	●	●	Ø	●	●	●	—	—	●	●	—	—	●	—	—	—	—	—	—	—	—	●	—
USA	15/0	15/0	5/0	●	15/5	15/0	●	15/0	15/10	15/0	15/0	15/0	—	—	15/0	5/0	—	15/0	15/10	—	●	●	—	—	—	—	—	—	—	—	—	—	15/0	—	—	Ø	15/10	5/15	●	25/15	Ø	—	—	15/10	15/—	—	—	●	—	15/0	—	15/0	●	15/0	15/0	—	●	—
USSR and Eastern Bloc	●	●	●	Ø	—	●	—	—	●	—	●	●/Ø	Ø	—	●	—	—	—	Ø	●	—	Ø	—	—	—	—	—	—	—	—	●	—	—	—	—	—	●	—	●	Ø	—	●	●	—	—	—	—	—	—	—	—	—	—	15/0	—	—	—	—
Argentina	Ø	Ø	Ø	Ø	●	●	—	—	●	Ø	Ø	—	Ø	Ø	●	Ø	—	Ø	Ø	●	Ø	—	●	●	●	—	—	—	—	—	—	—	—	—	—	—	●	—	—	—	—	—	—	—	—	—	—	—	—	—	—	—	—	—	—	—	—	—
Brazil	15/10	●	●	●	15/15	●	—	—	●	●	Ø	●	15/15	●	●	—	—	—	●	—	—	Ø	—	—	—	—	●	—	—	—	—	—	—	—	—	—	12.5/25	—	—	—	—	—	—	—	—	—	—	—	—	—	—	—	—	—	—	—	—	—
Bolivia	—	—	—	—	—	—	—	—	—	—	—	—	—	—	—	—	—	—	—	—	—	—	—	—	—	A	A	—	A	—	A	—	—	—	—	—	—	—	—	—	—	—	—	—	—	—	—	—	—	—	—	—	—	—	—	—	—	—
Chile	—	—	—	—	—	—	—	—	—	—	—	—	—	—	—	—	—	—	—	—	—	●	—	—	—	—	—	—	—	—	—	—	—	—	—	—	—	—	—	—	—	—	—	—	—	—	—	—	—	—	—	—	—	—	—	—	—	—
Colombia	—	—	—	—	—	—	—	—	—	—	—	—	—	—	—	—	—	—	—	—	—	—	—	A	—	—	A	—	A	—	A	—	—	—	—	—	—	—	—	—	—	—	—	—	—	—	—	—	—	—	—	—	—	—	—	—	—	—
Ecuador	—	—	—	—	—	—	—	—	—	—	—	—	—	—	—	—	—	—	—	—	—	—	—	A	—	A	—	—	A	—	A	—	—	—	—	—	—	—	—	—	—	—	—	—	—	—	—	—	—	—	—	—	—	—	—	—	—	—
Mexico	—	—	—	—	—	—	—	—	—	—	—	—	—	—	—	—	—	—	—	—	—	—	—	—	—	—	—	—	—	—	—	—	—	—	—	—	—	—	—	—	—	—	—	—	—	—	—	—	—	—	—	—	—	—	—	—	—	—
Peru	—	—	—	—	—	—	—	—	—	—	—	—	—	—	●	—	—	—	—	—	—	—	—	A	—	A	A	—	—	—	A	—	—	—	—	—	—	—	—	—	—	—	—	—	—	—	—	—	—	—	—	—	—	—	—	—	—	—
Uruguay	—	—	—	—	—	—	—	—	—	—	—	—	—	—	—	—	—	—	—	—	—	—	—	—	—	—	—	—	—	—	—	—	—	—	—	—	—	—	—	—	—	—	—	—	—	—	—	—	—	—	—	—	—	—	—	—	—	—
Venezuela	—	—	—	—	—	—	—	—	—	—	—	—	—	—	—	—	—	—	—	Ø	—	—	—	A	—	A	A	—	A	—	—	—	—	—	—	—	—	—	—	—	—	—	—	—	—	—	—	—	—	—	—	—	—	—	—	—	—	—
India	●	●	●	●	●	●	●	—	●	—	Ø	●	—	—	●	●	—	—	●	●	●	—	—	—	—	—	—	—	—	—	—	—	—	●	—	—	●	●	●	●	●	—	●	●	●	●	—	—	Ø	●	—	—	Ø	—	●	—	—	—
Pakistan	●	●	●	—	●	●	—	●	●	—	●	●	—	—	●	●	—	●	●	●	●	—	—	—	—	—	—	—	—	—	—	—	—	●	—	—	●	—	●	●	—	—	●	—	—	—	—	—	—	—	—	—	—	—	—	—	—	—
Sri Lanka	—	—	●	—	Ø	●	—	—	—	—	—	●	—	—	●	—	—	Ø	Ø	Ø	Ø	—	—	—	—	—	—	—	—	—	—	●	●	—	—	—	●	—	●	—	Ø	—	—	—	—	—	—	—	—	—	—	—	—	—	—	—	—	—
Honk Kong			Partial relief in some commonwealth countries but not U.K.														Partial relief in some commonwealth countries but not U.K.															Partial relief in some commonwealth countries but not U.K.														Partial relief in some commonwealth countries but not U.K.												
Indonesia	●	●	●	Ø	●	●	Ø	—	Ø	—	●	Ø	—	Ø	—	Ø	—	●	●	Ø	Ø	—	—	—	—	—	—	—	—	—	—	●	—	Ø	—	—	●	Ø	Ø	—	Ø	—	●	●	—	—	—	—	—	—	—	—	—	—	—	—	—	—
Japan†	10/10	0/10	10/10	10/10	10/10	10/10	—	10/10	—	—	10/10	10/10	Ø	10/10	10/10	10/10	—	10/10	0/15	10/10	●	●	0/10	—	—	—	—	—	—	—	—	0/0	15/0	10/10	—	10/10	—	0/12	10/10	10/10	10/10	—	15/15	0/10	0/0	—	—	—	—	0/0	—	—	Ø	—	0/10	—	—	—
South Korea	●	●	●	●	●	●	—	—	—	●	●	●	—	—	●	●	●	●	●	●	—	Ø	●	—	—	—	—	—	—	—	—	●	●	●	—	●	●	—	●	●	●	—	●	●	●	—	—	—	Ø	●	—	Ø	Ø	—	—	—	—	—
Malaysia	●	●	●	●	●	●	—	—	●	—	—	●	—	—	●	●	—	●	●	●	●	—	—	—	—	—	—	—	—	—	—	●	●	●	—	●	●	●	●	●	●	—	●	●	●	—	—	—	—	—	—	—	—	—	—	—	—	—
Philippines	Ø	●	●	Ø	●	●	—	—	●	—	Ø	Ø	—	●	●	Ø	—	●	●	●	●	—	●	—	—	—	—	—	—	—	—	●	Ø	●	—	—	●	●	●	—	●	●	●	●	●	—	—	—	—	—	—	—	—	—	—	—	—	—
Singapore	—	●	●	●	●	●	—	Ø	Ø	Ø	●	●	—	—	●	●	●	●	●	Ø	Ø	—	—	—	Ø	—	—	—	—	—	—	●	Ø	●	—	Ø	●	●	●	●	—	●	●	●	●	—	—	●	—	Ø	—	—	—	—	—	—	—	—
Taiwan	—	—	—	—	—	—	—	—	—	—	Ø	—	—	—	—	—	—	—	—	—	●	—	—	—	—	—	—	—	—	—	—	—	—	—	—	—	—	—	—	●	—	—	●	Ø	—	—	—	—	—	—	—	—	—	—	—	—	—	—
Thailand	15/15	15/15	20/15	15/15	15/15	15/15	—	—	15/15	—	15/15	20/15	—	—	20/15	—	—	15/15	15/15	—	●	—	—	—	—	—	—	—	—	—	—	15/15	15/—	—	—	15/15	15/15	15/15	15/—	15/15	20/15	●	—	Ø	—	—	—	—	—	—	—	—	—	—	—	—	—	—
Australia	—	15/10	15/10	Ø	15/10	15/10	—	15/10	15/10	—	15/10	—	—	—	15/10	15/10	—	15/10	15/10	15/10	—	—	—	—	—	—	—	—	—	—	—	—	—	—	—	—	15/10	15/15	15/15	15/10	15/10	Ø	—	—	15/15	—	—	—	—	—	—	—	—	—	—	—	—	—
New Zealand	—	●	●	●	●	●	—	—	●	—	●	●	—	—	●	Ø	—	●	●	●	—	—	—	—	—	—	—	—	—	—	—	—	—	—	—	—	●	●	●	●	●	—	—	●	—	—	—	—	—	—	—	—	Ø	—	—	—	—	—
Iran	—	—	—	—	20/10	20/10	—	—	—	—	—	—	—	—	—	—	—	—	—	—	—	—	—	—	—	—	—	—	—	—	—	—	—	—	—	—	—	—	—	—	—	—	—	—	—	—	—	—	—	—	—	—	—	—	—	—	—	—
Iraq	—	—	—	—	—	—	—	—	—	—	—	—	—	—	—	—	—	—	—	—	—	—	—	—	—	—	—	—	—	—	—	—	—	—	—	—	—	—	—	—	—	—	—	—	—	—	—	—	—	●	—	—	—	—	—	—	—	—
Israel	20/10	15/10	15/10	15/10	15/10	25/5	—	—	25/0	—	15/10	15/10	—	—	15/0	—	—	15/0	15/15	25/10	—	—	—	—	—	—	—	—	—	—	—	—	—	—	—	—	—	—	—	—	0/0	—	—	—	—	—	—	—	—	—	—	—	—	—	—	—	25/15	—
Saudi Arabia	—	—	—	—	—	—	—	—	—	—	—	—	—	—	—	—	—	—	—	—	—	—	—	—	—	—	—	—	—	—	—	—	—	—	—	—	Ø	Ø	—	—	—	—	—	—	—	—	—	—	—	—	—	—	—	—	—	—	—	—
Egypt	0/0	—	—	0/25	—	0/10	—	—	0/15	—	—	0/15	—	—	0/0	15/12.5	—	0/15	0/15	0/15	●	—	—	—	—	—	—	—	—	—	—	●	—	—	—	—	●	●	—	—	—	—	—	—	—	—	●	—	—	—	—	—	—	—	—	—	—	●
Ghana	—	—	●	—	—	—	—	—	—	—	—	—	—	—	●	—	—	●	—	—	—	—	—	—	—	—	—	—	—	—	—	—	—	—	—	—	—	—	—	—	—	—	—	—	—	—	—	—	—	—	—	●	—	—	—	—	—	—
Nigeria	—	—	Ø	Ø	—	Ø	—	—	Ø	—	—	Ø	—	—	Ø	—	—	●	—	Ø	—	—	—	—	—	—	—	—	—	—	—	●	—	—	—	—	—	Ø	—	—	—	—	—	●	Ø	—	—	—	—	—	Ø	—	—	—	—	—	—	—
Kenya	—	—	●	—	—	●	—	—	Ø	—	—	●	—	—	●	Ø	—	●	—	Ø	—	—	—	—	—	—	—	—	—	—	—	Ø	—	—	—	—	Ø	Ø	—	—	—	—	—	—	Ø	—	—	—	—	—	—	—	—	—	●	—	—	—
Zaire	—	—	—	—	—	—	—	—	—	—	—	—	—	—	—	—	—	—	—	●	—	—	—	—	—	—	—	—	—	—	—	—	—	—	—	—	—	—	—	—	—	—	—	—	—	—	—	—	—	—	—	—	—	—	—	—	—	●
Zambia	—	—	●	Ø	—	●	—	—	—	—	●	●	—	—	—	—	—	—	—	●	—	—	—	—	—	—	—	—	—	—	—	—	—	—	—	—	●	—	—	—	—	—	—	—	—	—	—	—	—	—	—	—	—	—	—	—	—	●
Zimbabwe	—	—	—	—	—	—	—	—	—	—	—	—	—	—	—	—	—	—	—	—	—	—	—	—	—	—	—	—	—	—	—	—	—	—	—	—	—	—	—	—	—	—	—	—	—	—	—	—	—	—	—	—	—	—	—	—	—	—
South Africa	—	—	—	—	—	15/14	—	—	—	—	15/14	—	●	—	15/14	15/14	—	15/14	15/14	●	—	—	—	—	—	—	—	—	—	—	—	—	—	—	—	—	—	—	—	—	—	—	—	—	—	—	—	15/14	—	—	—	—	—	—	15/14	15/14	—	—
Sudan	—	—	—	—	—	—	—	—	—	—	—	—	—	—	—	—	—	—	—	—	—	—	—	—	—	—	—	—	—	—	—	—	—	—	—	—	—	—	—	—	—	—	—	—	—	—	—	—	—	—	—	—	—	—	●	●	—	—

●: Tax treaty in force, including double taxation treaties; Ø: partial treaty *or* treaty negotiations pending; —: no treaties; A: Ancom Harmonisation Programme (Bolivia, Chile, Colombia, Ecuador, Peru, Venezuela). Where figures are given, the first figure represents the percentage tax payable on dividends under the treaty, and the second figure represents the percentage tax payable on royalties under the treaty. † Japan controlling parent rate shown.

If there is a continuous 'sub plot' to this book then it concerns the commitment of management to international opportunity and the structuring of the organization to find and use such opportunities. The optimum results will come not only from using professional people and methods, but also people who have the desire as well as the ability to understand any new environment that they are working in. Such professionalism aligned to the deeper understanding that arises from using local skills and knowledge will lead to better and safer research, which in turn will lead to sounder judgements and the presentation of better proposals to financial backers.

A great potential of pent-up activity, both financial and commercial will be released, not only through the more thoughtful application of the international 'techniques' outlined in earlier Chapters, but equally importantly through investors finding new understanding and confidence in the wider market-place. Cross-culture work can be a powerful diversification tool to handle both threat and opportunity, and is much to be preferred to staying behind the barriers of misunderstanding, ignorance, or prejudice, for, strong as they may seem to some managements today, such barriers will surely be crossed by others tomorrow.

Overall, there is a world of international business opportunity comprising many markets, far and near, which need research and assessment. There is no shortage of business methods to tackle these opportunities and without doubt skills can be improved by enthusiastic business people, who, with the full support of their organization, want to release the full profit potential of international opportunity, and to understand new markets and the culture of other managements. With few specific barriers to understanding there is no shortage of funds to support well-presented opportunities.

References

1 Annual Reports: The World Bank, The International Finance Corporation, and the International Monetary Fund.
2 'A Bank for All Seasons', *Economist*, Sept. 1982.
3 *The Export Credit Financing Systems in OECD Member Countries* (OECD Publications: Paris, 1982).
4 'International Capital Markets', *Financial Times* Survey, 17 Mar. 1986.
5 'Export Finance', *Financial Times*, 20 Apr. 1988.
6 'Management Buy-Outs', *Financial Times*, 13 Oct. 1988.
7 G. Fletcher, D. Paige, and G. Bond, 'Trade Finance: The Treasurer's Role in Exploiting Hidden Opportunities', *The Treasurer* (March, 1984).

APPENDIX I

Typical Contents Page to World Development Bank Report

CONTENTS

Index

X